IN
THE
SHADOWS

IN
THE
SHADOWS

TRUE STORIES OF HIGH-STAKES NEGOTIATIONS
TO FREE AMERICANS CAPTURED ABROAD

MICKEY BERGMAN AND ELLIS HENICAN

CENTER
STREET

New York • Nashville

Center Street
Hachette Book Group
1290 Avenue of the Americas, New York, NY 10104
centerstreet.com
@CenterStreet

First Edition: June 2024

Center Street is a division of Hachette Book Group, Inc. The Center Street name and logo are registered trademarks of Hachette Book Group, Inc.

The publisher is not responsible for websites (or their content) that are not owned by the publisher.

Center Street books may be purchased in bulk for business, educational, or promotional use. For information, please contact your local bookseller or the Hachette Book Group Special Markets Department at special.markets@hbgusa.com.

All photos unless otherwise indicated are courtesy of the author's personal collection.

Library of Congress Cataloging-in-Publication Data

Names: Bergman, Mickey, author. | Henican, Ellis, author.
Title: In the shadows : true stories of high-stakes negotiations to free
    Americans captured abroad / Mickey Bergman, Ellis Henican.
Description: New York : Center Street, 2024.
Identifiers: LCCN 2023051338 | ISBN 9781546004752 (hardcover) | ISBN
    9781546004776 (ebook)
Subjects: LCSH: Diplomatic negotiations in international disputes. |
    Prisoners—Foreign countries. | Political prisoners—United States. | Americans—Foreign
    countries. | Bergman, Mickey. | Richardson, Bill, 1947 November 15-2023. | Diplomats—
    United States—Biography.
Classification: LCC JZ6045 .B475 2024 | DDC 327.1/7—dc23/eng/20240130
LC record available at https://lccn.loc.gov/2023051338

ISBN: 9781546004752 (hardcover), 9781546004776 (ebook)

Printed in the United States of America

LSC

Printing 1, 2024

To my wife, Robin.
To my daughter, Noa.
To my family.
To my family of families.
To Guv.

CONTENTS

INTRODUCTION

WHAT COULD BE FURTHER FROM A HARSH RUSSIAN PRISON CAMP... than *this?*

The lavishly appointed power-breakfast room at the Hay-Adams Hotel, one block from the White House, with its hovering waiters, farm-fresh-egg-white omelets and postcard views of the blazing foliage in Lafayette Square.

Yet here *I* was, and, 4,915 miles away, there *she* was: Brittney Griner, WNBA superstar and two-time United States Olympic gold medalist, all six foot nine of her, already incarcerated for nine months on the most trivial charges imaginable, now on her way to the Stalin-era IK-2 female penal colony in Yavas, Mordoviya, three hundred icy miles southeast of Moscow, where she'd been ordered by a stern-faced judge named Sotnikova to spend the next eight-plus years of her life.

A hundred women per dormitory. Lines of identical bunk beds. Ten hours a day of work duty, most likely in front of a sewing machine, stitching uniforms for the prison service and fatigues for the Russian army in Ukraine. It was hard to say exactly how Brittney was adjusting. She got no regular calls with her wife, Cherelle, and her letters were censored. At this rate, Brittney would be forty before she had another chance to hug her twin daughters or thrill her loyal fans by slam-dunking a basketball.

And me?

I was in a black suit and tightly knotted tie—I hate wearing ties—a perfect two-egg omelet with thinly sliced tomatoes in front of me, enveloped by DC's finest patch of 8:00 a.m. hotel real estate. Joining me at the table was my seventy-five-year-old boss and mentor, former New Mexico governor Bill Richardson, whose bulging LinkedIn page also includes stints as a Democratic congressman, US ambassador to the United Nations, and US secretary of energy, as well as a fleeting run for president in 2008. But these days, the former governor is best known for getting people out of hellhole prisons in really complicated places around the world, which, thanks in part to him, had also become my life's work and the toughest job I'd ever loved.

Guv and I—that's what I call him, *Guv*—had come to the Hay-Adams to meet with the White House point man on the Brittney Griner case, Deputy National Security Advisor Jonathan Finer. Jon is a savvy, well-connected Democratic foreign-policy pro who'd held key posts in both the Obama and Biden administrations. We'd been going back and forth quite a bit with him, trying to come up with a plan that would bring Brittney and Paul Whelan, another wrongfully imprisoned American, back home to their families.

"Vinnik," I said as the waiter refilled my freshly squeezed orange juice.

The White House aide looked surprised. Clearly, that wasn't the name he had been expecting.

Three times he asked me: "Are you sure?...Are you sure it's Vinnik?... Are you sure the Russians want to trade Bout and Vinnik for Griner and Whelan?"

"I'm sure that's what they said. They were the ones who brought it up."

Guv jumped in right there: "Why, Jon? Is that a good deal? Would you take that deal?"

Finer stiffened at that. "Of course, I can't speak on the president's behalf, but...," he said. "This is very interesting, if true." He just let that hang in the air, as if to say, *You bet we'd take that deal* without quite saying so.

Clearly this was not the information the White House was hearing through the official channel at the State Department. But I'd just come back from Yerevan, the ancient capital of Armenia, where I'd met with people very close to Russian President Vladimir Putin. People who hadn't been too chatty lately with anyone in the Biden administration, as war raged in Ukraine and US sanctions squeezed the Russian economy. To me, the Russians sounded ready to make a deal. When I asked which prisoner they might like to trade for, they'd added the new name to their wish list: Alexander Vinnik, a Russian computer genius who'd been convicted in San Francisco in a $4 billion money-laundering scheme involving the BTC-e cryptocurrency exchange. I was in no position to say yes or no. I carried no authority from the US government. But I promised to deliver the name to the White House.

Though he sounded cheered by this new development, our Hay-Adams breakfast mate seemed a bit rattled by the way he was hearing it.

"Why *you*, Mickey?" he asked point-blank. "Why would the Russians propose that to *you*?" Someone entirely outside government. With no official title or legal authority. A *fringe diplomat*—my term for it—at a tiny organization most Americans had never even heard of.

"What sense does that make?" Finer asked.

Actually, it made perfect sense from the Russian point of view, proposing deal terms through a free agent. I presume they did it that way *exactly because* Guv and I didn't work for the US government. We represented Brittney Griner's family and the families of other imprisoned Americans. Unlike people in the administration, we weren't handcuffed by all the other issues that divided Moscow and Washington. All we cared about was bringing Americans home.

Were the Russians playing us? It was absolutely possible. But just a few months earlier, a similar message had helped bring home another American, Trevor Reed. No reason to believe this was any different.

Doing it this way also let the Russians deliver a message to the White House: *We don't always have to deal with you directly. We know some other Americans.* And Vladimir Putin didn't want to do anything that made Joe Biden look good, any more than Biden wanted to polish Putin's war-tarnished image at home or around the world.

So there we were, working both sides of this murky negotiation, doing what the two governments were unable to, wielding the awesome power

of fringe diplomacy, making every effort we could think of to get our
people home.

* * *

THIS IS THE INSIDE STORY OF OUR UNIQUE CAMPAIGN TO FREE IMPRIS-
oned Americans, men and women held wrongfully in some of the scar-
iest and most repressive countries on earth. And yes, much of it takes
place in the shadows. It's a story that's never been told before. The hidden
negotiations. The secret strategies. The unsung heroes who keep stepping up to help us. The mistakes we've made along the way. The courage
of far too many innocent prisoners, many of whose stories never appear
in the media. The heartbreaking pain and frustration experienced by
their families back home. The off-the-charts exhilaration that all of us
feel anytime another American is freed. And all the reasons that independent negotiators who don't work for any government are so important to the cause.

It's not that the US government doesn't try. Or try hard enough.
Our government does try. Really hard. But as we keep discovering, this
is extremely difficult work. Washington has complex relations with
all these countries and many other things to worry about in addition
to every innocent American languishing in a sordid jail cell somewhere.
While Brittney Griner and Paul Whelan sat behind bars thousands of
miles from home, the Biden administration was also trying to navigate
all the thorny issues surrounding Russia's costly invasion of Ukraine and
the loss of nuclear strategic coordination between the two nations.

One advantage we have: we can stay laser-focused on bringing Americans home.

I call this lifesaving mission of ours fringe diplomacy not just because
we operate so often in the shadows, but also because we work outside
official channels in ways that regular diplomats cannot. Our loyalty is
entirely to the families we work with, and no, we don't charge them a
dime. We prefer to work quietly, behind the scenes, often outside the
media spotlight, though we have learned that publicity can sometimes

be a valuable tool, if it's wielded carefully. We rely on our far-flung contacts, our diplomatic experience, and our hard-earned understanding of what motivates America's most ardent rivals. To be successful, we need to get inside the heads of some of the world's most infamous leaders and strongmen so we can figure out how we can most effectively influence them. To tap the humanity inside them. Yes, it can sometimes be dark in there. Some of these people you wouldn't want to invite home to dinner. But as we keep discovering, the world is often more complex than the simple dichotomy of good and evil. In fact, good and evil exist in most of us. Circumstances bring aspects of each to light. This is not meant to absolve anyone from the horrible acts they are responsible for. It is to say that accepting human complexities allows us to keep finding common ground. Seeking just the right incentives. Finding creative ways to steer reluctant leaders to *yes*. Not assigning blame, just bringing the innocent Americans home. And along the way, we've begun to establish a whole new discipline of foreign policy that emphasizes the role of informed, engaged citizens and recognizes how private, individual action really can change the world.

Diplomacy isn't just for government officials anymore. That's a story that needs to be told.

Under the umbrella of the Richardson Center for Global Engagement, Guv and I and a handful of others—local partners and veteran diplomats—have won freedom for dozens of Americans in some of the toughest countries in the world, including the regimes of most of America's fiercest competitors. Russia. Iran. North Korea. Venezuela. Somalia. Myanmar. You name it. If it's somewhere the State Department warns Americans against going, chances are we've been busy there. We don't win them all. We've fallen short and had some real heartbreakers. But when we take on a case, we devote every ounce of our energy and commitment. We now have the benefit of deep experience and a record of success that is second to none.

So how exactly do we do this? How do we find common ground with leaders who are often branded as terrible villains or simply dismissed as irrational? How do we convince these anti-American strongmen to do what's right this time? And how did I, a young Israeli soldier who fell in love with an American woman and decided that the United States was the place where he belonged, end up in the middle of such unlikely drama?

I will tell you exactly how all this happened and where I believe it's heading from here. It's a story that lives in the shadows of this fascinating, complicated, and sometimes terrifying world of ours, unlike anything you'll read in other books about war, diplomacy, or high-stakes negotiating. It doesn't get any more real than this. American lives hang in the balance. Hold on tight now! The unblinking details are in the pages ahead.

PART I
FINDING
THE
FRINGE

1 | BECOMING MICKEY

ALL MY LIFE, I'VE HATED TO MISS ANYTHING.

I burst into the world at Tzahalon hospital in Tel Aviv-Yafo on May 9, 1976, not quite two months before airborne commandos from the Israel Defense Forces staged a daring raid at Uganda's Entebbe International Airport to rescue 106 hostages being held by Palestinian and German hijackers.

I guess I didn't want to miss that either.

In many ways, we were a quintessential Israeli family. My mother, my father, my older brother, and I—and those who came before us. I am still amazed at how closely our family story parallels the national story of Israel, both the inspiring and the tragic parts. Ancestors on both sides came from the area around Lodz in central Poland, a former industrial center of grand mansions, redbrick factories, and dilapidated tenements that suffered a brutal German occupation during World War II. Lodz had the second-largest Jewish community in Poland, after Warsaw, and the Nazis were especially vicious there.

The local synagogues were set on fire. Jewish males over the age of fourteen were rounded up and shipped to forced labor camps. The Jews who remained were packed into the Lodz Ghetto. Many were eventually shipped 150 miles south to Auschwitz II-Birkenau in Poland, while others were sent to other German concentration and death camps in neighboring countries. My mother's family, the Homburgs, got out just in time, fleeing to the safety of Leeds in northern England, though many, many of their friends and relatives suffered terrible fates at the hands of the Nazis. The most reliable estimates say that 145,000 men, women, and children from Lodz perished in the death camps, and no more than

3

twelve thousand survived, most of them by escaping and starting new lives abroad.

The horrors of that time cast a long shadow over our family, as with the families of many European Jews.

My mother's father, Mendel Homburg, whose nickname was Mickey, became a well-known bodybuilder in northern England, not something you'd necessarily expect of a young Jewish boy. But that was his response to the death and disappearance of so many relatives: "We need to be strong. We need to be able to defend ourselves." He died before I was born. But I have seen photos, and I've heard stories, and I am told I have my maternal grandfather's smile. He and his wife, Rose, provided a warm and loving home in postwar Leeds for their two children, a son named Roy, who would go on to become a world-renowned fertility doctor in Israel, and an artistically minded daughter named Gabrielle, known by everyone as Gay.

My father's father, Michael Bergman, was an ardent socialist who caused quite an uproar in his family when he tried to organize the workers at a factory his father owned in the Polish town of Koło, demanding higher wages and shorter workdays. That went over about as well as you might imagine. Some say the idealistic young man was banished. He called it a liberation. Either way, my socialist grandfather set out for the untamed land of Palestine to live the socialist dream.

This may sound strange, but my family tree is actually shaped more like a circle. My mother and father were related—third cousins by marriage, I believe. They tell me this was normal for people whose families came from the tight-knit villages of central Poland. Maybe it was. Their two surnames said everything. Bergman is German for *mountain man*. Homburg is originally French for *man of the mountain*. It's the same name. My parents met in England. They clicked immediately. An aspiring teacher with an unabating passion for literature, theater, and the other arts, the adventuresome twenty-year-old Englishwoman moved to Israel in 1967 as a volunteer during the Six-Day War, staying to marry my father in 1969. They had my brother, Erez, in 1973, after the war in Sinai and seven months before the Yom Kippur War.

That's the thing about living in a tumultuous place like Israel. You can tie almost every family milestone to a war, an uprising, an invasion, or some other cataclysmic event.

When I arrived three years later, I was named for both my grandfathers, Michael and Mickey. Officially I'm Michael Bergman, like my father's father, though I've gone by Mickey, my mother's father's nickname, since the fifth grade. My parents clumped the names together, and that was me.

It was quite a legacy to carry on. These were the first people to inspire me.

* * *

My mother, Gay Homburg Bergman, had a larger-than-life personality and an amazing ability to engage and befriend people everywhere. While looking after her young family and all our craziness, she also held down a demanding career teaching English in elementary school and writing textbooks, eventually trading the classroom for a full-time marketing position with Israel's largest English textbook publisher. To survive all those years in a place like Israel in a family of three tireless males—my dad, my brother, and me—she had to be smart, stubborn, and strong. She was truly up for anything, buoyed by her quick sense of humor and relentless joy for life. "I was Gay before gay was cool," one of her favorite refrigerator magnets said. I don't think I've ever met anyone with more friends than my mother collected over the years.

My father, Baruch Bergman, was born in 1941, seven years before David Ben-Gurion proclaimed the establishment of the State of Israel and the American president, Harry Truman, recognized the new nation on the same day. All his life, my father liked to tell people he was Palestinian, and he had the birth certificate to prove it. "Born in Palestine," it said. (Years later, when I was negotiating in the Middle East and trying to break the ice with my Palestinian colleagues, I could say, truthfully, "My father was Palestinian.")

To me, he embodied everything good that the State of Israel was supposed to be. With a sharp mind, a serious demeanor, and a wicked sense of humor, he was humble and quiet in public but dynamic and assertive at home and in the comfort of friends. He was endlessly principled. Though he didn't make a big deal of it in conversation, he had a set of values and morals that he always lived by. He would do anything for his family. I admired and loved him dearly. He worked as a land surveyor but put his career aside each time the Israel Defense Forces went to war: the Six-Day War, the War of Attrition, the Yom Kippur War, and whenever else the army happened to call.

We lived frugally in a small apartment in Tel Aviv. With a socialist grandfather, I guess we couldn't really expect to be rich. But we weren't poor either. In 1982, when I was six years old and my brother was nine, my father's surveying work dried up in Israel. He accepted a position in Nigeria with a large Israeli construction company. After a few months, my mother and brother and I followed him there, living in Ibadan and Benin City for two and a half years. Though my father felt guilty for dragging his family so far from home, Erez and I had a blast in Africa. We played outdoors. We made friends from all over the world. I credit that time for sparking my lifelong love for travel and my eagerness to explore cultures everywhere.

Erez was a natural leader. Brimming with youthful charisma. Always surrounded by other kids. It was easy being his younger brother and following too. Our house was in a gated compound with a community swimming pool. Local workers cooked and cleaned for us. And my dad did well. While we were living in Nigeria, my father managed to save some money. When we returned to Israel, he invested in an apartment in Ra'anana, a well-off suburb twenty minutes north of Tel Aviv. Most of the other students in the local junior high school were wealthier than we were...with all the logos to prove it. That wasn't us, but we made do. While the other kids flaunted Reebok, Adidas, and Nike, my brother and I sported knockoffs like Robak, Adidos, and Mike. It was a valuable learning experience. I came to see that the brand-name status symbols really didn't matter much, and my father didn't have to say a word. His life lessons—about hard work, dignity, and good cheer, even under pressured circumstances—spoke for themselves. In good times and in bad, Erez and I always felt secure, comfortable, and thoroughly loved.

I was a dedicated student and a bit of a nerd. I almost always brought home high grades, especially in math and science, though reading was more of a challenge for me. I dreaded any assignments that required a big chunk of reading, never quite sharing my mother's passion for plowing through the written word. But I could ace anything involving numbers, charts, graphs, or formulas. Looking back, I can see that most of the pressure I felt to perform didn't come from my parents. It came from me. One term, I got a ninety in Torah studies, a low grade for me. I was worried about how my parents would react. I sat down with my dad as he looked over my report card. I squirmed as he lingered on my lowest grade.

"Mickey," he said in a tone unusually sharp for him, "if you ever come home again with a ninety in Torah studies, I'll throw you out of the house!"

"Oh-kay?!" I answered tentatively.

"You have to be *lower* than that."

Though he was proud I usually did well in school, his lifelong secularism gave me the perfect out.

I never really got in trouble as the years went on. When my friends started smoking, I didn't smoke. When my friends started drinking, I didn't drink, though my mother was always on guard for...*whatever.* One day, she marched into my bedroom with a scowl on her face while Michael, one of my classmates from Metro West High School, was there.

"What's that smell?" she demanded.

"Uh, cologne?" Michael offered.

"It smells like pot," my mother said.

I started laughing. "How do you know what pot smells like?" I asked her.

After a reflexive "Don't change the subject," even she recognized how unlikely it was that my friend and I were in my bedroom getting high. I just wasn't into that sort of thing. She shrugged and left the room.

* * *

METRO WEST WAS NAMED FOR THE JEWISH COMMUNITY IN NEW JER- sey whose generous donations had helped to build the brand-new high school. We were the first class. When I arrived, I was as shy and intro- verted as I was studious. But the principal, Avinoam Granot, must have seen something in me. He told me I should run for the student council, the last thing I ever imagined doing. "Just try it," he urged. "I think you'll find that people like you more than you realize." And without even look- ing, I found the leader inside me.

I was elected class representative, and I have to say the experience helped to pull me out of my shell. And it just started escalating. With Mr. Granot's encouragement, I ran for student body president against my friend Ofir, who was in with all the athletes and the other cool kids. I was astonished to win. It didn't make me cool, exactly. But it did sharpen my identity and give me a much-needed shot of self-confidence.

Our gym teacher, a warm and wonderful man named Eitan Sagi, also advised the student council. He was the one who encouraged me to run for the regional head of Israeli student councils and then the national head, both of which elections I won. I was exploring leadership and try- ing to figure out what kind of leader I could be.

Israel is a far more socialist country than most Americans realize, and there was a flurry of labor strikes when I was in eleventh grade. Our teachers stayed out for fourteen days in a wage dispute. The students were not at all upset by that. For us, it meant no classes. Time off. But when the teachers finally got their pay raise, there was a shocking conse- quence we hadn't considered—two weeks were added to the school year to make up for lost time. Suddenly the students were in an uproar. That was *our vacation!* From my perch at the student council association, I led a nationwide student strike against the extra days. Remembering the introverted boy I had been just a couple of years earlier, I could hardly believe that was me. But I was a pubescent Norma Rae! Eighty-six percent of high school students all across Israel skipped school those days.

I wasn't a brilliant orator. I wasn't a huge personality. But I did the work, I remembered my goals, and I liked working with others. I couldn't exactly define my style of leadership. But I was slowly learning how to influence people and how to get things done. And no one was more surprised at that than I was.

* * *

Military service is mandatory in Israel. At age eighteen, everyone, male or female, is expected to serve. The only questions are how and where.

Earlier in high school, I'd found the whole thing terrifying. With Israel's frequent skirmishes and short wars, odds were most of us would see real combat. *Maybe I can hide out in a technical position somewhere.* That was my default plan. But by the time I reached senior year, I had gained a bit of swagger and some eagerness to test myself. I was invited to apply for pilot training, the toughest and most selective course in all the Israel Defense Forces, followed by special forces, Artillery Corps (where my brother served), and then everything else.

I was sure I'd blown it just before the physical, when I sprained my ankle playing full-court one-on-one basketball with my best friend, Shelly Halevi. But the morning I was called in, I had just traded my plaster cast for an Aircast and was pretty much back on my feet. The written tests and the interviews were far less daunting than I'd expected. I got accepted. It probably didn't hurt that I was class valedictorian. Right after graduation, before we all had to report to various corners of the military, I flew to Greece with six of my closest school friends. Still, I didn't touch a drop of alcohol, not even in the all-night tavernas of Santorini with their famous lack of a minimum drinking age. But to all of us, that two-week blowout across the Mediterranean felt like the last wild gasp of our fleeting youth.

Yes, kids are expected to grow up quickly in Israel.

The two-year pilot course started with four hundred male recruits, including my friend Idan Ofir, who came from Ra'anana like me but had gone to a different high school. That year, 1994, the Israeli Supreme Court would hear a challenge from a woman seeking a place in the elite, all-male fraternity of fighter-jet pilot training. But for now, the room was filled with young men, and each of us was eager to earn a spot.

"Twenty of you will make it," one of the commanders said matter-of-factly the day we arrived. A quick calculation indicated that only 5 percent would be chosen. With such a steep washout rate, all of us were constantly wondering: *How much longer until I get booted out of here?* Everyone was judging us all the time and in every imaginable manner. Physically. Socially. Academically. Psychologically. We were expected to overachieve in every area. Overachievement: that was the culture of the pilot corps.

We lived together in ten-man tents and trained sixteen or eighteen hours a day. When we weren't training or sleeping, we passed the time guessing who was going to make it and who was not. My tentmate Nir Shreibman already had his pilot's license and seemed to carry himself with more confidence than the rest of us. Everyone figured Nir was in for sure.

After three months of basic training—just as grueling as you'd imagine—we were taught to fly single-engine Piper aircraft, making our way through an exacting series of fifteen one-hour flight checks. Anyone who failed to measure up was promptly sent home. A couple of people were dismissed after five months. My friend Idan was sent home after ten. And my tentmate Nir, despite his pilot training, surprised everyone by getting dropped after fifteen. Somehow I was still hanging on. By then, our ten-man tent was down to four guys, so we had to be combined with the guys from another depleted tent. Though I felt constantly exhausted, I could tell I was getting physically stronger, and I was keeping up with the aerodynamics classes and the other academics. Not so different from high school physics, really. Those of us still standing had developed a real bond, fortified by the knowledge that so many others had departed and we were still there.

I was beginning to grasp, even admire, the methodical way the Israeli army built strong warriors and fostered a deep camaraderie among them. And I understood the necessity. If we were going to be entrusted with the awesome responsibility of flying fighter jets in hostile territory, which was where all this was headed, we absolutely needed to be mentally unflappable and impeccably trained. There was no higher-pressure assignment in the army. The lives of our fellow soldiers truly were in our hands. People up and down the ranks would look up to us. Next up on our training curriculum: leadership. And how hard could that be?

Now, six months in, my teammates and I were handed a new responsibility: supervising the next class of pilot-training recruits. They weren't much younger than we were. I recognized a couple of them from my high school graduating class. And our group could hardly be called experienced. We'd started training only six months before they had. But we were their new commanders. That's where I really started struggling. Whatever I thought I'd learned up till now, I was still an eighteen-year-old kid. No one wanted to hear about my 100s in high school physics or my student-government triumphs. Whatever confidence I'd thought I had, it suddenly felt awfully thin.

We were learning higher-level navigation skills. I did well at that. But the mental burden was a lot for eighteen-year-old me, and the physical exhaustion was amplifying the mental burden. Then I sprained my ankle again. I went to the medical clinic, and the doctor told me, "You need to keep your foot elevated for three weeks."

Three weeks!?! I fumed to myself. *I can't possibly sit on my butt for three weeks! I have recruits to command. I have navigation techniques to learn.* So I asked the nurse for an ACE bandage, and I wrapped my ankle as tightly as I could. It actually felt OK.

I'll just tough it out, I decided. *No problem.*

I didn't tell my commanding officer about any of this. I wanted to be outstanding...at everything. I pressed on.

Well, that week, we were hiking deep in the desert, practicing long-distance navigation. Ten miles out, ten miles back. With loaded packs, heavy radios, and other gear. I made sure the ACE bandage was tightly wrapped, and I headed out with my partner. I did fine on the first half.

"I can do this, I can do this," I kept telling myself as we trudged through the heat and the sand. I was keeping up with my partner. So far, so good. But on the way back, I really began to suffer. My ankle was swollen. The pain was getting worse. Then the wind picked up, and rain began to fall. My partner didn't complain, but I knew I was slowing him down.

I can't tell you how relieved I was when we finally caught sight of the bus just before the cutoff time. It was on the other side of a little river, a ditch, really, that had filled with rushing water. By then the path was also beginning to flood. As we stared at the bus across this instant river, one of the commanders called out to us: "Change of plans. Because of the flood, you have to go back to the midpoint. We'll meet you there."

Ugh!

We turned around and started walking again. One excruciating step after another, as I tried to push the worst of the pain out of my head. We got there, eventually. But it was after the revised cutoff time.

A failure, in other words. This time, I definitely hadn't overachieved.

In my eight months of pilot training, I had never failed to deliver or showed up anywhere late. I felt devastated.

We had a formal debriefing when we all got back to the base, as we always did after any mission. That was the army way. Everyone needed to understand what had happened. And that's when I said, "My leg really hurt."

That's also when my commanding officer, Nahshon, went to the doctor and found out that I wasn't supposed to be on my leg at all.

I was sentenced to seven days in a holding cell at the base, not what I'd expected for my doggedness. If there was a lesson in there, I needed to think about it some more. I was given plenty of time.

For the next seven days and nights, I was separated from my team. I felt depressed and embarrassed for letting everyone down. I was assigned chores to complete every morning, useless chores. I cleaned a sewer canal that no one had used in twenty years...and no one would ever use again. And still, I kept telling myself, *I'll be the best damn sewer cleaner in the Israel Defense Forces.*

I knew it was coming. But only after I had served my sentence did my commanding officer break the news to me. I was being dismissed from the pilot course.

"You need to understand something," he said to me. "There is a difference between perfect and effective. You have to be effective. You don't have to be perfect all the time. You tried so hard to be perfect, you lost your effectiveness."

Now I knew I would have to pay the price.

2 AT WAR

THERE'S A SAYING IN THE ISRAELI ARMY: "ONCE A PILOT, ALWAYS AN artillery officer." That's how many washouts from the pilot course end up in an artillery regiment.

Well, I'd been booted out of pilot training. So here I was. After completing the sergeants' course at the Field Artillery School near Shivta, I was two weeks into the four-month officers' program at Ramon Airbase. A special infantry unit had tried to recruit me. But my brother, Erez, was an artillery officer. Artillery was where my friends Idan and Nir had gone when they too were bounced from pilot training. A couple of my other tentmates had made the same transition. I was relieved to join them.

"I need you to hear something," my new commander, Iftah, said to me after closing his office door so we could speak in private. He sounded serious.

Iftah was a character from Israeli central casting. Tough. Charismatic. Confident. His hat pulled down just so. I looked at him and thought: *Now that's the kind of leader I want to be.* After my inglorious departure from the pilot course, I was hungry for a new role model, which was part of the problem right there.

"What's that, sir?" I asked him.

"Don't fake it," he said.

"What do you mean?"

"I know you have an image of what an officer should look like and sound like. But if you fake it, everybody sees. At the end of the day, you need your soldiers to follow you under fire. If they think you're faking it, they're not going to stand up. You have to figure out who *you* are and lead with that. You need to be you."

I listened intently. I didn't love what I was hearing, all this about me faking it. But what he was saying made a certain amount of sense to me.

"You're not the tough guy," the commander went on. "You're the smiley guy who has the expertise. You are the cheerful guy who knows what he is doing. That's fine. Be that if that's who you are. You don't have to be the tough guy. People will follow you."

"The smiley guy"? I wasn't sure I'd put it like that exactly. But I had to admit my commanding officer was right. In a way, I also felt relieved. There was something deeply liberating and empowering about getting the space to be the real me. For the first time since my second sprained ankle, I had my confidence back.

By 1995, Israeli troops had been occupying a "security zone" in southern Lebanon for thirteen years, defending Israel's northern border and providing much-needed support to the often-hapless South Lebanese Army. In the years leading to the Israeli occupation, there'd been constant attacks by Palestinian militias from Lebanon against civilian communities in northern Israel. The Israeli artillery forces were a key part of the occupation, stationed in bases and outposts across the region and embedded in local villages and towns, living amid the beleaguered Lebanese people. We were there to fight the well-armed Hezbollah militias, who were tenaciously trying to spread their militant Shiite ideology and drive the Israelis out.

In an artillery unit, the soldiers are trained to make mathematical calculations, fire their heavy weapons at predetermined targets, and keep coming back with more. A smaller contingent of personnel is sent out with the troops in the field. It's their job to note the results of the incoming fire and order adjustments when necessary. I was one of those advanced forces artillery coordinators, along with Nir and Chen, another friend of ours from the pilot course. It was dangerous duty with the special operations forces in the violent eastern regional division of southern Lebanon. We all understood that. The missiles would be coming *our way*, and we couldn't afford to duck. We would need to radio the updated firing orders back to ground artillery. It was dicey stuff. At the

same time, the assignment was a dream come true for a young army officer like me. Exciting. Demanding. High tech. Taking the fight to the
fierce Hezbollah militias. Awesome responsibility for a nineteen-year-
old who, up until then, had spent very little time in an actual war zone.

Objectively speaking, we were occupiers in Lebanon. There was no
denying that. We were in a land that wasn't ours. But we had strong
beliefs about why we were there, and it was all very personal. We lived
in a battered village amid the Lebanese people. We trained and fought
beside the ragtag troops of the South Lebanese Army. We had an
up-close view of how a long civil war can wreck an ancient society, calling into question a nation's very identity. Each new week brought fresh
waves of hope and frustration. Every day was a collision of optimism and
fear. Sadly, the people of Lebanon never seemed to get the stability they
needed to live secure and happy lives. And I was gradually learning to
take command responsibility...*my way*. But tragedy was always waiting
for us, just over the next hill or just across the river.

* * *

For weeks, my good friend Nir Shreibman had been stationed
with his brigade at Beaufort Castle, an old Crusader fortress above the
Litani River on the eastern side of southern Lebanon. And I was stationed with my guys across the same river at the ancient town of Marjeyoun. With our state-of-the-art comms gear, Nir and I could speak as
often as we felt like it, and we could actually see each other across the
river and the rugged terrain of the Nabatieh Governorate. We passed the
hours joking on the radio. Humor, we had both learned by then, was a
blessed relief from the daily tedium of a long military occupation.

February 4, 1997, was the day my world blew up.

It was an evening like any other at our fortress-base in Marjeyoun
when, all of a sudden, the alerts started going off like Roman candles.
We jumped on our radios, trying to figure out what was going on.

"Oh, Mickey," my friend Idan said to me—*moaned*, really—when I
was finally able to reach him over the radio. He was commanding an

artillery brigade in northern Israel. "We just saw a huge explosion in the sky. We're off to do a search and rescue."

The first reports said a small helicopter had crashed. The truth was far more devastating than that.

Nir's unit had been about to come back to Beaufort Castle after a weekend at home. But the day was foggy, and they didn't want to risk the usual truck convoy. Too easy for the Hezbollah militias to plant explosives along the foggy road. The revised plan was to make the trip in two large Israeli Air Force helicopters, sixty-five soldiers and eight crewmen in all.

"When you get there," I told the obviously shaken Idan on the radio, "look for Nir. I'm worried about Nir." Idan promised he would.

It didn't take long to fill in the puzzle pieces. The two Sikorsky helicopters, numbers 357 and 903, had collided in midair over the She'ar Yashuv village in the Upper Galilee of northern Israel, violently jolting all seventy-three military personnel aboard and instantly igniting the munitions they had with them.

An army investigation later concluded that the rotor of helicopter 357 struck the tail of helicopter 903. Helicopter 357 crashed immediately. The crew of 903 struggled valiantly to regain control but couldn't, and 903 also fell from the sky. Though soldiers, firefighters, and other rescue personnel all rushed to the scene, and two mobile intensive-care units were up in a matter of minutes, there was nothing they could do. No one aboard either helicopter could be saved.

It was the longest night of my life, as the dire details trickled in. In all, I lost seven friends in that midair collision. Nir was my closest friend in service.

My parents saw the reports on the news. It took them a while to hear that I was OK. They couldn't get through to my little flip phone. I knew that Nir was gone before his family did. I'd lost other friends in combat, but this was different. When it's someone you know so well, that's a deeper kind of grief. I felt close to the entire Shreibman family, who were American Israelis. Nir's father, Amnon Shreibman, was a successful businessman who owned a large part of La Vergne, Tennessee. There are streets named after the Shreibmans. Nir was the oldest child. He had a younger brother, Sagi, and a younger sister, Tal. She was ten at the time. His death was traumatic for all of us.

Over the next year, I grew incredibly close to his girlfriend, Jessica. The shared loss drew us to each other. The closeness grew, and we would be a couple for the next two years. That helicopter crash was the largest loss of Israeli soldiers at one time ever. But for me it was more than a note for the history books. This was a real kick in the gut. The terrible grief that I felt—and, even more, the grief that Nir's family felt—it was almost impossible to get my head around.

That grief, seeing it and feeling it up close as I did, was something I knew would stick with me for the rest of my life. I was coming to understand what a family endures when a loved one is taken too soon under unimaginably horrible circumstances. It was horrible beyond words. I felt immense empathy at everything the Shreibmans had to go through. Trying to make sense of the loss they had suffered. Getting on with their lives, even though a part of them had been stolen and couldn't be retrieved. They had plenty of advantages—love, support, education, affluence, and each other. But part of Nir's parents died with their son. Part of me died too.

Nir's younger brother, Sagi, and I had intense conversations. "Nir's life cannot be in vain," I kept telling him. I didn't yet understand how or how much, but experiencing that loss would help to shape the person I would eventually become and many of the choices I would make. Living through Nir's death and seeing the impact it had on his family, there was no turning away from that, even as the war went on.

* * *

THREE MONTHS AFTER THE DEVASTATING HELICOPTER ACCIDENT, I joined a twenty-four-man special-operations unit of army paratroopers on a trip north, far outside the security zone, riding in fake cement trucks so no one would know we were coming. Our orders were to hide a load of explosives near the base of a large cliff, where a Hezbollah commander was expected to pass.

Because the location was so remote, there wasn't enough dark time for us to get in and out in a single night. So we traveled north one night, then hid amid the boulders on top of the mountain ridge the following day until night fell again. The twenty-four of us were split in groups of four. Our camouflage made us look like the boulders themselves. No one seemed to notice us, not even the local shepherds who led their flocks within a few yards of where we were. We had to remain perfectly still through twelve hours of daylight, crouched in our cloaks with our M16 assault rifles, our high-powered radios, and the rest of our gear.

The view was surreal. Pristine brown mountain peaks, crisp blue skies, contrasted with green, proud Lebanese cedar trees sprouting tall in the cracks of the sharp cliffs on both sides of the ridge. Less than a mile away, one on each side, two Lebanese villages. Pastoral. Peaceful.

"Hey," I whispered to Lior, who was crouched just next to me, "this is where we put the tourist shack." With so much time on our hands, it was easy to fantasize. "We will rent tubes. You can choose to slide down to the east of the ridge, where you will merge with the Hasbani River and flow for several hours to the Sea of Galilee. Or you can slide down the west side of the ridge and float on the Litani River for a day. You'll wash out to the Mediterranean Sea. But we'll need some refreshment shacks and campgrounds along the river...the journey will take more than a day."

I was on a roll. Lior smiled back.

"Oh, and we'll also need peace," I said.

These fantasy banters were a great way to pass the hiding time. We were living the Middle East sequel to Joseph Heller's *Catch-22*. I smiled as I gazed into the beauty in front of me until dusk fell and we began whispering into our radios again, folding our cloaks, prepping our gear, and starting to coalesce the dispersed atoms of four back into a single molecule, twenty-four strong.

Within seconds, the shots rang out.

A lot of them.

The rounds were flying straight toward us and ricocheting off the boulders...coming from who knows where. From the right? From the left? From above? From below? The sounds were echoing in all directions. It was impossible to tell. Was it Hezbollah? Was it "friendly fire" from someone on our side? This wasn't a movie. It was reality. Real combat is chaos and confusion. But we knew we had to get out of there, and we didn't have much time.

We radioed each other: "Is that you?" "Is that you?"

We could already hear voices shouting through the speakers at the nearby mosques, rounding up the neighborhood militias.

We knew. It wouldn't be much longer until the Hezbollah grenades and hand-launched missiles were raining down on us. With one quick look around, I could see that our unit already had three casualties. I couldn't tell how many more there might be. All I knew was that I had to help get our people out of there.

Our commander, Moti, was hit. I couldn't see how badly he was wounded. At least he was alive and able to move. As the deputy commander, Eran, stepped in and began to organize an evacuation, he too went down. His injuries looked far worse. Tzvika, our radio operator, took over from there, and he wasn't even an officer. But he began shouting orders: "Prepare to move the wounded! Gather the gear!" As soon as we could get some cover fire, we needed to evacuate. Ordering and directing that fire was my job, and it was sure to be a high-risk operation. The rounds had to come in low and close enough that they would ward off the advancing Hezbollah forces—but not so low and close that they would slam into us. We didn't need a suicide mission. Normally we maintained a one-kilometer safety zone. But there was no way a kilometer would be enough to hold back Hezbollah, avoid hitting the civilian villages around us, and give us the room to pull out. I was thinking, *One hundred meters max, one-tenth the usual distance...and hope for the best.* Playing it so close, a tiny splash of wind could be the difference between life and death. At least we had the boulders to hide behind, somewhere to duck as the rounds flew past us.

"Unless the shells fall directly on our heads," I assured my teammates, "we should be OK." I'm not certain how much that calmed anyone's nerves. And it didn't help when I added, "We'll probably get some shrapnel. But I think we can do this. What other choice do we have?"

No one liked my proposal, but no one had a better one. And there was one other factor to raise the temperature even more: my brother, Erez, was commanding the artillery unit that would deliver the fire our way. My own brother! But there was no time to reflect on any of this.

"Rescue fire," I barked into the radio.

I gave my brother the coordinates for the kill zone.

"Are you sure?" he demanded.

"I'm sure," I said. "Let's do three." That way we could see where the bombs landed and make adjustments from there.

The first three rounds hit where I'd hoped they would, about a hundred meters away from us. Unless you have lived through it, you have no idea how close that is. In all our practice runs, we'd always been back a kilometer. Now I could hear the whistle of the rockets passing directly over us, then the horrific blasts near enough for us to see the dust fly.

"Perfect," I radioed back to Erez.

Only then did I order seventeen more strikes. They began arriving, one by one, in a serial cacophony of shrieking rockets and pounding explosions, so powerful together I could see them begin to alter the rocky terrain. And we had only begun. But not everyone was pleased with the orders I'd made from the field, as I would discover soon enough.

The paratroopers' division commander was a man named Benny Gantz, who would later rise to the rank of the military's chief of staff and serve as Israeli defense minister and deputy prime minister. From his position at headquarters, he jumped on the radio and instantly overruled my orders—for just the reason you might expect: he thought it was too risky, failing to maintain the required safety zone. But as soon as Erez stood down, an order arrived from a higher authority. Amiram Levin, the commander of all North Forces, quickly joined his subordinates on the open radio. He said something I had never heard in the military before: "Disregard what the commander just said. The officer on the ground calls the shots. Renew fire."

I could hardly believe my ears.

Here we were, at this moment of highest drama on the battlefield, and I was making split-second decisions that could easily cost or save my teammates' lives. I couldn't guarantee success. I had used my best judgment. That was all I could say in my own defense. And I have to say I felt a small jolt of vindication when Commander Levin stood up for me. Now I could only hope for the best as the missile fire resumed.

The rockets started flying again, 330 additional rounds over the next three-plus hours, each explosion shaking the earth around us. With that awesome cover, our forces had time to regroup, take count of our casualties, and plan our much-needed exit. With all that firepower in the air, the Hezbollah forces didn't dare advance. That gave us a precious window of safety, and soon we could hear the telltale whirr of Israeli helicopters swooping beneath the artillery fire.

Our rescuers!

What a beautiful sound that was!

In those few hours of madness, we lost three members of our twenty-four-man paratrooper unit, including the deputy commander, Eran Shamir, and two warriors, Ran Mezuman and Ze'ev Zomerfled. The unit commander, Moti, and seven others were injured but survived. As we loaded the wounded and the dead onto the helicopters and climbed aboard ourselves, we were forced to leave some equipment behind. But we got all our people out. Air force bombers would return the next day and level the terrain. We couldn't risk the possibility that any of our lethal hardware might end up in the nefarious hands of Hezbollah.

During the postop debriefing at the Ministry of Defense, I was grilled by Minister Ehud Barak and a clearly perturbed Benny Gantz. I don't think he'd enjoyed being overruled by his Northern Forces commander, who took time to pull me aside.

"Look, Mickey," Commander Levin said to me, "you understand that the decision you made was extremely controversial."

I told him I did.

"And my decision to back you—that was also controversial."

I nodded.

"This is one of those situations where you either get an award or you get demoted—it all depends on the results," he said. "You saved forces on this one. So you would normally get an award. Except we can't give an award in an operation that had so many losses. Can't do it."

I told him I understood. I didn't need an award. "Given all we were up against," I said, "I'm just grateful that most of us got out alive."

"It could have been a whole lot worse," Commander Levin agreed. "Thank you."

I felt deeply relieved. But it wouldn't be correct to say I got through the day unscathed. Once the debriefing was completed, I was sent to the medical clinic for a thorough evaluation, as everyone in our unit was. Standard procedure after a direct encounter with the enemy. I knew I'd been banged around a bit. I was happy to be walking and talking. The tech had me strip down for a thorough set of X-rays. A few minutes later, the doctor walked in with a worried look on his face.

"See this?" he said, handing one of the X-rays to me.

It was a picture of my arm. I could see that the entire area around my elbow was riddled with chunks of metal and rock shrapnel, the kind that comes from an exploding grenade. "The Hezbollah fighters had grenade launchers," I told the doctor. "I know my radio was hit." He gave me a strange look. He was talking about my arm, not my radio.

"We're not going to start operating," the doctor said. "There's too much of it. For now, I think we'll just leave the shrapnel there. Go home. We'll decide later what to do."

When he said, "Go home," he didn't mean the base. I went back to my parents' apartment in Ra'anana and fell right asleep. I woke up the next morning feeling awful. My brother came home and found me with a high fever, 104 degrees. After I started turning yellow, he carried me to the car and drove me to the emergency room. The medical resident said I had a raging infection that had already reached my liver.

They pumped me full of antibiotics and decided that they would pull one chunk of shrapnel out of my elbow, the biggest piece in there. But that was all they could do. "Your system will have to flush the rest of it out," the young doctor said. "Eventually."

I was in the hospital for three weeks and out of commission for the next four months. Yet all I could think was, *I can't wait to get back to the unit.* My young brain was playing tricks on me. War was addictive, not rational at all.

3 GRAY SCALE

I LOVED MY TIME IN THE MILITARY, AND MOST DAYS, I GOT THE STRONG impression that the military loved me back.

Through all the highs and lows, I kept being told big things were in store for me in the Israel Defense Forces. "You could be a senior commander one day," I was reminded more than once by people who could actually make that happen. "Sky's the limit for you." I aced the advanced officer training course and, by 1999, was commanding a special artillery unit of 120 soldiers and twelve officers. Our special combat duty was to hide in strategic locations above the forces on the ground, overlooking the action. That way we could see what our soldiers couldn't, including who was advancing on them and from where. What made this new duty such a rewarding challenge was that we got to innovate new ways of camouflaging ourselves and develop other creative combat techniques. By then, I felt like I was really hitting my stride as a frontline military leader and doing it *my way*. I was taking what I'd learned from my own adventures in the field and turning my experiences into SOP, standard operating procedure. My confidence flowed from my growing expertise, just as my old commander had told me it would.

That summer I was offered the chance to fly to Warsaw and spend a week visiting the concentration camps in rural Poland.

"Or," I was told, "there's an opportunity to represent the army for a month at a camp in California." A different kind of camp. Every summer, it seemed, the Israeli army sent two or three younger officers to the Brandeis-Bardin Institute, a coed outdoors camp for college-age Jewish adults in Simi Valley, California.

A week in wet and chilly Poland or a month in sunny California?

Hmmm, let me think... "I'm going to California," I said to exactly no one's surprise.

Named for Supreme Court Justice Louis Brandeis and Jewish educator Shlomo Bardin, the institute was an amazing place, 2,200 rolling acres not far from the Ronald Reagan Presidential Library. Many movies and TV shows, including a couple of the *Star Trek* movies, have been filmed there. For me, having been raised in a nonreligious household, this Jewish summer camp was a chance to learn firsthand about American Jews, who are noticeably different from the Jews in Israel. It's no exaggeration to say that camp changed my life—and not only in ways I could have predicted.

In Israel, being Jewish is pretty much a binary thing. You're Orthodox or you're secular. There isn't much in between. And I was certainly on the secular side. In the United States, there are Reform Jews, Conservative Jews, Reconstructionist Jews—a whole rainbow of Jewish identities to choose from. To me, there was something freeing about that. I didn't need to squeeze into anyone else's box. I could pick the parts of Judaism that spoke to me—and I was discovering that some parts really did. At twenty-three years old, I was finally confronting my own Jewish identity. The values more than the rituals, but a Jewish identity nonetheless. Every weekend we had services at the camp in California. I sat with forty American Jews, and they knew all the words to all the prayers because they'd been saying those prayers in synagogue and summer camp all their lives. They might not know what the Hebrew words meant, but they didn't stumble over a single syllable. It was the first time I and the other two Israelis had heard some of those prayers. But having grown up speaking the language, we knew exactly what all of them meant. And I started thinking: *You know, I'm not feeling the clash like I used to.* I guess I had my version of a spiritual awakening.

When I got back to Israel and returned to my unit in Lebanon, I incorporated some of that spiritualism into my leadership. After a twenty-kilometer training march, I might lead the recruits to the top of a mountain at the break of dawn and talk to them about the miracle of nature and the unparalleled beauty of the sunrise. Some of my fellow officers rolled their eyes. But I was in the zone, and the recruits seemed to connect with it, and—well, that's what I did.

One day, my superior officers called me in. Not to complain about my glory-of-nature talks. Instead, they offered to invest in my mind. "Once you finish your sixth year," I was told, "you can go to university. We will pay for your degree, and you will pay us back with a year of service for every year of study." The simple math meant that three years at university plus three equal years of military service would put me into my thirties. To my twenty-three-year-old self, that sounded like a lifetime.

I have a better idea, I said to myself when I got out of the meeting and had a moment to think. *I will go to university, and I will pay the tuition myself. Then, if I want to come back to the army, I'll do that after I graduate.* It wasn't that I was itching to exit the military. I just wasn't prepared to commit three more years, three years away. I'd already agreed that I'd return to the Brandeis-Bardin Institute, as a counselor this time. Now my second summer of camp would mark my official departure from the army, at least for now.

I was a few days late getting to California, closing out my military career. But just as I was settling into my new role as a camp counselor and getting reacquainted with the awesome splendor of Simi Valley's rolling hills and mountainous peaks, one of the campers caught my eye. *I know…*there's always a girl involved. She was tall and dark-haired and pretty and standing off a bit from the other campers. A recent graduate from the University of Southern California, she was named, someone told me, Robin Levine. But when I tried to talk with her, she didn't want anything to do with me, which only made me more eager to get to know her. After some cajoling, she agreed to join me on a hike along a spectacular mountain trail. It turned out we had plenty to say to each other. The talk moved quickly from trees and birds to some serious human topics. Very serious. We talked about kids. We talked about adoption. And we kept talking for the rest of the four-week camp session.

Robin was a camper, and I was a counselor. So there was nothing physical between us yet. But we really did get to know each other in nature's hands. I had agreed to stay for another four-week session, and she planned her trip back to Los Angeles. Finally we had our first date. But that was more of a formality. I already knew I was falling in love.

I hated for the summer to end. But I returned to Israel to start my studies at Hebrew University of Jerusalem, where I began a dual major in physics and international relations. But I already knew I wanted to move to America to be with this extraordinary young woman. I worked really hard that year, piling up sixty college credits in two semesters and flying for long weekends to California every chance I got. Fifteen hours in the air each way. But she was worth it. I was soon exploring options to transfer to a school in Los Angeles, and we'd already decided to get married. We hadn't set a date yet when Robin called her mom and dad to break the news, which probably wasn't the best way to do it, especially since I was sitting beside her listening on the speaker. They laughed uncomfortably about the idea of their beloved American daughter marrying an Israeli army veteran/camp counselor who was just starting college at twenty-four—and tried valiantly to talk her out of her reckless plan. But love is love, and this was more than enough to overwhelm her parents' understandable skepticism. Soon Robin was flying to Israel so she would be there with me when I broke the news in person to my parents.

I asked her to wait in my childhood bedroom. "I'll tell them in the kitchen," I said. I hoped it would go more smoothly this time.

"Robin and I are engaged," I said to my mother and father, with no more buildup than that. "And I am probably going to move to the United States."

Without saying a word, my father stood up, walked into the hallway, and knocked on my bedroom door. When Robin opened, he gave her a giant hug.

"Finally!" he exclaimed. "I have a daughter!"

My father always knew what to say.

My brother was still in the army and still single. We had no sisters. And so began a lifelong love story between Robin and my dad.

My dad had only one piece of fatherly advice for me, and it wasn't marital. "Now that you are out of the military," he said, "you're going to be recruited by Israeli intelligence. I know you'll want to see if you can make it. Do the test if you want to. But you have to promise me that you will never, ever work for the intelligence community. It's a job where you need to lie to your family. It's a job where when you get caught, everybody denies knowing you."

"Don't worry," I told him. "I'm not doing that."

His prediction was right, of course. I was recruited. I did take the exam and sit for the eight-hour interview, including the lie-detector test, during which the operator seemed to think I was lying, even though I wasn't.

"Have you smoked cigarettes?"

"No."

"Marijuana?"

"No."

"Have you done other drugs?"

"No."

The operator shook his head. "No, no," he said. "You can answer truthfully."

"But I haven't done any of those things."

"It's not good to lie on the test," he emphasized. "We're just setting a baseline for the machine."

"I'm not lying," I assured him.

He still looked skeptical, but I must have made the initial cut because I got a letter the following week inviting me for another round of interviews.

I stayed true to the promise I'd made to my father. I put the letter aside and never called back. I'd taken the process far enough already. I'd bow out while they were still interested in me. I suspect there could have been some fascinating aspects to a career like that one. In later years

I'd even be accused—falsely!—of working for Israeli intelligence. But I already knew it wasn't the career for me.

* * *

NOW THAT ROBIN'S FAMILY KNEW ALL ABOUT ME AND MY FAMILY knew all about Robin and we were crazy in love and I was excited about making my life in America and I wasn't going to become an Israeli spy, there was really only one thing to do.

Get married.

And where better to do it than at the Brandeis-Bardin Institute, the camp where Robin and I had first met? The grounds were breathtakingly beautiful. We chose a late-summer date, August 25, 2002. We planned everything ourselves. My family and closest friends flew in from Israel. Robin's family came from New York. My brother was my best man. Robin's brother was hers. Many of the guests stayed overnight with us at the camp. It was all quite drama-free except for the fact that our wedding day was the first time in my life I actually wore a suit. And I didn't know how to tie my tie. I had a good excuse. I didn't come from a family of suit wearers. My dad and my brother didn't know how to tie their ties either. Robin's dad had to help all three of us, just before he officially became my father-in-law. And I was already pressing ahead with my new life in California.

The UCLA admissions staff wasn't nearly as impressed with my sixty credits from Hebrew University as I'd hoped they'd be. Before they'd accept me, they insisted I spend two semesters at Santa Monica College. And when I did turn up the following year at the big campus in Westwood, I was informed that a single major would be more than enough for me. I dropped physics and stuck with international relations, which required more dreaded reading but sparked a real intellectual curiosity in me. Things I'd thought I knew, I found myself questioning. Education does that.

All my life, I'd been hearing the narrative that Israel stood on the moral high ground and the Palestinians were our enemies. But the more I began to study and to read, the more I began to question some of those assumptions. When I was in southern Lebanon with the Israeli army, I had understood that we were occupying someone else's land, but I had never really thought about all the implications of that. Now I was forced to. With my coursework at UCLA—and the broader debates that had been raging since the 2001 attacks on the World Trade Center and the Pentagon—I was beginning to see Israel's place in the world in less black-and-white terms.

"You know," I said to my father on one visit home, "I'm learning all this stuff about how we actually pushed the Palestinians off their land."

"That's true," he said. "We did that. Some of them left for other reasons, but some of them, yes, we pushed them off their land. We love Israel and what it stands for, but Israel has also done some bad things."

I was perplexed. I'd fought for Israel. I'd fought the Palestinians. "How come you never told me that before?" I asked him.

My father thought for a moment before answering. "Well," he said finally, "we live in a harsh reality. When you go into the military, we need you to understand our narrative. We can't have you being confused about it."

I half understood and was half angered by that explanation. I knew I would have to process this some more. What I took from my studies and my conversations was that this world of ours, when you really got to know it, was far more complicated than it seemed at first. It wasn't so much a place of good and evil or right and wrong. Wherever you looked, the world presented itself in many shades of gray. This wasn't the first time this had occurred to me. I'd gotten some inklings of it in southern Lebanon, meeting with Lebanese families and living in their communities. But I was finally putting all this together in my mind, and I was telling myself, *It's too late to turn back now.* My understanding of the world and my place in it was being reshaped right in front of my eyes.

Coming out of military service, some people remain deeply committed to the power and effectiveness of the military, while others conclude that the use of violence is rarely a solution to the problems in the world.

As I adjusted to life after the army, I fell heavily into the latter group. Violence at times can seem like the only way to solve a problem. It certainly has drama on its side. But even if it appears to work in the short term, I was discovering, violence never really solves very much. I knew that somehow or another, I would want to incorporate that lesson into whatever came next for me. I also knew I had a whole lot left to learn.

I graduated summa cum laude from UCLA in four semesters and convinced Robin to move with me to Washington, DC, so I could pursue a master's degree at the Edmund A. Walsh School of Foreign Service at Georgetown University. I got a Wexner Graduate Fellowship, funded by the retailing titan whose empire included the Limited and Victoria's Secret, which covered my tuition, a Jewish scholarship to a Jesuit university. We were building bridges right there! Professionally, those two years at Georgetown were the best thing that ever happened to me.

The professors were brilliant. Washington was the ideal place to study international relations and diplomacy, so much of it happened there. My eighty-seven classmates were all so focused and talented, they sometimes made me wonder, *What am I doing here?* But they were just the kinds of peers I had dreamed about, friendly, supportive, pursuing their individual passions just as enthusiastically as I was pursuing mine. I knew from the start I'd be running into these people for decades to come, and they'd all be doing something interesting.

I made two really close friends, both from the Middle East. One was Bushra Mukbil, a Palestinian who shared a lot of my interests but from her own unique perspective. The other was Faisal Mansour, who was Lebanese and started out highly skeptical of me, the ex-Israeli military officer, the occupier in the class. I gradually forced my way into his heart, and we became the closest of friends. We even figured out that when he was a student at the American University of Beirut and he went to southern Lebanon to demonstrate against the Israeli occupation, there was at least one occasion when we were in the same place at the same time. Even as we grew closer, Faisal and I could never be Facebook friends. For him, any public association with me would jeopardize his professional future and potentially his safety. We joked about it privately, but I understood the severity of the risk. In fact, when I called his mobile phone, his caller ID was set to display "The Zionist enemy."

* * *

As MY SECOND YEAR AT GEORGETOWN BEGAN, ROBIN AND I WERE LIVing in a fourteenth-floor one-bedroom rental in the historic Ballston neighborhood of Arlington, across the Potomac River from Washington. "Honey...honey." Robin nudged me in the middle of the night. I am a deep sleeper. It was 1:30 a.m. "I need you to take me to the hospital. I don't feel safe."

I jumped. *What? What's happening?* The past few months had been tough. Like a hermit crab, Robin had been retreating into her own shell. Her personality seemed to be shrinking. She would spend hours crying in private while putting on a show of normalcy for everyone else. Just a few hours before waking me up that night, she had called me into the bathroom. She was scheduled to fly to California the next morning to see her brother, Jonas.

"I can't see myself getting to California," she'd told me in the bathroom, crying.

I tried to wrap my head around what she was saying, but I really couldn't. "So let's postpone your trip," I'd said. Then I'd added, "But we should acknowledge that you are spiraling, and we need to figure out what's happening."

We spent three hours that night in the emergency department waiting room at Georgetown University Hospital. Every twenty minutes or so, a nurse came out and asked Robin, "Are you suicidal? Are you homicidal?"

"No," Robin replied.

She still hadn't seen a doctor.

At 4:00 a.m., I jumped in when the same questions were asked. "Well, I'm not sure about *her*, but *I* am becoming a little homicidal. Can we get seen by a doctor?"

Weeks later, I would learn from Robin what she wouldn't admit that night. She *was* suicidal. She was visualizing jumping off our fourteenth-floor balcony. A small voice kept pushing her. *Wake him up, wake him up...*Thank God she did.

After finally being treated that night with an antianxiety medication, Robin sat down to make a plan. It was an amazing show of strength, composure, and resilience for someone who had been thinking of killing herself just a few hours earlier. I was in awe of Robin's self-awareness. After deciding on a facility in Southern California where she would be admitted for treatment, Robin looked at me and said, "This is not happening just to me. It's also happening to you. No secrets. No hiding. No shame. You can tell your friends and family. Be open about it. We have enough to deal with without the burden of hiding."

Her saying that saved us both. At the time I just didn't realize how true that was. Robin was diagnosed with severe depression, accompanying anxiety, and other "fun" stuff.

I'd never dealt with mental illness before, at least not that I was aware of. Honestly, I was clueless. I was terrified. *Look what you have done*, I thought to myself. *Two years of marriage, and your wife needs to be hospitalized.*

The next few months would be a steep learning curve for me. Learning about acceptance. Acceptance of our own limitations and the things we can't control. And I had a great teacher in Robin. I learned to accept that a healthy mind could never fully understand a sick one. I could try. I could get close. I could be helpful. But I could not genuinely understand the lack of logical progression. I constantly looked for reasons and triggers. "Why are you feeling down today? Did something happen?" That's not how depression works.

I would eventually learn that depression is not something you can *fix* and move on from. In most cases, at least with the kind of depression Robin deals with, it is a lifelong condition. You can learn to live with it. You can adopt tools to manage the dips. You can identify crises early. But you cannot solve everything. For me, that was an extremely hard pill to swallow. I was a problem solver. And now I had to accept that I couldn't solve the suffering of the person I loved the most. I had to learn to let go of control.

Robin could not tolerate living under "suicide watch," as she bluntly told me. I could understand that. But it was still hard to accept: someone I cared about might be determined to end her life, and I wouldn't be able to stop her, even if she was my beloved partner in life? Now, that was hard.

When I could see that Robin was hitting a dip, I would ask if she wanted to talk about it or if she wanted me to just sit silently with her. Or maybe she wanted me in the next room or wanted me not to be around at all. I had to accept her preferences without feeling rejection or resentment.

It would take me a long time to ease the guilt I was feeling. To recognize that being married to me was not the cause of Robin's depression. In fact, the safety of our relationship had allowed her to let go of her emotional guards and, for the first time in her life, treat her depression directly. That major depressive episode my second year at Georgetown was the first step toward healing—or at least learning how to live with this potent force in our lives.

Robin's recovery from that major episode would take months. For a while she remained an empty shell of her former self. Just surviving. But as time passed, her personality slowly started to reemerge. I was seeing the love of my life returning.

Over the years, we would remain extremely open about all this. We would develop systems between us. Levels of alert. Our own DEFCON system. That way, we could quickly communicate how severe a dip was, even if, physically, we were half a world apart. For each DEFCON level, we had a network of potential responders: Who could reach Robin in fifteen minutes? Who could be there in four hours? Who could be there in a day?

Beyond our dealing with the depression, this chapter of our lives would lead me into a world I would come to know as that of *emotional intelligence*. It would not only guide my personal and parenting life, it would guide my professional life too. I had no idea about any of this yet, but it would become the foundation of everything I was about to do.

* * *

My two years at Georgetown were packed with personal challenges and learning opportunities. It was a time of great excitement and tremendous growth. But what was next for me? I had no idea. As much as I loved the learning process, I couldn't stay in school forever. As graduation neared, I was proving myself to be the worst job hunter in the class, if not all of Washington. But with a week to go before graduation, I got a call. It was from Robert Malley, a senior director at the International Crisis Group, asking me to please call him, which I did right away.

"Why don't you come over tomorrow for an interview?" he said.

I couldn't believe the sudden turnaround. I would love to work for the ICG. I spent all night watching videos of Rob and learning about the organization's high-impact work in hot spots around the world. Rob headed the Middle East and North Africa programs.

"This is so exciting, everything you guys are doing at the ICG," I said to him after taking a seat amid the giant stacks of files, books, and loose paper in his office.

He looked up from his cluttered desk and said, "Yeah, yeah, forget about ICG. Think CGI."

CGI? What is CGI? Same three letters in a different order? I didn't ask, and he didn't say. He just handed me a four-page memo and said, "Take five minutes and read this."

There were other acronyms in the memo, including WJC and HRC. It took me a page or so, but I finally figured out that I was reading a plan for an incredibly ambitious foundation called the Clinton Global Initiative (CGI) that was being launched in September by Bill (WJC) and Hillary (HRC) Clinton and a small team of others that included former Clinton White House advisors Sandy Berger and Doug Band.

"This," I said, "sounds amazing."

"OK," he said, "you'll work on religious and ethnic conflict"—one of the initiative's four main areas of focus—"and whatever else comes up. We'll start tomorrow."

And so began my career in the field of international relations and conflict reduction, even before the ink was dry on my Georgetown diploma. I also learned something that week about how things really work in Washington. It's good to know people…even better if they know people that you know and they've had a chance to see your work…and they like it.

4 BABY DIPLO

No one at the Clinton Global Initiative was thinking small. In fact, the mission could hardly have been any more ambitious: recruiting innovative leaders from business, academia, media, and the nonprofit sector to confront some of the most daunting challenges in the world. Ethnic conflict. Sustainable growth. The ravages of war, climate change, and infectious disease, plus whatever other catastrophes happened to bubble up along the way. Why should these challenges be left entirely to government officials? Wasn't there a crucial role to be played by the strongest leaders and best thinkers from other realms? It wasn't as if government had solved *everything*. That was the core idea behind the Clinton Global Initiative.

And there was more: The participants wouldn't be addressing these challenges nation by nation. They'd be encouraged to think—and *act*—globally. And the small team of staffers had just three months to organize the initiative's first major conference, which would be held that September in New York City beside the sixtieth session of the United Nations General Assembly.

How hard could that be?

I assumed I'd get pigeonholed into working on Middle East issues, but that never happened. Even when I was a junior staffer, my portfolio was truly worldwide. I spent long, intense days recruiting the CEO of Nike and a wide range of other top leaders and making sure they joined the initiative in the right frame of mind. Sandy Berger told me exactly what to say: "President Clinton is very excited that you're coming aboard (and that you're paying the fee). However, this is not just talking heads. The president is expecting you to make a personal commitment to address one of the global challenges."

I found it inspiring how many of these brilliant and busy people responded with an immediate yes. I was so inspired, in fact, I even convinced myself. If I was going to be asking all these world-renowned leaders to make personal commitments to the global cause, I figured I should probably make a commitment of my own. Make an impactful difference, as I was asking others to. So I did.

"Immediately after the conference," I declared, "I will go to the border between Sudan and Chad," which was just then being overrun with refugees from the western Sudanese province of Darfur. Half a dozen militant rebel groups were challenging the iron-fisted military government of Omar Hassan al-Bashir. "I will interview the refugees and figure out what they need most. Then I'll come home and raise fifty thousand dollars and apply that to whatever I learn."

The crisis in Darfur was incredibly complicated, a long-running clash over land, identity, and self-determination. It had already claimed more than two hundred thousand lives and driven some two and a half million people from their homes. What was happening in the region, international human rights groups were calling genocide.

Darfur was certainly in a crisis. The crisis was undeniably global. What I didn't know for sure was how much difference someone like me could possibly make there, one engaged individual representing no one but himself. We'd just have to see how that worked out.

* * *

IN THE SECOND WEEK OF JULY 2006, I FLEW HOME TO ISRAEL TO PARticipate in a conference in Herzliya. On my way to the conference, I decided to visit my mother and father and brother and spend some time relaxing at the beach. Nothing clears my head like a gentle breeze off the Mediterranean. I woke up in my parents' apartment my first morning in Ra'anana, borrowed my mom's car, and drove to Herzliya Beach, arriving well before the crowds did. At that hour of the morning, only the jelly-fish and the windsurfers were out.

I had no idea what I was about to be drawn into.

All of a sudden, seemingly out of nowhere, the morning calm was burst by the roar of low-flying military helicopters, more than a dozen of them, streaming up and down the coast in rapid succession.

Wow, I said to myself. *If we hadn't withdrawn six years ago, I could swear something was happening in Lebanon.* When I was in the army, that was the sign: helicopters hugging the coastline, rushing to reinforce Israeli troops on the ground somewhere beyond the horizon.

I got back to the car in time to hear Hassan Nasrallah, the gray-bearded secretary-general of Hezbollah, come on the radio and announce a daring raid: a squad of his heavily armed militants had crossed from Lebanon into Israel, ambushed two Israeli army Hum-vees, killed three Israeli soldiers, and captured two others, hustling them across the border back into Lebanon. Soon news would break that five more Israeli soldiers had been killed in Lebanese territory in a failed res-cue attempt. But for now, everyone was focused on the two Israeli hos-tages, reservists on their final day of operational duty.

This was a stunning triumph for the anti-Israeli militants and a ter-rible black eye for the Israeli army. There was nothing the Israelis hated more than a well-armed enemy taking an Israeli soldier alive. In the past, the Israeli military had reflexively blown up vehicles and raided safe houses even when that meant certain death for their captured country-men. Better a brother soldier be dead than alive in enemy hands. That was the thinking, anyway. Two years earlier, 450 Lebanese prisoners held in Israeli jails had been traded for one captured Israeli colonel and the bodies of three Israeli soldiers, one of the most lopsided prisoner exchanges in the history of human warfare. And just two weeks before the Hezbollah raid, an Israeli soldier named Gilad Shalit had been cap-tured in a cross-border raid by Palestinian fighters from the militant group Hamas. It was anyone's guess what condition he was in. But the Israeli military and Israeli politicians were already in a frenzy over the

Shalit kidnapping. No one in Israel wanted a repeat of that at the border with Lebanon.

The spokespeople for the Israel Defense Forces weren't saying much in the media about this latest raid. But I had studied Nasrallah while I was in the army, and I knew he didn't lie. He might exaggerate. He might embellish. But he prided himself on not lying outright. If the leader of Hezbollah said he'd grabbed two Israeli soldiers, he had them for sure.

As soon as I got back to my parents' apartment, I called my Lebanese friend from Georgetown, Faisal Mansour. He was in Washington. He picked up before the second ring.

"Mickey," he said, without saying hello. "Have you heard?"

"I heard."

"What do you think will happen?" Faisal asked me.

I answered my friend without hesitation: "There is going to be war. Tonight."

"War? Come on. It's just one incident."

"No, no," I cautioned. "You need to understand. First, it's a kidnapping. You know how Israel reacts when its soldiers are kidnapped. And second, it's not an isolated thing. Hamas has Gilad Shalit. Hamas and Hezbollah are different, I know that. As different as Palestinians and Lebanese."

I was trying my best to convey the Israeli perspective. "For an Israeli," I said, "a live kidnapping means we've lost the deterrence. There's only one way to bring the deterrence back. That's to show the enemy we're crazy. Israelis will stop at nothing. We will do anything to get our people back, including go to war. Israel will declare war tonight. I have no doubt."

People often have trouble understanding why Israel responds disproportionately to an attack. When a terror attack kills several Israeli citizens, why does Israel launch a war that kills hundreds or even thousands? I can't remember where this came from, but here's the best explanation I ever heard for that: "In Israel, we do not count casualties one, two, three. We count six million and one, six million and two, six million and three." The collective Israeli sense of trauma is a direct result of the Holocaust. Once you understand that, you can begin to understand decision making in Israel.

I was long out of the military, but I felt my heart racing. I worried about the civilians who would be caught in the crossfire. About the possibility of hours, days, weeks of sleepless nights as air-raid sirens and the sound of exploding artillery kept everyone on edge. As always, I worried about my family.

I wasn't sure if Faisal was convinced by my analysis or if he just saw there was no point in debating with me when I was so obviously revved up. "How far do you think the IDF will go?" he asked. "A little bit of artillery bombing? Something like that?"

"More," I said, "Much more. This will be significant. A significant military operation. I think they'll go all the way this time. I wouldn't be surprised if they bomb the airport in Beirut."

"You really think they'll bomb the airport?"

"I could be wrong, but yeah, that's exactly what I think."

Before night fell in Washington, Faisal was interviewed by the BBC as an expert on this latest crisis in the Middle East. Asked what he was expecting next, my Lebanese friend referred to our call without giving my name. "I don't know exactly what will happen," he told the British correspondent. "But I have sources. They are telling me that, potentially, the Israelis are going to declare war tonight. They might even bomb the airport. This could escalate very quickly."

And that evening, that's exactly what occurred. Israel declared war on the forces of Hezbollah and bombed the airport in Beirut. Later that night, Faisal and I got a chance to speak again.

"Mickey," he said, "this is disastrous." There was no denying that. "Do you think there is anything *we can do* to try and stop this or control it?"

"I don't know. What do you have in mind?"

We were just a couple of foreign-policy graduates, barely a year out of Georgetown. We had no authority or responsibility to do anything. Our diplomatic portfolios were—well, actually, we didn't have diplomatic portfolios. We had entry-level jobs in the field—and let's be honest, we were lucky to have them. But Faisal had obviously given all of this some thought.

"My family is good friends with the prime minister of Lebanon," he said to me. That would be Fouad Siniora. "And I know you have a friend in the Knesset who is very close to the prime minister." Which was true.

Ami Ayalon was a legendary Israeli general, a decorated warrior who had gone on to be commander of the Israeli Navy and director of the Shin Bet, Israel's secret service. The true embodiment of a strong yet moral leader, he was now a key Labor Party member of the Knesset and an influential ally of Prime Minister Ehud Olmert. With Olmert's support, he'd been advocating for a peaceful solution to Israeli and Palestinian land issues. Ami and I had met at an event in Washington in late 2005, just as he was starting his political campaign. I had been like a child meeting his hero. I'd helped him organize visits with policy leaders and potential donors in Washington.

As I pondered Faisal's question—*What can we do?*—the thought did occur to me that we were very well positioned here. There was only one person between me and the prime minister of Israel, my friend Ami. There was only one person between me and the prime minister of Lebanon, my friend Faisal. Here we were, just a couple of overgrown adolescents. But if we chose to reach out, we might actually have some access here.

"You want to give it a try?" Faisal asked me.

That was an easy question. "Absolutely."

* * *

I reached Ami right away on his cell phone. Though he was clearly busy, he was his usual friendly self. I explained the situation to him. "Through a good friend of mine, I believe I have access to the Lebanese prime minister. Is there some way we can set up a back-channel line of communication between the two sides, a way of passing messages back and forth—in hopes of limiting the damage here? As you know, these explosions don't usually end well."

My question certainly caught Ami's attention. How did he react? I would say he sounded interested but noncommittal. "Let me get back to you, Mickey," he said.

"There is a chance I can be useful here," I said. "I'd certainly like to try."

A few hours later, Ami was back on the phone. By now he was in full government mode. "Mickey," he said sternly, "we need some demonstration that your contact is what you say it is. Here is what I would like you to do. At five o'clock this afternoon, the Lebanese prime minister is making a speech. In that speech, I would like him to use a certain phrase." Ami shared the very simple phrase with me. "Somewhere in his speech, he should repeat that phrase."

Oh-kay...

As far as I could tell, the phrase was entirely benign. It had no meaning...except that it would prove Faisal and I could reach the Lebanese prime minister and get him to do something. That would confirm our contact.

"I will convey that," I said to Ami. "Let me see what we can do."

Could Faisal and I really drop a phrase into the speech of Lebanese prime minister Siniora and do it on just a couple of hours' notice? We were about to find out.

I called Faisal and told him about Ami's request. He actually sounded confident. "I don't see why that should be a problem."

At five o'clock, I turned on the TV and waited for the prime minister to speak. I had no idea if he would use the phrase that Ami had planted through Faisal and me. Along with everyone else, I was about to discover how strong our contact was.

Fouad Siniora used the phrase.

Less than a minute after those words were out of the prime minister's mouth, my phone was ringing again. It was Ami.

"I guess we have proof of concept," I told him.

"This is good," he said.

I'm not sure which of us was more pleasantly surprised.

That wasn't Ami's only request. He was back on the phone the next day. "This time," Ami said, "when the Lebanese prime minister refers to the UN authority that governs the rules of engagement, it would be very helpful if he avoided citing Resolution 425. He should refer to Resolution 1559 instead. If he can do that, it will help us empower the government of Lebanon over Hezbollah."

I made no promises. But as I had the first time, I passed the request through Faisal to the Lebanese. This time, Faisal heard back immediately: "That's fine." And as promised, in his press conference the next day, the Lebanese prime minister referred to UN Resolution 1559.

* * *

AND SO BEGAN A RUNNING DIALOGUE BETWEEN THE HIGHEST-ranking officials in the governments of Lebanon and Israel, coordinated through a couple of twentysomething foreign-policy nerds who lived 5,900 miles away in Washington, DC, one Lebanese and one Israeli. Faisal and I might be baby diplomats, but we were right at the center of the action at an especially dicey moment for the tinderbox of the Middle East. And people far more powerful than we were appeared to be relying on *us*. This was no graduate school exercise. This was as real as the real world gets.

The next request came to Faisal from Prime Minister Siniora. If the Israelis could take advantage of our back-channel communication grid, so could the Lebanese. This time, the Lebanese prime minister asked if the Israelis would scale down a certain area in their military campaign. It was, I understood, an area that was not of crucial importance to the Israelis, and they agreed to the Lebanese request. Faisal and I didn't weigh in with our own opinions about whether these requests were wise or whether they should be granted. That wasn't our role. We were there to foster communication between the two sides in hopes of reducing the violence and easing the conflict. We were convinced that had real value of its own. And honestly, if we didn't do it, who else would?

"Can you believe this?" I said to Faisal in one of our many calls that week.

"Isn't this the shit?" he said.

We had no actual authority. We didn't represent anyone beyond ourselves. We were just a couple of engaged civilians who were trying to be helpful at a very difficult time. And I had no doubt that indeed we were.

This kept going, back and forth, as the fighting intensified, then eased, then intensified again. The Lebanese had some influence over the Hezbollah fighters but not full influence. The Israelis, as Israelis do, were debating among themselves. And the entire Middle East remained on a knife's edge. Would the two sides find a way to dampen the hostility? Would the declared conflict explode into all-out war? We would just have to see.

Seven days in, Faisal called me and said, "I have a big one."

"What's that?" I couldn't wait to hear.

"The Lebanese have a cease-fire proposition," he said. "They want to see if the Israelis will accept it. We need to pass the Lebanese proposal to the Israelis."

Holy shit! We'd just hit a whole new level here.

"Faisal," I said, "this needs to be in writing. This isn't something we can just pass on verbally."

"I can't have a paper trail indicating this is from Lebanon," he said. I could tell he was smiling at that. "What if you draft it as if it is your idea and send it to me for review? Once we know the draft is accurate, you can take it to your channel."

And there it was: a seven-point cease-fire proposal from the sovereign government of Lebanon to the sovereign government of Israel… to be delivered through Faisal and me. The United Nations wasn't even involved.

The proposal was as remarkably detailed as it was simple. It laid out a full cease-fire and a pathway to resolving a long-term dispute over demarcation lines. It discussed the pullback of soldiers from each side. Under the deal, the prime minister of Lebanon would be empowered to seek Hezbollah's return of the captured Israelis. He would then negotiate with Israel for the terms of their release.

At this point in the conflict, Israel had beaten up on Hezbollah pretty badly, as often happened in the first few days of a war. But Israel now appeared to be running out of preidentified targets, and mistakes were being made. Was the tide shifting a bit? It seemed to be. This was, without a doubt, a significant cease-fire proposal...and time sensitive too.

As Faisal directed, I forwarded the Lebanese proposal to Ami. He acknowledged receipt and wrote back, "Let me take it up to the cabinet." Now it was in their hands.

I had no idea whether the cease-fire would be adopted, though I did have the impression that the proposal was being seriously reviewed. That was good news, and that seemed clear. I was certainly eager to hear what the Israeli cabinet would decide.

Ami called late that afternoon. He sounded exhausted as he delivered his report.

"We sat for four hours," he said. "We had an intense conversation about the cease-fire proposal." He said the group had included Prime Minister Ehud Olmert, Foreign Minister Tzipi Livni, and Defense Minister Amir Peretz, along with several top Israeli military officials.

Ami described what had happened. Tzipi Livni, the foreign minister, had loved the agreement. She'd said, "This is the best we can get. We should grab it right now." The defense minister wasn't so sure. "We haven't pounded them enough," he said. "We're doing really well with our targets. We should keep going. It's too soon to stop." The two of them, the foreign minister and the defense minister, argued back and forth for quite a while. Tzipi was adamant. "No," she said, "we're doing really well *now*. We always do well at the beginning. But we know from history, these things turn. Let's take advantage of where we are now. Let's sign this." The defense minister kept saying, "We have further to go." It was clear that neither one of them was going to budge.

Therefore, the decision was up to Prime Minister Olmert. He had to break the tie.

And...? I couldn't wait to hear the rest of the story. "The prime minister sided with the defense minister. So they voted two to one against it. Sorry, Mickey. The answer is no."

Ugh! We'd been so close. That was how it felt, anyway. I knew what more war meant. It meant more death. I called Faisal and broke the news to him. "Two to one," I said. "They voted no. The fighting continues."

Both of us understood that we were only the messengers here, the conduits for the cease-fire proposal. We weren't the decision makers. At the same time, we did have an interest in the outcome. Both of us were strongly hoping that the two sides could find their way to a deal, the sooner the better as far as we were concerned. Israeli and Lebanese lives were in the balance. We didn't want anyone else to die.

We did what we could to console ourselves.

"We did our job," Faisal said.

"We have a right to be proud of that," I agreed.

That's what Faisal said, and that's what I said. But it still wasn't enough to convince ourselves. Speaking just for me, I desperately wished our conduit had led to a prompt cease-fire. This was personal for me. Though I was Israeli, I had spent enough time in Lebanon to know that both nations were populated by decent people who were tired of war and craved peace and stability so they and their families and their neighbors could get on with their lives. Every extra day of war was a tragedy for them. Especially since we had the means to avoid it. But Israel, my country, had refused to go along.

I hated that.

And the next day I applied for United States citizenship.

It wasn't the specific decision that had me so upset, though I was plenty upset about that. It was also everything that seemed to be swirling around it. The politics of Israel. The iron grip of the military. The refusal among Israeli officials to recognize the suffering and rights of others, as we insisted they recognize ours. Even with civilian overseers, the military remained firmly in charge, and that, I knew, was seldom the best route to peace.

So the fighting went on.

Instead of seven days, the war lasted seven weeks. Fifty-five Israeli soldiers were killed, along with thousands of Lebanese. And the cease-fire agreement that was eventually brokered by the United Nations was almost exactly the same as the Lebanese draft that Faisal and I had delivered to the Israelis.

PART II
TAKEN
ABROAD

5 THE GUV

THE DO-MY-PART MISSION TO THE CHAD-SUDAN BORDER, THE ONE I'D promised the Clinton Global Initiative, was just as intense as I'd imagined it would be. I focused my fundraising in the Washington Jewish community, where the small checks began trickling in. Then Dennis Ross from the Washington Institute for Near East Policy wrote a nice check. I got an even larger one from S. Daniel Abraham, who founded the company that sold SlimFast diet products and funded the S. Daniel Abraham Center for Middle East Peace. His check came with a generous match and immediately put me over my goal. He promptly recruited me to work with his group, assuring me I could also remain involved with the Clintons.

For guidance on the ground, I teamed up with the International Medical Corps, a wonderful nonprofit doing lifesaving work with some of the world's most threatened populations. Robin's dad, Richard Levine, a fantastic photographer, came along to record the mission. I interviewed dozens of desperate Sudanese refugees and the kind people who were hosting them in Chad. I decided to help establish a health clinic that would not only tend to the medical needs of the refugees but also treat the local villagers who were taking them in. These generous souls had been largely overlooked in the flow of international aid.

Did we solve the crisis in Darfur? Of course not. This was a drop in a very large bucket. But we did make a difference, and we proved once again something that was becoming a theme of mine: that engaged individuals could play an important role in helping to confront some of the largest challenges in the world. One by one by one, people did matter. Governments could never do everything. That was one of the key lessons of the Clinton Global Initiative. On a far smaller scale, it was becoming one of mine.

A few months after I got back to Washington, Danny Abraham got a call from someone I knew nothing about, New Mexico governor Bill Richardson. This was early January 2007. The governor, it seemed, had been asked by the Save Darfur Coalition to fly to the Sudanese capital of Khartoum and try to negotiate a cease-fire between President Omar al-Bashir and the rebel factions in Darfur. The two sides, each accusing the other of horrific atrocities, were deadlocked on a number of issues, including who should police the embattled region. President Bashir was adamantly opposed to the introduction of peacekeeping forces from the United Nations. Only four months earlier, Richardson had successfully negotiated with President Bashir to free Paul Salopek, a *National Geographic* reporter who'd been ambushed and imprisoned by progovernment forces. Naturally, the Save Darfur Coalition figured the governor might also be able to help in this new mission. And the governor had his own agenda.

"You should support this effort," he said to Danny. "It's very important." Perhaps the SlimFast founder would lend the governor his corporate jet?

The executive balked at that request, as any sensible aircraft owner would. "You're not taking my jet into Khartoum," he said, though he did offer to help pay for a chartered flight. "And oh, by the way," he told the governor, "there's this kid, Bergman, who works for me. You really should take him with you. He's a Sudan expert."

Really? I couldn't believe he'd said that. But my phone rang first thing the next morning. I heard a gruff voice on the line.

"Is this Mickey Bergman?"

"Yes?"

"This is Governor Richardson of New Mexico. I need you to pack your stuff and get your ass to Santa Fe. We're leaving for Khartoum."

I really thought it might be a prank. And if it wasn't, did Governor Richardson really believe I was an expert on Darfur? Did he know anything about me? Did he realize I was Israeli? And Jewish? How would that go over with the fiercely dogmatic Muslim generals in Sudan? From what little I knew, this sounded like a highly delicate mission at an especially dicey time. Robin had her doubts from the start. When I hung up the phone and told her that the governor of New Mexico had asked me to go with him to Sudan, she was—let me put this gently—not entirely certain that was such a wise idea. I told her, "Out of respect, I'll go to Santa Fe and meet with him. Once he learns about my background, I'm pretty sure he'll decide I shouldn't go."

Governor Richardson was a natural raconteur. I had a fascinating lunch with him as he opined on the world's greatest challenges and recounted some of his adventures as a congressman, United States ambassador to the United Nations, secretary of the US Department of Energy, and a kind of private diplomat, taking on thorny missions like negotiating the 1996 release of the first American civilian to be arrested on espionage charges by North Korea since the end of the Korean War. And now, while also serving as governor of New Mexico, he was wandering into the Sudanese civil war.

As a lunch companion, the governor certainly had plenty of material to pull from.

Joining us at the table was Amjad Atallah, a Palestinian American I'd gotten to know in Washington. He and I had actually written an article together about the Israeli-Palestinian conflict.

"What are you doing here?" I asked him.

He said he'd gotten so frustrated trying to improve relations between the Israelis and the Palestinians that working on the Darfur genocide felt like a break to him. "At least there's some reason for hope in Darfur," he said with a shrug.

I listened more than I talked. But as our lunch was winding down, I finally brought up the topic of my own background. "Governor," I said, "I need to tell you something. I'm not only Israeli. I was an officer in the Israel Defense Forces. I don't want to risk the mission."

Once he heard that, I figured he would find some way to ease me out of the trip. Instead, he totally dismissed my concern. "I vouch for you," he said. "If Bashir complains, I'll tell him we've known each other for years. You have your British passport, right? You have your visa. You're part of the delegation. If they have a problem with you, they have a prob-lem with me. They don't separate us. You're coming. That's all there is."

He stopped right there, and a big smile slid across his face. A smirk, really. "Mickey," he said, "do you know what I'm famous for?"

I shook my head. I had no idea where he was going. "What is that, Governor?"

"I get people out of prison."

He let that sink in, and then he continued. "So, worst comes to worst, you spend a couple of months in a Sudanese prison. Think what that would do for your career."

He was laughing so hard by then, he could hardly continue.

"I'll get you out...eventually."

All I could think was, *I might regret it, but no way am I skipping this adventure!*

I called Robin from the tarmac and told her, "Honey, I need to go with this guy. I'll just go to Khartoum. I won't go on to Darfur."

Two days later, she'd been at home watching CNN when a few sec-onds of B-roll came on the screen: a short video clip of Governor Rich-ardson in Darfur. And yes, standing right behind him in the shot was her Israeli husband, just where he'd assured her he wouldn't be. I don't believe she was comforted by that. But in my defense, it did give her a small preview of what our lives together had in store.

* * *

WE SPENT FOURTEEN HOURS ON OUR CHARTERED FLIGHT TO KHAR-toum, including a refueling stop in Iceland. Besides Amjad, Governor Richardson, and me, our small group included Calvin Humphrey, who'd been a staffer on the House Intelligence Committee when the governor was in Congress. Calvin was now handling the logistics for this trip. There were also a couple of other aides. The flight gave me a chance to study firsthand how the governor organized an international mission like this one.

He did it, first of all, by assigning roles to everyone.

He looked at Amjad on the plane and said, "Amjad, you're going to be the expert on gender-based violence." The lawless Janjaweed militias had been using rape as a weapon in Darfur. That would certainly come up in our discussions.

He turned to me. "Mickey," he said, "you'll be the expert on the African Union and their role in all this."

I thought, *Oh-kay...At least now I have my homework for the rest of the flight.*

As soon as we landed in Khartoum, we went to see Cameron Hume, the US chargé d'affaires and the highest-ranking American official in Sudan, who'd known the governor from their time together at the United Nations and from various other adventures since then. The governor seemed to know a lot of people, and he clearly had his own ways of doing things. Hume struck me as a fascinating person. While he certainly participated in the choreographed dance of diplomatic procedures and formalities, he had a certain edge to him. He was able to find openings in things that weren't said in meetings—discovering hidden doors, then boldly marching through them. I hoped I'd have other opportunities to learn from such an obviously brilliant diplomat. Little did I know that years later, I would be working closely with him.

As we began to meet with Sudanese officials, I noticed that Governor Richardson liked to make up names for the people on his team. He kept referring to Amjad as Dr. Atallah. "Well, Dr. Atallah, as a world-renowned expert on gender violence..."

The first time I heard that, I shot a quick glance at Amjad. I knew he wasn't a doctor. Like me, he didn't even have a PhD. And even though he had never been on a trip with Governor Richardson before, he just shrugged and smiled back at me. Whatever the topic, I noticed that the governor kept deflecting the conversation to one of us, his subject-matter experts. My first reaction to that was, *Oh, that's nice. He's so inclusive. He's bringing in the staff.* But I quickly came to see the real purpose of all that deflecting: the governor was using us to create a buffer between himself and whichever Sudanese official we were engaging with.

Whenever the African Union was mentioned, he deferred to me. "Mickey, how do you expect the union to respond?" So I was the one going back and forth with our Sudanese counterpart—not the governor. I stated our position. I asked questions about theirs. It was almost as if the Sudanese official were negotiating *with me.* Then, wherever the discussion landed, the governor came in at the end, offering his reaction to whatever understanding had been hammered out.

"OK, I like it," he might say. Or "No, that's not good enough. We can do better than that." And he'd push some more. With us, his expert associates, he always had a buffer between himself and the person on the other side. Structuring the negotiations that way, I realized, made him the ultimate judge and jury. If he had been the one expressing our position, he'd have been stuck wherever the conversation happened to land. This one last step gave him additional leverage at the end. All appeals went through him.

I would later come to understand that this wasn't necessarily a conscious strategy on the governor's part. It was more of an instinct, something he did because it worked for him. I was attending a master class in international negotiations just by being there. I knew there had to be other techniques, conscious or not, that I could study and maybe copy one day. I didn't have to wait long.

We were sitting with Foreign Minister Lam Akol Ajawin in advance of our big meeting with President Bashir. A protocol meeting. We were methodically working our way up the chain of command. The foreign minister was basically the president's right-hand man. The meeting seemed to be going well when Calvin walked in.

"Governor," he said, "we just received something from the office of President Bashir. It's a draft of the joint statement to be released at the conclusion of our visit."

These statements matter. Since this was a private mission and we weren't there representing any government, we couldn't sign official agreements. The joint statement at the end of the trip—that would be the strongest record we had, the mutual understanding that would define the mission's accomplishments.

Calvin handed the draft to Governor Richardson. As the foreign minister continued speaking with the rest of us, the governor began to read.

His face quickly hardened into a scowl. It hardened even more as he read to the end.

"Excuse me, Mr. Foreign Minister," he said, starting softly, "I have to stop you here for a second. I need to deal with this." What he said next, he said to Calvin, sharply. "Calvin, I'm reading this statement. Am I missing something? This is nothing. This letter says that we came here for no reason."

As he spoke, the governor's voice grew louder and harsher. His tone was plainly angry. He was still addressing Calvin, his own staff member who'd had zero to do with drafting the statement. "Calvin," the governor snapped, "this is embarrassing. We might as well stay in Khartoum. I can't go back to the United States with this. This is terrible."

Calvin didn't really answer. He just kind of stammered. The foreign minister said nothing. Things had escalated to the point where it was genuinely uncomfortable in the room.

"You need to fix this," the governor demanded, as if the statement were all Calvin's fault.

With the temperature in the room still at a boil, I was thinking, *The governor's really pounding on Calvin. This is totally unfair. The statement came from President Bashir.*

As the governor pounded on, the foreign minister turned in his desk chair and quietly picked up the phone. I wasn't sure at first who was on the other end of the call or what exactly was being said. The foreign minister spoke in Arabic. But right then, I noticed the governor glancing at Calvin and tossing him a little wink. Then it all made sense: Governor Richardson was telling Calvin, *Thanks for playing along*, while Foreign Minister Akol was on the phone with President Bashir, informing him, *This is a disaster. You have to fix this. Now!*

I was learning quickly. I immediately understood why the governor had chosen to play it like that. If he had directed his anger at Akol, the foreign minister would almost certainly have dug in on the statement, and that would have been the end of it. Take it or leave it. That would be the choice. But, experienced negotiator that he was, the governor directed his reaction at his own guy, showing his own displeasure indirectly, while also making sure the message landed exactly where it was intended to, with the foreign minister, who'd just passed it on to the president.

That way, the problem could be fixed.

And by the time this meeting was over, it had been. We had a brand-new draft from the president's office with language the governor could almost have dictated himself.

* * *

OUR FACE-TO-FACE ENCOUNTER WITH PRESIDENT BASHIR, THE MEETing that really mattered, went very much as we'd wanted it to. He already seemed to have bought into the terms of the updated statement. The governor deferred to each of us, his subject-matter experts. One by one, we engaged with the strong-willed Sudanese president, explaining our thinking and determining how much ground he might be willing to cede. The governor spoke up later, running the ball a few more yards down the field. The president even agreed to make some more tweaks to the joint statement we would share with the media, reflecting the late round of progress we had made.

As we'd hoped, the Sudanese president agreed to a twenty-one-day cease-fire, a proposal all but two of the rebel factions happily signed on to. It gave the rebels time to work on their own internal disputes. Though the president clung to his opposition to United Nations peacekeepers, saying they'd be seen as "non-African colonialists," he did agree to halt military operations long enough to give a political settlement time to emerge.

Was it a perfect agreement? No. Would it end the Darfur crisis once and for all? Not even close. But it was, as the governor told the New York

Times on the way home, "a step in the right direction"—and a whole lot better than throwing up our hands and trying to forget about the horror of Darfur.

On the long plane ride home, I couldn't help but marvel at everything I'd just seen and been a part of. This was my first time on a diplomatic mission of any sort. I was still a wide-eyed newbie, less than two years out of graduate school. And I was already learning some important lessons about diplomacy from someone who'd been through this many times before and really seemed to know. The importance of advanced planning. The distinct roles of team members. The power of structuring the negotiations a certain way. Knowing when to come at the other side directly and when to try more of a bank shot.

I loved all the little tricks and tools of the diplomatic trade I was picking up. Watching the governor operate was an education in itself, whether he did all those things consciously or not. And I learned something I didn't even realize I was learning at the time: the vital role that private individuals can play in shaping the world.

When I asked the governor about some of this on the flight home, he waved me off immediately, as if I was trying to intellectualize things that just came naturally to him. But there was no denying this much: He—and therefore we—didn't represent a government in any of this. We had no official role in Sudan and no actual power. And yet there we had been, negotiating with all the major players, inserting ourselves in the middle of this, having an undeniable impact on one of the most daunting challenges in the world.

Personally, I found that inspiring, whatever anyone else might say.

6 BORDER RAID

I GOT BACK TO WASHINGTON ON A HIGH. THAT GOVERNOR RICHARD-
son was an amazing character, I decided, like no one I had ever met
before. Everything I had learned at Georgetown—and in my brief time
at the Clinton Global Initiative and the Abraham Center for Middle East
Peace—had suddenly come alive. This was no academic exercise. We had
flown into one of the most challenging corners of the planet, a place of
famine, genocide, and tribal warfare, and we had actually made a difference there. And I was a genuine part of the team...an esteemed expert on
the African Union, from what the governor had proclaimed. We'd created a space for the rebel parties to organize for negotiations. At least for
a minute. Brokering a temporary cease-fire, cooling a hot war. People who
might have been killed before wouldn't be killed now. I couldn't say how
many. No one could. The war might resume at any moment—and probably would. But none of this would have happened if we hadn't gone. And
we'd done it all as freelance diplomats, not working for any government
or wielding any actual authority. Just a small band of individuals trying to
do some good. As far as I knew, there wasn't even a job title for that. Who
knew it was even allowed?

So as I settled back into my life in DC, the thought naturally occurred
to me: *It's a big world out there. There must be stuff like that to do in other
places. Why stop with Sudan?* That's what happens when you are young
and idealistic and you haven't learned yet all the things that can't possibly
be done. You decide to do them.

That's when a name popped into my head.

Gilad Shalit.

I'd read about what happened to him. I didn't know all the details, just what had been written in newspapers back home in Israel. I knew what an awful situation it was.

A nineteen-year-old corporal in the Armored Corps of the Israel Defense Forces, Shalit was just a kid. He was on duty near the Kerem Shalom border crossing, which connects Israel with Egypt and the Gaza Strip. On June 25, 2006, armed Palestinian militants marched across the border through an underground tunnel, engaged in a bloody firefight with Israeli troops, grabbed the young soldier, and dragged him back to Gaza, where he was now being held at an undisclosed prison.

The cross-border raid caused an immediate uproar. It was the first time an Israeli soldier had been captured by Palestinians in twelve years. Using terms like *kidnapping* and *abduction,* Israeli leaders vowed to do whatever it took—*whatever!*—to get Corporal Shalit safely home. Quickly, human rights groups were also denouncing the capture, calling it contrary to international law. The Red Cross was not permitted to visit the Israeli, which was alarming right there. The groups holding him wouldn't even say where he was being held. He wasn't allowed to communicate at all with his family, which the Israelis termed a violation of his rights as a captured soldier under the Geneva convention.

For their part, Shalit's captors said they wouldn't even discuss the case until Israel released all female Palestinian prisoners and all those under the age of eighteen. The statement was issued by the Izz ad-Din al-Qassam Brigades, the Popular Resistance Committees (which included members of Fatah, Islamic Jihad, and Hamas), and a previously unknown group calling itself the Army of Islam.

Things escalated quickly. Three days later, Israeli forces rolled into the southern Gaza city of Khan Yunis in response to repeated cross-border rocket attacks. Israel demanded that Mahmoud Abbas, the president of the Palestinian National Authority, order Shalit's release at once. Four Israeli Air Force planes flew over Syrian President Bashar al-Assad's palace in Latakia, as Israel charged that Syria was a key sponsor of Hamas.

Prime Minister Ehud Olmert demanded Shalit's unconditional

release. "There will be no negotiations to release prisoners," he said. "The government of Israel will not give in to extortion by the Palestinian Authority and the Hamas government, which are headed by murderous terror organizations. The Palestinian Authority bears full responsibility for the welfare of Gilad Shalit and for returning him to Israel in good condition." On July 1, Israeli authorities threatened that the "sky will fall" if Shalit was harmed. In those first days after the kidnapping, more than 150 Palestinians were killed. The two sides were still trading threats and insults. And they seemed to have made no progress at all on getting the young soldier released. Despite Israel's best-in-the-region intelligence sources, no one in the government knew exactly where he was being held. The best anyone could say was that the young Israeli soldier was probably still alive.

I kept putting myself in young Gilad's shoes, imagining that I was he in captivity. How he must be feeling. All the uncertainty. The constant fear. What were his captors telling him? He knew from his own military briefings that *a kidnapped soldier is worse than a dead one.* He knew that if he was tossed in a car, the Israeli army would bomb the car if it was able to. He understood that his own military might be OK with him being dead. Was that the war he heard raging outside? As soldiers in southern Lebanon, we'd often thought about the nightmare of being captured, and it hadn't been just an abstract possibility. The risk had always been near. These thoughts about Gilad haunted me. Later, I would learn that the empathy I was feeling helped to direct my own future and the work I decided to take on. I just didn't know it at the time.

I had recently been to a talk at the Washington Institute for Near East Policy, and that got me thinking. One of the speakers was Rob Malley, the International Crisis Group director who had brought me to the Clinton Global Initiative when I was desperate for a job. I still felt grateful to Rob for that. We had become good friends since then. I admired the way his mind worked. When something happens, most policy analysts try to find the *What should we do next?* answer. Not Rob. Rob's mind goes right to *Where do we want to be in ten years?* From that vision, he walks back to his recommendation of next steps. It takes away the immediate emotional response to what are sometimes terrible events.

At the Washington Institute, Rob had spoken about Hamas, the fundamentalist Islamic group that held a majority in the Palestinian parliament. After hearing Rob's talk, I went home and wrote a memo to Governor Richardson, "Israel-Hamas Prisoner-Exchange Deal, Mediated by Governor Bill Richardson," laying out six steps that I believed could lead to the return of Shalit. They included gauging the feasibility of a deal, initiating contact with both sides, concluding negotiations, and implementing the exchange to bring the captured Israeli soldier home.

It was a very straightforward memo. *Here are the steps that need to be taken…Here are the risks…Here's how we mitigate those risks.*

After my experience in Sudan and with the attempted cease-fire in Lebanon, I realized I had contacts that could be useful here. Danny Abraham, my boss at the Center for Middle East Peace, was close to Prime Minister Olmert, who had voted against the cease-fire agreement in Lebanon. Rob Malley knew more about Hamas than almost anyone in the American foreign-policy world. Unlike most US government officials, he had excellent sources inside the group and was in regular contact with them. And now, with Governor Richardson, I had an American presidential candidate who was an experienced crisis diplomat and was willing to get involved, as long as his campaign schedule allowed.

Wow, I thought to myself, *these are three contacts I need to get something going on Gilad Shalit.*

My basic idea was that Governor Richardson—or Rob and I on his behalf—could mediate—more mediate than negotiate—between Israel and Hamas over the terms each side would accept to bring Gilad Shalit back home. Suggesting a framework. Running proposals back and forth. Being the link that these two hostile parties so obviously lacked. That was the simplistic thinking behind my memo and my ideas of what we could achieve.

But would Governor Richardson agree to help?

By then he had already announced his candidacy for president.

He was running hard for the Democratic nomination against Hillary Clinton, Barack Obama, John Edwards, Joe Biden, and a mob of other candidates. Instead of mailing or emailing my memo, I figured I might as well show up at one of the governor's campaign events in Washington.

After he finished speaking, I handed him a manila envelope with the memo inside and said, "Hey, take a look at this and let me know what you think."

My cell phone rang at six thirty the next morning.

"Hello?"

"Mickey, are you asleep?"

I recognized that gruff voice immediately. Of course I was sleeping!

"No, I'm up," I assured the governor, a reflexive lie on my part, as he barreled right ahead.

"Good. Get off your ass and get working on this. It is a good idea. This is the governor."

"OK," I mumbled, still shaking the sleep out of my head.

"Go do it," he said.

"What do you mean, 'Go do it'? I wrote it for *you* to do."

"Mickey," he answered, as if he were talking down to a six-year-old, "I'm running for president. I don't have time for this. You staff it. I'll back you up. You do it on my behalf."

And that's how our involvement in Gilad Shalit's case began.

Rob Malley was game. He thought the idea sounded promising. The governor was on board, though not out front initially. And I knew what I had to do next: reach out directly to the Shalit family. I didn't want to do anything without their blessing. I was already planning a trip to Israel to visit my parents and my brother. Gilad's family lived in Mitzpe Hila in the western hills of Galilee near the Lebanese border. I was able to reach his father, Noam Shalit, and awkwardly got myself invited to visit him at their home. At that point the Shalits still hadn't heard from Gilad. The father was racked with grief and worry, as any parent would be. And feeling frustrated too. His son's case was very much still in the news. It was still a topic of grave concern in Israel. But no one had any reason to feel hopeful about the young soldier's release.

I was feeling sick to my stomach as I drove to meet the Shalits. How was I supposed to start a conversation with them? How could I explain what I was suggesting? How could I build sufficient trust with them? Would Gilad's parents think I was a crazy kid? I was asking them to trust me with the life of their son. While Governor Richardson was an old hand at cases like this one, this was my first time. And I had no one with me. I was all alone.

When I stepped into the house, what I noticed first was the heavy silence, as if the entire household were frozen in time. The family's life was on hold. But in Noam's eyes, I saw something familiar. His voice I also felt as if I recognized. It took me a few minutes to place what was familiar. But it was the same emotion I had felt from Ruth and Amnon Shreibman when their son, my friend Nir, was killed in Lebanon. It was grief. It was sadness. It was helplessness. All rolled into one. Gilad Shalit was not dead, but the feeling of his family was almost the same. I was certain at that moment: I had to find a way to help.

As a first step, I told Gilad's father, we should try to get a letter from his son. That would at least provide some contact and prove that Gilad was alive.

I'm not sure how much faith Noam Shalit had in our efforts. But no one else had achieved much progress. I guess he just figured, *Why not give it a try?*

"Do what you can," he said to me. "We will cooperate however you need us to, but please make sure to coordinate with the authorities. We don't want anything to damage other efforts, if they even exist."

* * *

ONLY AFTER WE GOT STARTED DID I COME TO UNDERSTAND HOW important the Egyptians were. Israel and Hamas had no direct line of communication. Egypt was the main channel between them. As a result, if the Egyptians didn't like the direction of the negotiations, they could easily manipulate things. Gaza, which Hamas controls, sits between Israel and Egypt. Egypt has its own interests in Gaza and wanted those addressed as part of any prisoner deal, which meant that no deal between Israel and Hamas could be concluded unless the Egyptian government of Hosni Mubarak signed on.

Welcome to the Middle East, where nothing is ever quite as straightforward as it should be!

This wasn't going to be a bilateral conversation between the Israelis and the Palestinians. It would be *trilateral* from the start. Thankfully, as I learned through my contacts, the Egyptians seemed open to dealing with us...as long as they were convinced they'd get credit if we succeeded in hammering out a deal. They had political and security interests in Gaza, and they wanted to be part of any agreement. But credit was very important to them. And all of this was in the hands of Omar Suleiman, the legendary Egyptian general who now directed the Mukhabarat, the nation's intelligence service.

I reached out directly to him.

When I was in high school in Israel, I had learned to fear Omar Suleiman. He was, we were taught, a ruthless mastermind of terror and torture. Now here I was, trying to figure out how we could persuade him to help us make a hostage-release deal. We didn't meet in person initially, but over those first couple of weeks, he and I spoke several times on the phone...until one day, without warning, his cell phone went dead. I kept trying, but I couldn't get through. Had he changed his mind about cooperating with us? Had I offended him somehow? I hoped not. Finally I reached him through his office in Cairo. He was in New York. I was on a weekend retreat with my Georgetown friends in a remote part of the Shenandoah Valley of Virginia. I was just happy to get him on the phone again.

"General, I've been trying to reach you," I said at midnight from the parking lot of the water park at a Yogi Bear's Jellystone Park Camp-Resort, the only place I could get reception. "Your phone number doesn't work."

"Mickey," he said, "what do you want from me? I'm a spy. I change my number every two weeks."

Oh-kay...

That was the kind of guy Suleiman was. Blunt. Busy. And always on the move. I kept the governor in the loop, and he kept telling me we needed to meet the general in person. "The Egyptians are delaying us," the governor said. "You have to play hardball with him." I left the Georgetown retreat early and flew to Kennedy Airport in New York, where Rob Malley and I were ushered into a private side room in the Egypt Air first-class lounge. The general was sitting there, waiting for us.

He looked exactly as he did in photos. He was almost bald with a little tuft of hair around the sides, a sharp mustache, and a prominent birthmark on his face. A *falula*, as it's known in the slang of both Hebrew and Arabic. When I was a boy, visions of that falula had given me nightmares. Now I had to stop myself from staring at it. The three of us spoke for two hours, floating various scenarios, while the airline kept delaying the general's flight to Cairo. I don't believe the other passengers had any idea why.

"You know, Mickey," the Egyptian intel chief said to me at one point, "you need to understand. Violence is the only thing these people understand. You need to bring them to their knees. Then you will get what you want."

I knew he meant Hamas. But I looked at him quizzically, and I said, "When you say *these people*, do you mean Hamas, Palestinians, or Arabs?" Of course, that pissed him off. But in a funny way, I think he also liked my chutzpah. The point I was trying to make to him was, *Listen to what you are saying here.* "We're trying to make a deal," I told him at one point. "You're trying to break their knees. That's no way to get this done."

There was plenty of back and forth now that the Egyptians were on board. What there wasn't was any real progress with the leaders of Israel and Hamas, the ones who would eventually have to reach a deal. Mostly they were expressing ancient grievances, complaining about each other and talking in circles about the issue at hand, getting an Israeli soldier freed from Palestinian custody in the Gaza Strip. As our efforts continued, it became clear that Governor Richardson needed to travel to the Middle East and meet in person with the prime minister of Israel and the president of Egypt. If we were going to make any progress, we needed clear blessings from above. Rob would continue to handle Hamas.

To justify such a trip for the sitting governor of New Mexico, his staff arranged an economic-development mission to Israel and Egypt. The mission was real. We began in Israel with meetings at the Weizmann Institute of Science, with Foreign Minister Tzipi Livni, with opposition leader Benjamin Netanyahu, and with the prime minister, Ehud Olmert. In each session the governor dutifully pitched economic opportunities in Albuquerque, Santa Fe, Taos, and Las Cruces. He may have mentioned his campaign to become the US president. He slipped a note to the prime minister, asking for some one-on-one time after the economic-development conversation broke up. That's when he made the pitch he had really come for.

"Enough of the talking around this," he said sharply to Prime Minister Olmert. "I think we can get an agreement on Shalit. But I need you to tell me that you want this deal done and that you want me involved. I want you to appoint your chief negotiator to be the liaison with my team."

In fact, the prime minister wasn't that hard a sell at all. He agreed to all of it. The plight of Shalit was both a concern to the Israelis and an embarrassment to a country whose military had so much strength and pride. "Governor," he said, "we welcome any help you and your people can provide. We would very much like to get this resolved."

We flew overnight to Cairo and headed straight to the Heliopolis Palace to meet with Egyptian president Hosni Mubarak. Another person I'd seen on TV and never imagined I'd be meeting, much less negotiating a highly emotional prisoner exchange with. Though I was Israeli and he was Egyptian, I have to admit I was starstruck. It was just the four of us, President Mubarak, Governor Richardson, Rob, and I. The president was nearly eighty by then, but he was extremely sharp and thoroughly knowledgeable about the case. He was just as encouraging as Olmert had been, though he did largely defer to his intelligence chief. "Go see Omar Suleiman," he said. "He knows everything."

So that's what we did. The three of us, the governor, Rob, and I, piled into a van for the short ride from the Heliopolis Palace to Mukhabarat headquarters. Now the governor seemed to be in a jovial mood.

"Where to?" he asked me.

"You know where we're going, Guv. We're going to meet Omar Suleiman."

"I know, I know," he said. "But *where* is the meeting?"

"At his office in Cairo."

"But *where* exactly? Tell me."

What was he getting at? Was this a game? I couldn't tell.

"Guv," I said, playing along, "we'll know we are there when you hear the yelling and the screaming from the dungeons of the people who are being tortured by him."

The governor lit up at that. "Oh, that's good," he said. "That's good."

When Guv and I walked into Suleiman's large office, he wasn't alone. He had at least ten aides there. And to me, every last one of them looked just like him. Most of them had his mustache. At least they didn't all have his prominent birthmark.

He had set up a long conference table with a pen, a notepad, and a water bottle at every seat. His guys filled the seats on one side of the table. It was just the three of us on our side until the governor quickly called Marcus, the New Mexico state trooper who was handling security, to fill another seat.

"Reinforcements," he whispered under his breath.

Suleiman began with a long, formal monologue, packed with history and grievances, going back almost to the days of the pharaohs. His main point seemed to be that Egypt had to be involved in everything, and there was no way we could possibly make a deal anytime soon.

It was not the message any of us wanted to hear.

We weren't expecting everything to be settled in a day. But we were hoping to get the space we needed to begin productive talks. That didn't seem like too much to hope for...until, suddenly, it did.

I looked at the governor. The governor looked at me. I could see the wheels spinning in his head. He didn't like how this was going any more than I did. He interrupted Suleiman in midsentence.

"General, General," he said. "I'm going to let you get back to your speech. But I have to tell you, when I was driving over here, I asked Mickey, 'Where are we going? Where is the meeting?' He said, 'You'll know we're there because you'll see the dungeons and hear the screams of the people who are being tortured.' But your office is pretty. You have a beautiful office over here."

I couldn't believe it. The governor was throwing me under the bus. Was he trying to get me killed? I could only imagine how the Egyptian intelligence director would look at me after that...and what he might be thinking.

I could see Suleiman's head turn slowly in my direction. I thought, *Shit, I'm gonna end up in his dungeon now.*

It was probably just a couple of seconds before he responded, but to me it felt like an hour or a week. Suddenly he cracked up laughing. And as soon as he started laughing, so did all his twins in the room.

And then the governor brought everyone back to why we were there: "General," he said, "why don't I send my team out? You send your team out. You and I, we need to talk." All of us left, and in the next few minutes, Governor Richardson and General Suleiman reached some understanding. That sudden break in the action had turned everything around.

We left that meeting with the approval of the Egyptians to go ahead and try to mediate directly between Israel and Hamas. Now all we had to do was bring these sworn, bitter enemies together on one of the most emotionally fraught topics of the past generation in the Middle East.

How hard could that be?

* * *

EARLY ON, THE LEADERS OF HAMAS NAMED A PRICE.

In return for Gilad Shalit, they said, *Israel needs to release eleven hundred Palestinian prisoners, plus, plus.* The *plus* and the *plus* were actually three things: the female and teenage Palestinian prisoners who'd been mentioned right after Shalit was taken, as well as a couple of dozen Hamas parliamentarians imprisoned by Israel a few months earlier.

In our role as independent mediators, it wasn't our job to declare the demand reasonable or unreasonable. We just needed to get the two sides engaged. The first step was to deliver the Hamas proposal to the Israelis.

The Israelis didn't respond immediately. It took a couple of months. Every day of delay, I knew, was excruciating for the Shalits. Finally the Israelis said, *We'll give them twenty prisoners.* It was a long way from 1,100, but it was a start.

We took the Israeli offer to Hamas. And Hamas responded, *OK, eleven hundred, plus, plus.* Hamas hadn't budged at all.

We brought that back to the Israelis, who spent some more time thinking and then responded: *All right, we'll give them fifty.* A pattern had now been set.

We kept carrying proposals back and forth. Israeli officials kept inching up with their number. Hamas kept repeating, *Eleven hundred, plus, plus.*

I could feel the frustration rising. And after a while, the Israelis threw up their hands.

Hamas isn't negotiating, they complained to us. *Nothing is being achieved.* And Hamas kept repeating, *Eleven hundred, plus, plus.* Their method of negotiation was not *We will meet you in the middle.* Their approach was *We will give you the time you need in order to come to our conclusion.* And that's exactly how things proceeded. Yes, the two sides were getting closer, ever so slowly and ever so slightly. But at this pace, a deal could take decades to achieve. We'd all be dead by then. Rob and I began looking for a way to speed things up.

It seemed to us that, if the price was going to be the price, we needed to find a way to structure the deal differently, maybe separating the women, the teenagers, and the parliamentarians from the rest of it. "If the price is going to be eleven hundred, plus, plus," Rob said, "what if we're able to convince the Israelis to do the plus, plus outside this deal?"

I liked the sound of that. They could release the women and children and Hamas parliamentarians, but only to the more moderate wing of the Palestinian Authority, headed by Mahmoud Abbas. "The Israelis want to empower him," I said.

If this worked and we could remove the plus, plus from the equation, the Israelis could feel progress was being made. Hamas wouldn't add new demands. We'd just narrow the deal and achieve the same things. That was the idea, anyway.

We counted on Rob to float the idea with Hamas. It seemed unwise for me, an ex-Israeli army officer, to travel to Syria or somewhere similar for in-person meetings, especially with an Israeli soldier still in enemy hands. We didn't think we should double the number of hostages they held. So Rob handled that part, meeting with Hamas leaders in Syria and elsewhere.

When Rob traveled to Syria to meet Hamas's chief, Khaled Mashal, the trip was always mired in security measures. Hamas wanted to make sure even Rob did not know where he was taken. One such visit was in the summer of 2008. While at Mashal's office, Rob received a text from his son's summer camp in Canada. Fearing an emergency, Rob asked Mashal if he could use his office phone to call the camp to make sure his son was OK. He was. But we couldn't stop laughing thinking of American and Israeli intelligence analysts trying to make sense of a sudden call about medicine from Khaled Mashal's Hamas office in Syria to a summer camp in Canada.

Rob and I did have a few useful sessions in Vienna and Geneva, trying to push the deal along.

We had one especially tense meeting with the Israelis.

"You're not doing a good job," Ofer Dekel, Prime Minister Olmert's envoy, thundered at me. "You can't bend Hamas on anything. Where's the compromise?"

I didn't disagree. I too was frustrated. But I could read the reality.

"We hear you," I said. "You can yell as much as you want to. But if you want to know what is possible, this is what is possible. Are you up for getting there or not?"

Clearly we needed a break. The Israeli officials stood up at the table. "You and Rob, you can stay and talk," Dekel told us as he and his team headed to the door. "You can call Hamas if you want. We'll take a walk. We'll be back."

Then I looked at a pair of sunglasses they'd left on the table, and a thought occurred to me: *Are they still listening to us?* I gave Rob a *shhhh* sign. "Not here," I whispered. We found another spot to talk.

Eventually we got an answer to our proposal. The two sides agreed with our idea of separating the plus, plus into a side deal. For their part, the Israelis kept bringing their number up. Not quickly. But still. To seventy-five. Then to one hundred. Then to two hundred.

As predicted, Hamas remained at 1,100.

We had other small achievements along the way.

We arranged an exchange of letters—"terms of reference"—between Prime Minister Olmert's envoy and Khaled Mashal, the head of Hamas. Believe me, those two were not regular pen pals. As slow progress continued, everyone stuck with the framework of the divided deal, which was a huge achievement right there. There were protracted discussions about who should count among the 1,100 Palestinian prisoners to be released—what crimes, which prisoners, who should decide, and anything else that could be debated.

Since the two sides refused to speak with each other directly, everything took far longer than it needed to. Interestingly, one of those released prisoners, Yahya Sinwar, would go on to head Hamas in Gaza.

And then came the 2008 election for president in the United States. When Barack Obama won, he nominated Governor Richardson as his secretary of commerce. At that point, the governor called me with an urgent message: "Mickey, we have to bow out from this. We can't be negotiating between Israel and Hamas, not if I am going into the cabinet. We can't do it."

Dealing with Hamas was still a huge taboo in Washington, even if the goal was getting the group to release an Israeli prisoner.

I hated the message, but I suspected the governor was right.

Rob and I thought about pressing on without him, and with Guv's blessing, we did...for two more months. We knew our time and our influence were limited. Violent conflict flared again between Israel and Hamas in Gaza. We decided to try to hold "proximity talks" in Egypt, in which a delegation from each side would stay on a separate floor of the same hotel and Rob and I would run between them with offers and counteroffers. Hamas and Israel wouldn't engage directly. But that way we could accelerate the negotiations.

We managed, with much difficulty, to get both sides to agree to the talks. But Rob and I confronted a major dilemma. In our private conversations with Hamas and Israel, we saw they were still nowhere near an agreement on the minimal requirements for a deal. We had two options. We could use "constructive ambiguity" in our language to make the gaps less obvious. That would get us to the talks in Cairo. Or we could be honest with everyone and tell both sides that with their current positions, there was simply no formula for an agreement. Prime Minister Olmert was clearly not willing to trade 1,100 prisoners for Shalit, and Hamas was still adamantly refusing to lower its long-standing demand.

Our objective was to get a deal. Proximity talks were just a tool, not an end. What would be the point of getting the sides to Cairo if the talks were certain to blow up? And if the talks blew up, and each side blamed the other, how much more violence would ensue in Gaza? Wouldn't that be on us? So at the end of December 2008, after eighteen months of painstaking effort, Rob and I decided to send a clear and honest letter to both sides.

We mediators, we said, had come as far as we were able. It was up to the two sides now. We still hoped we could help them reach a deal in the near future, even if it was without us. But the next steps would have to come from them.

As things unfolded, the governor was never confirmed as secretary of commerce. Washington politics interceded, and not for the first time. But just as we hoped, the negotiations continued in the Middle East. Not quickly, but they did press on. In the end the deal was made almost exactly as we had structured it. It would just take another three years. The Israelis would release 1,100 Palestinian prisoners. The women, teens, and parliamentarians would be dealt with separately. The Egyptians would get their credit. And the Shalits would get Gilad home, safe and free at last.

7   NORTHERN EXPOSURE

"Oh, quit feeling sorry for yourself."

That's always good advice, and it's never fun to hear. But I definitely needed to hear it this time.

Early January 2009. I had just spent a dreary week in full sulking mode, pretty sure that I'd been robbed of my future and that my promising career had been sidetracked before it had even begun. In the thirty-one days between Governor Richardson's nomination as Barack Obama's secretary of commerce and the governor's decision to withdraw, he and I had been mapping out a great adventure. He'd asked me to go with him to Commerce and manage a large part of the department's international portfolio, a sprawling responsibility with tentacles everywhere. Not a bad entry-level position for someone who had assumed he'd never work in government.

I was gearing up. I was making plans. I was totally psyched about the unexpected opportunity. Then, *bang*—just like that, it was gone. An old pay-for-play investigation was dragged back into the news and tied to Richardson. Nothing ever came of it or ever would. But the governor decided he didn't want the controversy to be a damaging distraction for his friend, the incoming president.

So he bailed.

The news hit me hard. I'd just run into Corner Bakery that Sunday afternoon. When I got back to the car, I must have had eighty texts, calls, and emails on my phone. Richardson was out, which meant, of course, that Bergman was out too.

A gut punch...for both of us.

But when the governor and I finally got to speak, he sounded totally at ease as he admonished me for being so self-focused. "This is just politics," he said, as if this sort of thing happened to him every week or two. "Sometimes we win, sometimes we lose. You need a thick skin. There's nothing in that investigation, but I had to withdraw. It was becoming an issue for Obama. So get over yourself. We have work to do."

That was Richardson. He was the one who'd lost the cabinet post, but *he* was picking *me* up off the floor. And I wasn't exactly on the street. I still had a job, working for Danny Abraham at the Center for Middle East Peace. I'd also picked up a small contract with the Aspen Institute, setting up private-public partnerships in Palestine, and a second side gig with the Clinton Global Initiative. And I would also be volunteering on projects with the governor, who had two years left in office but was constantly getting calls about thorny issues overseas. An American held hostage in some far-off country. A government needing advice on how to stage a democratic election. A tense ethnic conflict about to erupt into civil war. From his time as UN ambassador and some of the other crises he'd managed, he'd developed a reputation for being the diplomatic equivalent of an urban firefighter, rushing into international hot spots and trying to cool things down. He still had his day job. He'd be serving the people of New Mexico until the start of 2011. But he also hated saying no when a call for help came in and the cause struck him as important. I felt the same way when he called me from time to time and asked if I could pitch in.

Sure.

While still governor, he led a private mission to North Korea and hammered out a deal that allowed international inspectors to enter the controversial Nyongbyon nuclear facility and send fuel rods to an outside country for enrichment. Both were historic firsts. The North Koreans also agreed to send the remains of some Korean War soldiers back to the United States. Soon after leaving office, Richardson was busier than ever. He was appointed as a special envoy for the Organization of American States. He joined the boards of the World Resources Institute, the National Council for Science and the Environment, and Refugees

International. Clearly this was not a man who wanted to sit still. He joined the Inter-American Dialogue, a Western Hemisphere think tank. And—this is the big one—he established the Richardson Center for Global Engagement, a nonprofit foundation that would become a central focus of his life…and mine. I helped with much of this and was happy to be involved.

I certainly believed in the Richardson Center's primary aims: responding to international crises, working to free the wrongfully imprisoned, and helping to spread democracy around the world. It was an ambitious agenda. Then again, no one ever accused Bill Richardson (or me) of thinking small. All along, I was still doing projects for the Clinton Global Initiative, the Aspen Institute, and the Abraham Center for Middle East Peace. But I did notice I was being pulled deeper and deeper into the high-stakes world of Bill Richardson.

This would only get more interesting.

* * *

KENNETH BAE WAS A KOREAN AMERICAN MISSIONARY HELL-BENT ON spreading evangelical Christianity in North Korea, where communism is really the only faith allowed.

Bae, who grew up in Northern California, was arrested in the North Korean capital of Pyongyang in late 2012 for "hostile acts against the republic." The authorities said he'd been preaching against the regime from pulpits in the US and South Korea even before he decided to try saving souls in the isolated communist country. "I knew that Jesus wanted me to be a 'channel' to the North," Bae was quoted as telling a Korean congregation in St. Louis. "This year, I'm working at taking several short-term missionary teams into North Korea."

The government of Kim Jong-un didn't like the sound of any of that. In the supreme leader's view, the Christian missionary was up to something more than preaching. He was accused in a North Korean court of leading a Christian coup d'état, intent on overthrowing the entire North Korean government.

Since Washington had only limited diplomatic relations with Pyongyang, there wasn't all that much the US government was prepared to do, other than denounce Bae's imprisonment and call for his release. Kenneth's son, Jonathan Bae, and Kenneth's sister, Terri Chung, contacted Governor Richardson right away. We jumped in immediately. "We reached out to our official contacts in North Korea and further inquired and pressured them on progress with Kenneth's proceedings," I wrote to Terri. In the second week of January, the governor asked to meet with Bae in prison and to deliver a letter from the missionary's son to the North Korean government.

Both requests were ignored.

That April, Bae was sentenced to fifteen years of hard labor at a high-security prison farm. Things had escalated quickly. That's when the governor asked me to join him on a trip to North Korea. Clearly there was no way to make progress on Bae's case from thousands of miles away. We had to go there. And we wouldn't be traveling alone. Coming along on the trip was Eric Schmidt, who'd just gone from CEO to executive chairman of Google.

This was a plus all around.

Schmidt, whose company played such a crucial role in organizing the internet for billions of users, was eager to get a look inside one of the world's last closed-off nations. North Korean officials had forbidden their citizens to use his ubiquitous search engine. But they were still fascinated by the technology Schmidt had unleashed on the world, almost as much as they were resistant to it. They very much wanted to meet the man behind the internet's most popular search engine. Our hope was that we could leverage all that and somehow use it to win Kenneth Bae's early release.

And how exactly would we do that? It would be my job to sort that out.

The way I saw it, the Google chairman could be our prisoner-release Trojan horse, getting us into North Korea and making the nation's leaders excited about engaging with us. Once we were there, we could get around to our first agenda, trying to speed the release of the American missionary. That was our plan, anyway.

"It's worth a try," the governor and I agreed.

You can't just buy a few airline tickets and take a group to North Korea. Not if you're an American. Arranging a trip like that requires painstaking planning and about ten levels of permission. Mainly it requires patience. I got busy arranging everything. Though it would take a full eight months to get everything in order, everyone would assure me that was fast, given what we were trying to achieve. Aiding us in all this was a leading Asia expert and think-tank researcher named Tony Namkung. Tony had forty-five years of experience in various aspects of US-Asian relations, having worked in everything from academics to public policy to business and nonprofit consulting. He had deep contacts and a long history with key North Korean officials. We were fortunate to have him on our team.

Officials in the US State Department seemed to hate the idea of an independent mission like ours, and that was part of what dragged things out. Secretary of State Hillary Clinton called the governor in early December and asked him to put the trip on hold, saying our visit to the north could complicate elections in South Korea, which were being held on December 19. It was not clear exactly how. But this was an ask from an old friend, and the governor reluctantly agreed.

"OK," he told the secretary. "We'll put it off a month. But don't ask again, unless there is a very good reason."

But you guessed it: as the second week of January 2013 grew near, we received another call from the State Department. This time it was Wendy Sherman, the under secretary for political affairs. She asked us to postpone again.

"Why?" the governor wanted to know.

Wendy didn't offer much of a reason. South Korean elections were over by then, and Kenneth Bae was still behind razor ribbon. "You just don't want us to go because you don't want us to go," the governor told her. "We're going."

The under secretary didn't seem to appreciate the governor's insistence, and she found a public way to express her displeasure after the phone call. She told the media that our independent mission on behalf of the Bae family was ill advised, adding that the State Department didn't "think the timing of this is particularly helpful." She still didn't say exactly why.

Was that how she wanted to play it? The governor delivered his own message through the media. "They shouldn't be that nervous," he said on CBS *This Morning*. "I've been dealing with North Korea for fifteen years. I've brought back American servicemen. I've brought back American hostages, I've negotiated for the remains of our soldiers from the Korean War. Food aid. I know the North Koreans." In other words, *What's the problem?* "It's a private mission. We're not representing the State Department."

As I was learning, it's good to be independent. True, we didn't have the gravity and the heft of the United States government behind us. At the same time, we didn't have the handcuffs either. If the US government couldn't help Kenneth Bae, maybe we could—and, with Eric Schmidt along, also leave at least a tiny crack in North Korea's closed society. It all seemed possible as we changed planes in Beijing.

There was a cartoon in one of the Chinese newspapers. It was a drawing of the North Korean leader, Kim Jong-un. He was asking one of his aides: "Who is this Eric Schmidt person who is coming and visiting us?"

The aide shrugged and replied, "If only there were a way to look him up online…"

I thought that was funny. As no one knew better than the Google chairman, there was no way to search for what might happen next.

* * *

THE VISIT TO NORTH KOREA, WHEN IT FINALLY HAPPENED, WAS AN eye opener for all of us—and, I suspect, for the North Koreans too.

It was my first time in the country, but Pyongyang was just as gray and orderly as I'd seen in photographs. Everywhere we went in the ancient riverside capital of three and a half million residents, people were unfailingly polite. Despite not seeing many Westerners on the streets, the local people appeared thoroughly unfazed by our presence. Later I would come to understand that in a society so focused on productivity, being distracted is a sign of weakness. We were a distraction they wanted to avoid. As for Eric Schmidt, he struck me as a man of great curiosity, and he seemed to love engaging with the North Korean leaders, all of whom seemed in awe of him. It was strange: they wouldn't permit his search engine in their country, but they obviously respected the tech-savvy American capitalist who led the company that had created it. He was "Mr. Google" to them.

We visited labs and universities. We had several large, formal dinners. Almost all of it was done through Korean-government translators, who I had to assume were taking notes on everything we said in English while omitting any comments in Korean we weren't meant to hear. The topics ranged from telecommunications to data security to the internet. Our hosts showed us the carefully controlled *intranet* search engine that North Korean students were allowed to use, which sifted through a relative handful of preapproved PDFs. No wide-open internet for them. There was a whole department dedicated to vetting those pages.

We met with the head of the Korean Committee of Space Technology, North Korea's NASA, who expressed great pride over a recent satellite launch. "Why are you looking at satellites?" the Google chairman asked the agency chief.

"We need telecommunications," the Korean space boss said.

Eric shot him a quizzical look. He knew all about the closed system the North Koreans were using—*Kwangmyong*. "Satellites for telecommunications?" he asked. "The future is fiber optics. Why don't you lay fiber optics across the country? I know you want *intranet* and not internet. But you still want productivity. You have to assume that some of your best talent is outside Pyongyang. If you're able to lay fiber optics, that will give you better access to the talent and give them better access to the tools they need."

The Koreans looked intrigued.

As we made our way around the capital, we stepped into a cell-phone store that rented phones to visiting foreigners. Eric picked up one model and began poking at it. "Of course, the data is turned off," he said.

After another minute of poking, he looked up and told us, "I just turned the data on. I'm connected to the internet now." He lowered his voice so our minders wouldn't hear. "You don't think the local kids already know how to break this? Come on, it's intuitive."

Being around Eric Schmidt was a constant learning experience. But I also had something to share. "There are three main pillars to the way North Koreans see the world," I said to Eric, the governor, and the rest of our group at the end of our third day in Pyongyang. We were sitting in the official guesthouse, where we were being hosted.

"What are those?" Eric asked me.

I laid out my three. "First," I said, "I think the North Koreans believe that the world is out to get them. And they have the historic evidence to prove it. They really believe that when Americans discuss North Korea, we discuss how to invade Pyongyang. And they aren't bluffing. It's a genuine belief that is very difficult to dismiss. Even when we tell them that Americans don't really spend time thinking about North Korea, the North Koreans believe we are just telling them that so they will lower their guard, and then we will invade them."

Eric listened intently as I pressed on.

"Second," I said, "the North Koreans see themselves as a small country surrounded by enemies: Japan, South Korea, with the US hovering over them. They don't even fully trust the Chinese or the Russians. That creates a sense of constant siege. And third…"

This was the most interesting part, I thought, and the most important too. "If my first two pillars are correct," I said, "I have to believe that the North Koreans genuinely believe that the *only* way for them to survive as the state they currently are…is to have an asymmetric threat toward the rest of the world—hence their nuclear program."

"That's quite a lot," Eric responded. "What have you learned from that?"

"Well, two main lessons," I answered. "First, if I am correct, then our expectation of a complete nuclear disarmament by the North Koreans is unrealistic and unreasonable. We can aim for freezing of further development, tests, and proliferation. But there is simply no way to get the North Koreans to give up their existing stockpile, at least not in the near or medium term. Insisting on that as a precondition to engagement is miscalculating how the North Koreans see the world. And second"—here I couldn't help but smile—"I was trying to figure out why it is so easy for me to empathize with our North Korean hosts. I realized that I was born and raised in Israel, where I have three main pillars to the way I grew up seeing the world: First, the world is out to get us, or as it is often referred to in Israel, *Everyone is an antisemite*, and we have the historic evidence to prove it. Second, Israel is a tiny country surrounded by enemies. And third, the only way for Israel to survive as a Jewish democracy is to have an asymmetric threat over our neighbors. Even those who've made peace with Israel did it only because they feared Israel's military."

I knew that was a lot to take in. I also knew that those Israeli pillars I had just described were objectively not true. After all, I had engaged deeply with colleagues and friends from the Arab world. But I also knew how powerful that narrative had been for me growing up and how powerful it still is with Israel.

Eric grasped exactly what I was saying, and he offered a piece of practical advice. "Now, that's an op-ed I do *not* think you should publish," he said to me. He was the one smiling now.

"I'm not comparing the Israelis to the North Koreans," I said half-defensively, "but the national emotional experiences have similarities."

I knew Eric was teasing me, but I also felt that I needed to explain it to myself. Empathy is a tricky thing.

* * *

I HAD ALWAYS ASSUMED I WOULD BE A FATHER...ONE DAY. ROBIN AND I both loved kids. But while we got married young, it took us time to become parents. Robin was always set on adoption. She was adopted herself. It took me some time to love the idea. When I was growing up, adoption was not a familiar concept to me. I am so happy Robin insisted!

We put in our application in November 2009, after we'd been married for seven years. The process took another four years. Before approving a family for adoption, the agency went through an intricate assessment protocol that included interviews, home visits, and a deep dive into the medical and personal histories of the potential parents. And Robin's mental-health challenges made our home study more intense than usual. We understood all that. But since adoption was our first choice, not something we'd come to as a last resort after failing to get pregnant, we didn't harbor the impatience and frustrations that some prospective parents feel. We expected and accepted that the process might take longer than usual. Then, suddenly, the day arrived.

It was a Friday in November 2013. I had just returned from a mission to Colombia, and Robin was driving to New York for a few days when she got a call from the adoption agency. "A baby girl was born in Baltimore ten days ago," the woman from the agency said. "She is in interim care, and the mother has chosen you as adoptive parents. You have twenty-four hours to decide. If you accept, you will need to pick her up on Monday."

Wow!

Robin called me from the road. Though we'd been working toward this for four years, it still felt like a shock to me. Everything was happening so quickly! One day to decide! Three days to pick up our little girl! "Our. Little. Girl." It felt so strange, saying those three words together. But we knew we'd say yes. We already felt as if she was part of our family.

We had to get ready. Physically and mentally. I panicked much more than Robin did. Being an instant father was a lot to wrap my head around so quickly, even if I had taken four years to get here. As I was flipping out, Robin was shopping for baby formula and a car seat and working through a thousand other details.

It was a real role reversal—and just in time.

Because of Maryland law, we couldn't take our baby home until she was three weeks old. The wait was to give the biological parents time to change their minds. So even though we lived just across the river in Virginia, we had to stay with our newborn daughter at a friend's house in Maryland. At first we thought about naming her Shai or Adi, after our grandmothers. But after meeting her and absorbing her frenetic energy, we went with Noa, a Hebrew name that comes from the same root as the word for movement.

Until I held Noa for the first time, I think I had held one baby in my arms: Tom, my brother's firstborn. There was no forgetting this! Robin and I were both overwhelmed with excitement and happiness. Over the previous four years, Robin had said to me more than once, "The universe is waiting for us to get the right baby. When that baby comes, it will be the right time and the right baby."

It was one of the truest things Robin ever said.

* * *

WE NEVER GOT TO MEET WITH KENNETH BAE IN NORTH KOREA. That was a disappointment. We asked. We asked again. Always politely. It didn't happen. And we didn't get to meet with Kim Jong-un. We had requested an audience with the supreme leader even before we left home. We were told it might happen. But after Wendy Sherman labeled our trip "ill-advised," we got an updated message from the office of incoming foreign minister Ri Su-yong: "The leader was looking forward to the meeting. But he saw the comment by the Department of State, and he doesn't want to upset the US government. So he is not going to meet."

A missed opportunity for us and for Kenneth Bae.

Still, we did achieve a couple of steps forward—in part, I have to admit, because of the goodwill generated by Eric Schmidt. Before we left, the billionaire tech exec made a humanitarian contribution to the nation, ten metric tons of corn to a North Korean orphanage. We were able to impress on North Korean officials how eager we were to speed the American missionary's release, suggesting they might like to think of his early release as their own goodwill gesture. We got no promise about that. But at least we planted the idea. And we figured out something that would end up being vital to our efforts.

Wheelchairs.

The North Koreans needed wheelchairs. Wheelchairs for children especially.

It may sound basic. But with their shaky manufacturing sector, their lack of hard currency, and their heavy emphasis on military spending, they hadn't been able to get enough wheelchairs to meet the needs of their people. The topic was just something that came up in conversation with our North Korean hosts. But we noted it, and I'm glad we did. Wheelchairs weren't the only thing the North Koreans needed. Not by a long shot. But wheelchairs were definitely high on their list.

How much could wheelchairs cost? They couldn't be *that* expensive. I knew we'd have to sort that out after we all got home.

On our way back to Beijing, we flew Air Koryo, the North Korean national airline, where I learned that flight attendant is a highly sought-after job in North Korea. Air Koryo flight attendants got the unique opportunity of overnighting in Beijing and other Asian capitals. As for us, our seats on the Russian-made aircraft were in first class. And that, right there, felt to me like an interesting detail. I thought communist North Korea was supposed to be a classless society. Not on Air Koryo it wasn't. Our seats were especially roomy, and the service from the cheerful flight attendants was impeccable.

* * *

"Find a Christian charity that focuses on accessibility."

Shortly after we got back home, I could almost see the wheels spinning in the governor's head.

"Tell them we'll raise the money. We'll deliver the wheelchairs. We'll facilitate all of it. But we need them to be the ones to sponsor the gift. That will give us leverage with the North Koreans."

With the help of Michelle Welby, a trusted advisor to Governor

Richardson who'd traveled to North Korea on his behalf in 2014, we found an excellent group called Joni and Friends. The charity had been founded and was led by Joni Eareckson Tada, who suffered a diving accident when she was seventeen that left her without normal use of her arms or legs. The group's International Disability Center had been providing wheelchairs around the world since the 1990s. They were a perfect fit, and they loved the idea of donating wheelchairs to disabled children in North Korea. But getting it done was going to be ridiculously complicated. I could see that already. We had to special-order the chairs in China and then get special permission to ship them to North Korea. More patience. More time. Thankfully, the State Department didn't seem too inclined to stand in our way. As I made slow progress on all that, another force was bouncing around in the background. That force was Dennis Rodman.

The tattooed, rainbow-haired, thoroughly outspoken former NBA star had struck up a personal connection with Kim Jong-un. It turned out that the North Korean supreme leader was a huge fan of the 1990s Michael Jordan/Scottie Pippin Chicago Bulls, one of Rodman's teams. And that had given the ex-player and reality-TV star access that no other American had. He was back and forth to Pyongyang all year.

In February 2013, Rodman met with Kim, his new "friend for life," and staged a basketball exhibition. In May, as I was just starting to round up the wheelchairs, Rodman agreed to send a tweet asking Kim to release Kenneth Bae, which we very much appreciated, even though it didn't produce an immediate result. Rodman was back in Pyongyang in September to meet with Kim and then again in December. Watching all the back-and-forth, I couldn't help but marvel: *You know, Rodman is a little different, but so is Kim, and so is North Korea.* This, I decided, was one of those cases where we had to welcome whatever allies we could find. Eric Schmidt had proven unexpectedly valuable. Maybe Dennis Rodman would prove valuable too. The unique NBAer might be a fringe character, but hey…fringe isn't necessarily a bad thing. And the usual approaches weren't exactly delivering instant results.

Knowing that Dennis wanted to stage a large-scale basketball tournament in North Korea, we met with his people late in the year and made a suggestion: "The next time he meets with Kim, what if he says to him, *Can you do me a solid? Give me Kenneth Bae, and let me take him home. Because if I come back with Kenneth Bae, I'm a hero in America, and all these people who criticize me for coming to see you, screw them!*"

Dennis's people loved the idea. He was working with Vice Media at the time. Vice loved the idea. We broached it with the North Koreans. They too were encouraging...with a couple of tweaks. "Here's how it has to go," the North Korean representative said. "We'll send an invitation to the US government, asking them to send a US official to visit us. The US government wants to engage. They can come and engage. The release of Kenneth Bae will be one of the things they ask for. We won't give an answer. But when Dennis Rodman comes and asks for Bae, we will release him to Dennis Rodman. We are open to this, but it has to be done in a package like that."

"Sounds good to us" was the message I sent back. It was crazy. Almost as crazy as the always-entertaining former basketball pro. But it just might work.

The North Koreans sent an invitation to the Obama White House. The invitation landed on the desk of White House National Security Advisor Susan Rice. Coordinating with the State Department, the White House said it would send someone. And that's when it became suddenly clear that someone in the White House or the State Department didn't fully grasp the win/win proposal. The American official they chose was a hard-line human rights activist and special representative of the State Department, Sung Kim. Someone the North Koreans absolutely detested. There was no way the North Koreans would welcome him to Pyongyang.

The North Koreans were furious when they heard the name.

"We do what you tell us to do, and the US government slaps us in the face," a highly perturbed official said to me on the phone. "The deal is off. Forget it. Kenneth Bae can stay in prison for the rest of his term."

Very frustrating.

We circled back to Dennis's people to let them know the deal was off. "Actually, we don't have access to Dennis," I was told.

"Excuse me?"

"He's in rehab."

"Oh, great."

At least we didn't have to worry about him turning up in North Korea while the Kim government was angry at us and at Obama and probably at Kenneth Bae as well. Or so we thought. Dennis being Dennis, he had already skipped out of rehab and flown to North Korea without the benefit of knowing that the deal was off. He did exactly what he was supposed to do—if the deal had not been trashed. He went there. He played basketball. He asked Kim Jong-un to do him a solid and give him Kenneth Bae.

"I was going to give him to you," the leader said. "But the White House screwed us over and tried to send a human rights activist to embarrass us."

No Kenneth Bae.

On his way home, Dennis stopped in Beijing, just as we had, where he held a press conference in the airport.

"What about Kenneth Bae?" one of the reporters asked him.

"Why don't you ask Obama, the *asshole*," Dennis sneered.

That was the headline back home, and it made the White House even more suspicious of independent emissaries in North Korea. You can question Dennis's style. His words certainly weren't the best way to express the frustration all of us felt. But he wasn't totally wrong either. He hadn't blown it. The Obama administration had.

All I can say is that I was glad we had connected with Joni and Friends. With the media focused on Dennis Rodman and whatever feud he was having with Barack Obama, we were diligently working with the Christian disability group on those made-in-China wheelchairs. Finally, after numerous delays, the shiny new chairs were set to roll off a Chinese cargo ship into North Korea. And that's when the long-awaited moment of leverage arrived at last.

The kind of leverage the governor had imagined at the start.

By then the North Koreans had also detained Jeffrey Fowle, an American tourist who was arrested for purposely leaving a Bible in the restroom of a foreign sailors' club in Chongjin, the country's third-largest city. His family never contacted us, so we were focused on Bae.

I sat at a restaurant in New York City with Jang Il-hun, the North Korean ambassador to the United Nations, and his counselor, Kwon Jong Gun. "Mr. Ambassador," I said, "we're pleased to know that the wheelchairs are finally on the way from China. But this is really tough. The wheelchairs were donated by a Christian organization, and people keep asking Governor Richardson, 'How come the Koreans are OK receiving those donations from a Christian organization while they're holding Kenneth Bae in prison for spreading Christianity in North Korea?' The governor doesn't know what to say."

The ambassador did not answer directly. He just nodded as if he was considering my question but wasn't prepared to respond. He had to send it up the government chain. So I can't say exactly how everything happened, who spoke to whom, who gave what permission, how the decision was finally made. But I know this much: from that meal on, the wheels, literally and figuratively, started spinning. On October 21, 2014, Jeffrey Fowle was returned to his family in Ohio. Then, on November 8, after some dialogue between the two governments, Kenneth Bae was released from the North Korean prison farm and returned to his family on the West Coast.

With 735 days' captivity, he had been held prisoner in North Korea for longer than any American since the Korean War.

When Kenneth Bae came home, there were two other American prisoners we weren't officially working with but whose cases we'd been trying to push along. Matthew Todd Miller and Merrill Newman were released as well.

8 POSTER BOY

"This is pretty gruesome," I warned Rick Downes, the president of the Coalition of Families of Korean & Cold War POW/MIAs.

Rick was three years old when his father, US Air Force Lieutenant Hal Downes, went missing ten kilometers outside Pyongyang. Rick had dedicated his life to finding and repatriating his dad's remains, as well as the remains of the more than five thousand other American servicemen lost in North Korea.

I was back in North Korea, without Governor Richardson this time. Rick and I were at Pyongyang's Victorious War Museum, which commemorates what Americans call the Korean War and North Koreans call the American War. That right there says volumes about conflicting perspectives, how two nations can take the same piece of history and interpret it in such radically divergent ways. The war story told in North Korea could hardly be more different from the one that's been drilled into generations of American schoolchildren.

On this early fall afternoon, Rick and I were staring up at a larger-than-life wax statue of a decaying US soldier with a raven pecking at his eyes.

"Definitely gruesome." Rick shuddered.

It was Sunday, September 25, 2016. I had returned to North Korea's ancient gray capital to negotiate the release of Otto Warmbier, a twenty-two-year-old University of Virginia undergraduate who'd been arrested almost nine months earlier at Pyongyang International Airport as he and the other members of his budget tour group were preparing to fly home.

The charge: that after a night of drinking near Kim Il-sung Square, young Otto had stolen a propaganda poster from the Yanggakdo International Hotel...or, as the North Korean authorities described the offense, that the American college student had engaged in "subversion" and committed a "hostile act against the state."

Clashing perspectives, again.

What struck Otto's family in Cincinnati as a dumb college prank—unwise, certainly, but far from dire—the North Koreans were treating like a genuine threat to their national security. After getting nowhere with the Obama State Department and desperately worried about their son, Fred and Cindy Warmbier, Otto's parents, reached out to Ohio Governor John Kasich, who told them to contact his friend Governor Richardson. The governor and I immediately agreed to help. We met in New York with two high-ranking diplomats from North Korea's mission to the United Nations, pressing for Otto's speedy release, which seemed to have no impact at all.

Just a few hours after that meeting, Otto was put on trial in Pyongyang for subversion "pursuant to the US government's hostile policy toward North Korea in a bid to impair the unity of its people." After barely an hour of testimony that featured grainy surveillance video and the allegedly stolen poster ("Let's arm ourselves strongly with Kim Jong-il's patriotism!"), Otto was convicted by the court and sentenced to fifteen years of hard labor in a North Korean prison. Fifteen years in a North Korean prison...*for this?*

Once that happened, we knew the only way we'd make any progress on the case was by going to North Korea. After we tried for months to find the justification for a visit, the North Koreans finally issued the desired invitation—though not without a caveat: they did not want Governor Richardson to come, not then, anyway. *Too high profile. Trip needs to be discreet.* Those were the explanations they offered. Richardson authorized me to go without him. So I rounded up Rick Downes and P. Willey, a forensic anthropologist from Chico, California, and the three of us flew to Pyongyang.

Governor Richardson remained closely involved. But for the first time ever, I'd be the one leading an overseas mission to bring an American prisoner home. Thankfully, after Kenneth Bae, I had some idea what I was getting into. Everything in North Korea would have its own unique rhythm and require its own special choreography. Which was part of the reason we were spending this Sunday afternoon gazing at a grotesque wax statue in the War Museum and why our escorts were also dragging us through a packed week of monument tours, music-and-dance performances, multicourse banquets, hand-shaking sessions with midlevel bureaucrats, even a dolphin show, all designed to disguise the real purpose of our visit.

And what did any of this have to do with Otto Warmbier? Well, everything.

* * *

YOU CAN'T SIMPLY GO TO NORTH KOREA TO NEGOTIATE THE RELEASE of a political prisoner. To begin with, the North Koreans denied that Otto *was* a political prisoner. Therefore, in their eyes there was nothing to negotiate. Just as importantly, I did not work for a government, nor did I have the authority to negotiate on behalf of one. And, of course, the North Koreans could not afford the perception, external or internal, that any such negotiations were taking place at all.

Officially, we were there to assess the need for humanitarian assistance in flood-stricken areas in the north of North Korea. We were also there to negotiate the return of remains of US service members who had died in the Korean War but had never been repatriated. And, while there, we would privately and discreetly raise Otto's case. I was careful to call it "a package of unrelated, mutually beneficial humanitarian gestures." It was the only way to negotiate Otto's release.

Negotiations in North Korea are very different from what we are used to in the United States. In the United States, when you come to negotiate, you sit around a table, exchange opening statements and positions, discuss, and argue. Then you take a break, during which time the two sides trade information more informally and try to figure out each other's flexibilities. In North Korea, things go almost in reverse.

"Mickey, look at this," Willey said to me as we were reviewing the itinerary the North Koreans had given to us at the start of the week. "Our meeting with the vice-minister of foreign affairs is scheduled for the afternoon of our last day here. We will not have time to negotiate in any real way. Why are we going to museums, monuments, and a dolphin show? They can't be serious."

"Think about it, P," I responded. "The vice-minister is not really empowered to negotiate with us. He does not have the authority. His team, our minders, first have to mine us for all the information they can as to what we are authorized to negotiate and offer. They then need to prepare a memo for their boss, the vice-minister, who then needs to take it up to the leader to get his response. Only then will the vice-minister be able to meet with us, knowing what the leader has authorized him to say. Consider this cultural tour part of the negotiations."

They split us into separate cars, asking each of us similar questions and comparing our answers for consistency.

"How do the three of you know each other?"

"Have any of you worked for the US government?"

"Who exactly is paying for your trip?"

Their assumption: if we were lying, we'd have trouble keeping our stories straight.

It was just one of their soft, indirect interrogation techniques as we passed the hours touring landmarks and sharing meals. Realizing this, we used the faux-casual exchanges to deliver messages of our own.

Kim, my minder, was a young foreign-service officer in the North Korean ministry. So often, we focus on relationships with the leaders, the higher-ups. But the connection you strike with staff can actually have a huge impact. This might have been one of Kim's first assignments. He seemed as anxious as I was feeling. I tried to spark a conversation as we were driving through the dark roads in Pyongyang on our way to the official guesthouse. I soon learned that Kim had a young daughter. I pulled out my phone and showed him a picture of my toddler daughter, Noa. Robin and I had adopted Noa nearly three years earlier. Though born in the United States, Noa is ethnically Guatemalan.

In fact, just before departing on the mission to Pyongyang, I had taken Noa to the playground. "You know how I have to travel for work sometimes?" I asked her. "Well, tomorrow I need to go again for a few days." Up to that point, when I went on work missions, I had downplayed the goodbyes. I'd told myself it was best for Noa, but I suspect it was just easier for me. Robin had told me that when I traveled, Noa acted out much more than usual. We'd figured, *Let's try a different approach.*

"Where are you going?" Noa asked.

"To a faraway country called North Korea on the other side of the planet."

"But why?"

"Because there is a boy there. He is in trouble, and I am trying to bring him back to his parents."

"What's his name?"

"Otto."

"Will he be my friend when he comes home?"

"Yes, he will. I am sure of that."

Robin would later tell me that during my mission to North Korea, Noa seemed different. She was behaving and even helping Robin. Kids, even little ones, understand so much more than we give them credit for!

"Is she one of ours?" Kim asked me as he looked carefully at Noa's picture.

"Oh no...you don't get to claim her," I said with a smile. "Noa is Guatemalan." I laughed. It was not the first time one of my diplomatic counterparts had asked if Noa was one of theirs. It had happened to me in Myanmar too. It was also not the first time I'd used a photo of my daughter to break the ice with someone. Leaning in with your own personal story, your own vulnerabilities, that can create intimacy, I had found. It's an invitation for others to share their own feelings and connect.

Kim and I talked about the special bond between fathers and daughters as he showed me pictures of his own young daughter. You see? Humans are similar on so many levels.

"I have to tell you, Kim," I said, switching the topic just a little, "I am really nervous."

Kim looked at me. "Why is that?"

"Well," I told him, "because this is the first time I am leading the negotiations by myself." I looked directly into Kim's eyes. "If I screw this up, Governor Richardson will kill me!"

Kim's eyes opened wide. Yes, "kill me" was an exaggeration. But that was intentional. Knowing this was one of Kim's early assignments, I was sure that the accuracy of the memo Kim would prepare for his bosses could have grave consequences for his career—maybe even his livelihood. If he told his bosses that I would say one thing, but at the meeting I said something different, then Kim would pay a high price. I also knew that if that happened, the vice-minister would not have the authority to improvise, and my mission could be wrecked.

"So, Kim," I continued, "please tell me exactly what information you need from me. I will not mislead or surprise you. It is in my interest that you are able to do your job as well as possible so that my mission can be successful." Despite being on opposing sides, Kim and I had a joint objective, and we were building a personal bond around it.

It was during the dolphin show, sitting with hundreds of North Korean schoolkids at the Rungna People's Pleasure Ground Dolphinarium, that I shared with my minder Kim that, as a nongovernmental organization, we could pay no more than $7,000 to $10,000 per set of human remains and that I could do ten of those right away. I mentioned this under the pretense of casual chitchat as we watched dolphins, sea lions, and synchronized swimmers dressed as mermaids. The real art of negotiating with the North Koreans is finding just the right openings in conversations to insert our priorities while paying careful attention to everything we hear.

As our official guide was showing us through the Victorious War Museum, she pointed out some random pieces of American military hardware: parts from a crashed US Air Force fighter jet, charred metal from a busted US Army tank, a collection of left-behind combat helmets, each of these a symbol of some American setback, failure, or mistake during the Korean War.

"Of the four and a half million Koreans who died in the war," she said, continuing with her scripted presentation, "nearly half were—"

I interrupted her there.

"I'm sorry," I said, "I don't think I heard you correctly. How many Koreans died during the war?"

"Four and a half million Koreans died in the war."

Four and a half million?! Could that be true?

It felt as if someone had just punched me in the stomach. A very physical sensation. My mind was running numbers and timelines. That was in the early 1950s, less than a decade after the Holocaust, wherein six million of my fellow Jews were killed. I knew very well what the Holocaust meant to me—in my life, my family's life, and my nations' lives. It was not *that* long ago. My grandparents had escaped the Holocaust. And as a Jew, I knew what it meant for all that to be acknowledged. I'd been through reconciliation with Germany. I'd commemorated International Holocaust Remembrance Days. I had visited Holocaust museums in many capitals around the world. Had this Korean loss ever been acknowledged?

The Holocaust was an intricately designed system of annihilation. Although the Korean War was a war of political ideology, the immense loss to the people of this peninsula was truly difficult to comprehend. Numbers so unfathomable! We were two people who culturally seemed to have little in common, an Israeli American and a North Korean. But in that moment, I realized that despite all our differences, there was an agony of loss that we shared, as individuals and as nations.

There is a difference between empathy and sympathy. Empathy is putting oneself in the shoes of another. Sympathy is aligning your objectives with another's. The two are often confused. In my line of work, empathy is a necessity, while sympathy is a trap. Understanding why the North Koreans do what they do is different from justifying their actions or aligning their objectives with ours. In today's political discourse, these two concepts are often conflated to attack those who are looking to engage with rivals. Remember this whether you're dealing with your neighbor of the opposite political party or the head of a hostile government. It can go a long way in either case.

* * *

Two days later, it was finally time for our official meeting with Han Song-ryol, North Korea's vice-minister of foreign affairs. As I was about to walk into the grandiose headquarters of the North Korean Foreign Ministry, Kim, my minder, gave me a smile and wished us luck. He was not included in the meeting. But by this point, Kim and I shared a bond and a hope for a productive meeting. I thanked him before I was directed down a long marble hallway toward the vice-minister's high-ceilinged office.

I'd barely taken a seat in the office, and Vice-Minister Han was already lecturing me. "You are the reason for the state of affairs. Your aggression towards the Democratic People's Republic of Korea is the source of the suffering. Your government just plotted to kill our leader. We uncovered it. Otto Warmbier is a prisoner of war."

What was all this *you...you...you?* I didn't do any of those things, even if they were true! This is how formal meetings in North Korea usually go. The first part is scripted, in Korean, with a translator. Harsh language and accusations, for the record. You sit. You listen. And then you respond, in English, just as harshly. That's the formal part. But after the harsh formalities are over, a meeting with North Koreans typically breaks into the informal part, where the faces become friendlier, the language turns to English, and, typically, a glass of cognac is raised.

This time, I went a bit off script. "Mr. Vice-Minister," I said when it was my turn to talk, "I will get to my points and respond to yours shortly. But I first have to tell you something." I described our visit to the museum two days before and the conversation with our guide. "Minister, I am Jewish. I was born and raised in Israel before moving to the United States. I know what six million deaths means to me, to my country of birth, to my people. Despite working with North Korea for more than six years, I never knew that four and a half million Koreans died in the war. I now understand much better what you, your family, and your people experienced. I now understand better the canyon that exists between us and what it might take to build a bridge across it. I understand the mistrust you must feel. And I can assure you, Mr. Vice-Minister, that most Americans have no idea. Most of those who can recall the war think of it as a small war between World War II and Vietnam. They don't understand its gravity."

I paused. I looked at him. I could see his demeanor begin to shift. Quieting down, then lightening up. I did not apologize for the Koreans' loss. I just acknowledged it. And that seemed to matter...a lot. The dynamic of the meeting had changed completely.

That was the power of empathy and emotional intelligence, the ability to recognize and understand emotions in yourself and in others and the ability to use this awareness to manage your behavior and relationships. Emotional intelligence, I kept learning, was the most critical skill in engagement and negotiations. We are all taught to believe that national interests are the sole drivers of international affairs. In reality, they are just one part of the game.

When I brought up Otto Warmbier and the severity of the young American's punishment, the vice-minister was actually responsive. I did not get Otto Warmbier released with that meeting. I knew that was not a realistic expectation. The purpose of the meeting was to chart a path toward Otto's release. And while the meeting was productive, I still felt disappointed.

"Are you OK?" Kim asked me as I walked out of the meeting. I've never had much of a poker face. "There is a saying in my country," Kim continued. "'It takes one hundred hacks to bring down a tree.'" I knew Kim was disappointed too, and I understood what he was conveying to me.

"Thank you, Kim," I said with a sad smile. "I sure hope I don't need to come back ninety-nine more times before we can get this resolved."

Kim smiled without saying anything else.

9 TRAGIC TWIST

THE WHEELS TURNED SLOWLY FROM THERE...BUT TURN THEY DID. Though we didn't get an answer by the time we left Pyongyang, we seemed to have made a real connection in North Korea. I could definitely feel the difference—at least I thought I could. As if we'd made genuine progress on both our reasons for being there: getting a deal to bring Otto home and also arranging for the return of US service members' remains. So when would it happen? We were waiting for the same trigger the North Koreans were: the expected victory of Hillary Clinton over Donald Trump. And that almost seemed like a lock. What better way for these two nations to start fresh than with a couple of high-profile humanitarian gestures? That really could set these two ancient enemies on a whole new path, just as a new American president was being sworn in.

Oh, were we ever in for a big surprise! And not just the unexpected victory of Donald Trump.

On a cold December night, Governor Richardson and I hosted a dinner at New York's Sparks Steak House in honor of Jang Il-hun, the North Korean ambassador to the United Nations for American affairs, who was just then leaving his post. As Guv and I sat with Ambassador Jang, North Korean Counselor Kwon, and their families, I was still stunned by Hillary Clinton's defeat and still struggling to grasp what it meant for our negotiations with the North Koreans. Despite the nice bonding opportunity, we didn't really have a game plan for what to do next.

"I am worried," I said to our North Korean colleagues, "that when Donald Trump steps into the presidency in January, he will look to demonstrate his 'strength.'" I put air quotes around the word, a gesture the North Koreans seemed to understand. "Since ISIS will be largely defeated by President Obama, Trump might look for another target. He will probably turn to Iran, but the Israelis might argue against that. So he will look further, and I am afraid he will set his eyes on you, North Korea."

Guv turned his head toward me. He liked where I was going with this. His raw instincts were on display.

"Mickey might be right." The governor took over. "Trump might see you as a convenient and manageable target." Neither Guv nor I had thought much about this scenario before. We were certainly not confident in the prediction. But suggesting it opened up an opportunity in our minds.

We were in a race against time. If our crazy idea for a deal to bring back Otto Warmbier were to succeed, it had to happen before President Trump's inauguration on January 20. The idea was to simply execute our planned agreement, but instead of doing it in the context of the Hillary Clinton presidency, what if we did it using a Trump Organization plane? That way, President-elect Trump would get a clear win—and a powerful TV visual—before he even got to the White House, and the North Koreans would get the symbolism of a Trump plane arriving in Pyongyang's International Airport. Win-win. But this could happen only *before* Trump actually assumed the presidency. Once he was in office, the government bureaucracy would take over and we'd have to use an air force plane, which would make the operation all but impossible.

"We have a very short window," I said.

The North Koreans gave us a soft nod. The Warmbier family was soon on board. We had to get this in front of President-elect Trump. Not just an aide. The president-elect himself. Despite my contempt for much of what Trump represented, I strongly believed that this would be something he would go for, if it was presented directly to him. The famous dealmaker could get Otto out and say to the world, *Hey, I'm not even in*

office yet, and look at the deal I just made. I was confident. We just needed
to get this in front of Trump.

And boy, we tried!

We approached the chief of staff to the vice president elect, Mike
Pence. We reached out to Ivanka Trump, Jared Kushner, and Rudy
Giuliani. We got nowhere. The transition team was in major disarray
and time was running out. A couple of people on the transition team
expressed interest. But sadly, there was no follow-through. And the clock
ran out on us. I still think that was a missed opportunity. On January 20,
Donald Trump replaced Barack Obama in the White House. Rex Til-
lerson took over John Kerry's position as secretary of state. And we were
dealing with large bureaucracies again.

* * *

EARLY IN HIS TERM, TRUMP SPOKE HARSHLY ABOUT THE NORTH
Korean leader, Kim Jung-un, just as Barack Obama had. Later in his presidency, Trump would cross the border into North Korea and meet with
Kim. The two men would exchange warm letters. But in these early days,
the US administration did not have much success nudging the Kim government on Otto's release. That still felt like *our* job. What would finally
end this nightmare? When was Otto coming home? As April turned to
May and then June arrived and Otto remained in prison, those answers
were still frustratingly vague. But we kept pushing, and we kept being
assured by our North Korean sources that progress was being made.

I was just as impatient as ever, but this felt better than the
alternatives—complete silence or outright hostility. I know Fred and
Cindy Warmbier thought so. Otto had been in prison for almost seventeen months by then. So when was he coming home?

* * *

"MICKEY, IT'S FRED AND CINDY."

It was 5:15 on a cool June morning, one of the last cool mornings
before summer turned DC into soup. I was still in my car when I got

the call from Otto's parents. I had just dropped Robin and our now three-and-a-half year-old, Noa, at Reagan National Airport. They were flying to the Adirondacks to spend two weeks with friends. This would be my first staycation since becoming a father, a blessed break of solitude, golfing, and TV binge-watching from the couch. But instead of the flight update I was expecting from Robin, I heard Fred's voice, quaking with urgency.

"Give me the great news," I said excitedly.

"He cleared North Korean airspace," Fred said.

Immediately I felt such a high! I had been dreaming of this moment since we first began negotiating with the North Koreans for Otto's release. For an entire year and a half, Otto's release had consumed me, emotionally and professionally. Days and nights. I had literally been dreaming about flying back home with Otto. I had nightmares too. In one of those I was standing beside him in a North Korean prison, watching while he was executed. I woke from that one in a cold sweat. My family saw how obsessed I was, how focused and intent I was on the need to bring this young man home.

All along, we'd been working around the clock, pulling every lever and pushing every button we could think of, analyzing and reanalyzing the internal dynamics based on partial information and misinformation. There'd been intense moments of optimism, punctuated by repeated setbacks—during my trip to North Korea and after I got home. I had spent countless hours speaking with Cindy and Fred. They had become like family, trusting me with their most intimate personal tragedy. My heart ached for them. Their anxiety sapped me emotionally. Now I smiled alone in my car. It was the start of a bright new day. Otto Warmbier would soon be reunited with his family.

"But there is a complication," Fred said cautiously.

A complication?

In all the scenarios I had played out in my head, Otto's return was always met with joy. It had never occurred to me that I should prepare for any alternative reality.

"He is in a coma," Fred said quietly.

My heart sank.

"We don't know any details, but it sounds serious."

"Was it an induced coma? What do we know?"

"Not much at the moment," Fred said. "They will have a stopover in Japan and then head back to Cincinnati."

So many questions were racing through my head. How long had he been in a coma? What was the medical issue? Why hadn't my North Korean counterparts shared this information with me? Could this coma have been induced to obscure the details of his release? How could I spin this devastating development into something more emotionally manageable?

The few details we had didn't answer any of this. All the Warmbiers had been told by the State Department was that their son had at some point been moved from a prison cell and was now being medically evacuated from the Pyongyang Friendship Hospital. Otto would be arriving in Cincinnati on the evening of June 13. They wouldn't know much more until he was taken to the University of Cincinnati Medical Center, where doctors would assess his condition and try to determine what had brought on the coma. Would he recover quickly? Would he recover at all? They didn't know anything…yet.

I drove home in deflated silence. All I could do was wait for time to pass. But at the heart of an international and diplomatic crisis, I had come to learn, time plays an excruciating game of cat and mouse, hope and loss. And it didn't seem as if there'd be any winners here.

The sun was barely making its way over the horizon, but my world felt dark. I tried catching my breath as my head began to throb with anger and then guilt. I'd imagined triumphantly bringing Otto home with me on a commercial flight. Now I just didn't know. Never had I imagined that Otto would be returned in what the doctors would call a persistent vegetative state.

I was furious.

* * *

JONG KWON WAS MY NORTH KOREAN COUNTERPART IN NEW YORK. As consul at the Permanent Mission of North Korea to the United Nations, he'd been very helpful when we set up my last mission to Pyongyang, sharing his valuable guidance about how I should approach the regime. Over the past few years, Jong and I had developed a friendship. I liked him a lot. While politically inferior to Pak Song-il, North Korea's ambassador for American affairs, Jong had excellent access and a bright future inside the North Korean Foreign Ministry. He was effective and genuine. We had a shared sense of humanity, both of us loving our families deeply, and we would swap stories of parenting and talk about socializing together with our wives one day.

I sat down to draft an email to Jong. Various drafts rambled on with emotional accusations, confessions of anger and fury, and demands for an explanation. Ultimately I fell back on one of my favorite principles of emotional intelligence: only get angry with purpose. So in my email, I opted for simplicity and directness: "This is not good, Jong...I am really worried about what comes next."

Jong's response came within ten minutes. "Dear Mickey," he wrote, "I understand what you mean and feel sorry for that. I hope it won't drive our relationship to a bad condition." In the moment, I was so raw that I interpreted his reply as flippant and disrespectful. The nature of rage clouds judgment. So I decided to wait to respond. *Only get angry with purpose*, I kept reminding myself.

I headed to Cincinnati the next day to see Fred and Cindy. I waited until I was at the airport to answer Jong, though I had not been able to think about anything else over the previous thirty-six hours. "Our relationship will maintain, as I know this was not your intention or responsibility. I know you would have liked things to go down very differently. To be honest, I am emotionally torn. I spoke with Cindy and Fred Warmbier early morning yesterday. They called me as soon as they were allowed to and shared with me what they knew about Otto's condition.

It was a heartbreaking conversation. I am frustrated and angry. No matter what language we refer to—prisoner of war, student detainee—Otto was under North Korean custody, and therefore his health was your government's absolute responsibility. His reported condition is a terrible violation of conventions and more importantly, humanity."

My heart was pounding. Was I burning bridges here? I sure felt like I wanted to. More than six years of relationship tending, humanitarian engagement, and trust building was quickly deteriorating. Were all those efforts even worth it? How could I justify such a relationship to the Warmbiers? What about the thousands of families of US Korean War service members whose remains we were still trying to bring back from North Korea? I was ethically and emotionally torn. Otto was twenty-two years old, just about the same age as many of those dead American soldiers.

"But again," I continued in my answer to Jong, "I know you would have never wanted this to be the case. I know you did and continue to do everything you can to improve the relationship between our countries, and I really appreciate you as a person and friend. Maybe we can get a visit by the governor approved?" I tried to add purpose. "Maybe we have a visit focused on the recovery and return of U.S. servicemen from the war?"

Jong did not reply.

* * *

Once I landed in Ohio, I headed straight to the hospital.

"I am so sorry, Cindy," I said as I shared a long, somber hug with Otto's mom.

Even as I heard myself utter those four simple words, I knew they were entirely insufficient to ease a mother's pain. But they were all I could manage to whisper through my tears.

We were standing at Otto's bedside.

I was devastated. I felt that I had failed Cindy and Fred. I had failed Otto. For the past year and a half, I had gotten to know him through the stories Cindy and Fred shared with me. Although we had never met, Otto lived inside me, slowly becoming a friend I needed to rescue. But this young man, lying in the sterile hospital bed in front of me—he was nothing like the Otto I had slowly gotten to know, the cherished brother and son, student and friend. He had been a vibrant, energetic, and charismatic athlete. He was tall and handsome, a natural-born leader with a fervent curiosity about the world. That was the Otto I had promised my daughter she would meet one day, the Otto I had promised Cindy and Fred I would bring home to them. Clearly I had failed.

Cindy was kinder to me than I was to myself. She didn't seem to blame me, which I deeply appreciated. She seemed thankful for all I had done and tried to do. "Thanks to your efforts," Cindy said through her tears in the hospital room, "I got a chance to hug my boy while his body is still warm."

"His body." His broken and empty body. I don't think she heard her own tragic words. But those words ripped at my soul.

Just heartbreaking.

I didn't know what to say to that. I didn't say anything. I didn't know what to do. I simply stood at her side. I didn't know what to think or feel. But I knew that my eyes were still teary. I couldn't help but question myself. Question my life's work. Question my whole worldview.

The next six days were an international media frenzy. Everyone, it seemed, wanted to know about the comatose University of Virginia student. Had he been tortured in North Korean custody? Had he fallen ill? Had something else happened to him? Round-the-clock reporting on Otto's condition dominated the news. Governor Richardson was interviewed on all the major networks. There was a report saying that North Korean officials had advised US State Department Special Representative Joseph Yun that Otto had contracted foodborne botulism shortly after his sentencing and that he had fallen into a coma after taking a sleeping pill. I had never been told any of this. Nor had Otto's family. Was it true? Was it the whole story? Were there key missing details? There had to be something more. If not, why all the months of silence from the North Koreans? All those questions hung in the air. The Koreans were not coming clean. Americans were outraged. Personally, I was seething along with Guv, who was busy expressing his anger in the media. He called for accountability and even used a couple of demeaning adjectives in reference to the North Korean leader, Kim Jong-un.

I finally got an answer from Jong. He blamed his silence on Governor Richardson. "Sorry, the governor disabled us," Jong began his email. "We are unable to make any more excuses to meet anyone connected with him." That certainly included me. "His speech not only struck my people enough to get upset but also pulled down all the things we had built up in the meantime. Forgive me if my words were too immoral or insulting."

Jong was obviously upset. To me, he sounded personally and professionally nervous. I could only imagine what North Korea's supreme leader was saying as his country was rightfully being vilified over Otto's ordeal.

"I guess this chapter of our work is over," I said to the governor after I showed him Jong's note.

"How are you going to respond?" Guv asked me. "Remember, with the North Koreans, there is always a next round." He should know. The governor had been negotiating with them since 1994, when the original Kim leader, Kim Il-sung, the founder of North Korea, was still in charge. He'd kept negotiating as Kim's son and grandson, Kim Jong-il and Kim Jong-un, took over.

"I'm going to think about it for a day," I responded. I really didn't know what else I could say or do.

Jong's message stayed in my inbox. To me it seemed as if the door had been shut. Jong's language was very clear. Even if I wrote back, chances were he would not respond. Maybe he would not even read my answer.

Still, one line in my friend Jong's message kept nagging at me. "Forgive me if my words were too immoral or insulting." Was that Jong trying to express exactly what I had tried to say six days before? Was he torn between reflecting the pressure he was under, the anger of his superiors

about what Governor Richardson had said on TV, and his own desire
not to burn bridges? Was it possible he was trying to leave the door open
just a crack? Was he hoping I'd also keep that same door open...just a
crack?

The day I decided to write back to Jong was truly one of the most difficult days of my life. I was heading back to Ohio, this time to attend
Otto's funeral.

In communication with the North Koreans, writing has some advantages over talking. Even when their English is good, as Jong's was, the
accent can be challenging, especially on the phone. The last thing I
wanted at such a dicey moment was any confusion in our back-and-forth.
Even a tiny word change, I knew, could leave one of us with a drastically
altered understanding. Plus, writing gave me an extra moment to reflect
on my message and also to remain calm even as so many of my emotions
were still heightened.

I started my reply, "Thanks for your note, Jong. Last Friday, I spent
the day with Otto Warmbier at his hospital bedside in Ohio. A young
healthy 22-year-old man was reduced to an unresponsive body."

I continued to describe, in very graphic detail, what I had witnessed. I
wanted to share with Jong the trauma I had personally experienced.

"Otto had been in that state for over a year," I continued. "Imagine
your child like that. Imagine the pain of his parents sitting next to him
in his final days, knowing he's been like that for over a year, in a foreign
country. No visits. No loved ones around. When he was arrested, he was
healthy. Jong, you know me well enough by now. And I know you well
enough to know that this was not what you would have wanted to happen. You know that my sincere intention is to help prevent escalation and
maybe get something positive between our countries. I am on a plane
now, on my way to Otto's funeral. I had never met him before Friday, but
this work is personal. Emotions, on both sides, are very raw and intense.
Nothing like this has ever happened before. It is very, very serious." I
was hoping my sincerity would come across. Next I addressed Jong's concerns about Richardson. "You know I'm not a fan of media and public

exposure," I wrote. "But you have to know that there is no way around it, in these circumstances."

I hoped I was conveying the enormous betrayal I felt. The stated lies and ones told through omission. There had been days, weeks, months, a full year, when the Koreans could have told us the truth and allowed Otto to come home to his family. I understood that we all had roles here. We all had jobs to do. But this went so far beyond anything professional, I didn't know how we would ever recover. What kind of future association could possibly survive this level of dishonesty? I decided I was comfortable with my direct language. I thought my words were necessary and justified.

I had one last point I wanted to make. "If our ability to communicate is now gone," I continued, "it is not because of words said by the governor in one interview or newspaper. We have thicker skin than that. If our ability to communicate is now gone, it is because of the actions taken, not the words said. I'm still struggling with the fact that while I was in Pyongyang, meeting with the Vice Minister, he knew Otto's status. It is devastating." Again, I made it personal. "I am being very honest and transparent with you because I feel that we have developed a friendship and trust. I hope we can talk and process this together, since we both know and believe that engagement and dialogue is more important in a crisis than ever."

I pressed *send* without rereading my message. The governor seemed to believe there was a tomorrow in this relationship. I wasn't nearly as sure. But I'd said my piece. I didn't know if my email would even be opened, if Jong would ever read what I'd written. In fact, I genuinely believed this entire ordeal constituted my last interaction with the North Koreans.

* * *

A WEEK AFTER OTTO'S FUNERAL, I DID AN INTERVIEW WITH MY friend Sarah Wildman for Vox Media. Her piece was published in early July, a little less than a month after Otto's return. The article had been live for more than four hours, though I hadn't even read it yet. Robin, Noa, and I had just landed in Los Angeles for a much-needed break. I had a scholar-in-residence position at a summer camp in Malibu, where we planned on spending three relaxing weeks. That's when a text from Jong showed up on my phone.

We should meet.

I stared at the phone for a moment, then typed two letters.

O and *K*.

Why don't you come to see us in New York tomorrow morning, Jong texted back.

Hmmm. I wasn't quite sure what to make of that.

"What do you think they want?" Guv asked me on the phone after I shared the text with him.

"I have no clue."

"You should go. See what they have to say."

Some days, I felt as if all I did was disappoint people. This would be one of those days. Despite my repeated promises to improve my work-life balance, interrupted family travel plans were a dance that Robin and I continued to struggle with. After a familiar sigh of frustration and about ten seconds of thought, she told me to go.

"I have to go to New York tonight," I tried to explain to Noa, who was three and a half years old. "But I will be back tomorrow night."

We got into a rental car, and I drove my understanding wife and sad daughter to the camp. We got settled in. Then I headed back to LAX for a red-eye to New York.

Jong didn't come to our meeting alone. He brought his boss, Ambassador Pak. The North Koreans never meet one-on-one. They always conduct their meetings in pairs. Maybe it is to have two sets of ears confirming the substance of the conversation. Perhaps it is to make sure that one of them does not stray from the official message or get tempted by the Americans to "turn."

We met in the garden of a restaurant near the United Nations. Ambassador Pak started the conversation.

"Pyongyang read your interview," the ambassador said.

"They did?"

I was genuinely surprised at that, and now I was concerned too. I knew the North Koreans followed the governor's media appearances… but mine too? Even on Vox?

I steeled myself for a lecture. It wouldn't be the first time, and I knew I could handle it, though my own emotions were still raw from the events of the past month.

"Pyongyang found your interview harsh but nuanced," the ambassador continued. "So they authorized us to reopen our channel."

This was not going the way I'd expected it to. I do not have a poker face. I was sure they could read my surprise.

"I'm glad," I began. "I try to be very honest. It is important to me that people understand that this is complicated and—"

"But for now," Pak interrupted me, "we cannot meet with Governor Richardson."

"I think that is OK," I said. Then I quickly added, "As long as it is clear that I am working on his behalf. I am not doing this independently." I felt that I had to clarify my allegiance.

The ambassador nodded.

"This was the first message we wanted to convey to you." Pak kept going. "The second one is a personal message from the vice-minister. He personally wanted you to know that when you were negotiating with him in Pyongyang eight months ago, he did not know of Otto's medical condition."

Really?!

This was huge—and not only huge. It was validating to me in a way I had not expected—in a way I hadn't even realized I needed. I was relieved to hear it. For the past month, I had felt so betrayed by the vice-minister. It had made me question my intuition about people, something I have always considered critical to my success. Of course, there was no way for me to know whether the vice-minister was telling the truth now. But he could be. Understanding the North Korean system of information control, I thought it was plausible that the Foreign Ministry had not been brought into the loop about Otto's condition by the security forces who'd held him during his captivity.

The most important part of this revelation was that the vice-minister felt compelled to let me know that he had not negotiated in bad faith. That meant two things: First, the connection we had established in Pyongyang eight months earlier was real. And second, the vice-minister saw value in our relationship continuing. Otherwise he would not have bothered delivering this kind of message. It was unusual.

"Thank you for that, Ambassador," I responded. "I will take the vice-minister at his word."

"Now for the third message," Pak said. "We have a proposition for de-escalation."

Ambassador Pak described a proposal by which we would take a small group of American leaders to Pyongyang, and in return the North Koreans would allow us to repatriate several sets of remains of US service members from the Korean War.

This was significant. It made sense on several layers. Symbolically, it was a gesture used previously by the North Koreans in 2007, when seven sets of remains were given to Governor Richardson on a bipartisan mission under President George W. Bush. I cannot overemphasize the meaning of repatriating remains. Bringing the remains of service members home, even after sixty years, was priceless to grieving families and valued by Americans at large. After Otto's death, the rhetoric between President Trump and Kim Jong-un had escalated dangerously. If we had an opportunity to douse the fire with genuine diplomacy, I was going to work tirelessly to do so.

This could change what appeared to be an inevitable collision course for the United States and North Korea. It could even lead to a start of negotiations and collaborations.

I felt both the hope and the weight of the moment.

"You know I have to take this to the White House with Governor Richardson, right?" I told Ambassador Pak. I wanted to make sure it was clear that this could not be done without the US government's approval. "This will need to go to the national security advisor, H. R. McMaster."

"Do what you need," Pak responded with a nod.

Otto's tragic return would stay with me forever. There was no dampening the harsh reality or the feeling of loss. But there was also no question that the world was better off if the United States and North Korea were talking again.

PART III
BEST
OF
FRENEMIES

10 JAILED JOURNOS

"Guv," I said, "this letter will get you arrested."

We were sitting in Governor Richardson's room at the resort in Naypyidaw, the capital of Myanmar. Our heads were still spinning from the cascading events of the last twenty-four hours. Despite the sense of urgency, I was struck by how surreal this moment felt. The luxurious cabins spread around the manicured grounds of the resort. Lush green grasses peppered with flowers and a lavish pond. Whatever serenity could be found in this idyllic setting was in stark contrast to the reality on the ground in Myanmar.

"*Nah*...do you really think so?" Guv asked with surprise in his eyes and his signature taunting smile.

"You are exposing Aung San Suu Kyi's hypocrisy publicly," I reminded him. "I am pretty sure the Myanmar government will detain you for a while. It will make her look strong."

Our colleague and Myanmar expert, Steve Ross, agreed.

The letter in question was the governor's resignation from the international advisory board that was assembled by Myanmar's Nobel Peace Prize–winning leader, Daw Aung San Suu Kyi. Publicly the board was tasked with resolving the conflict in Rakhine State, a conflict the international community had already recognized as "the Rohingya Genocide." The governor's letter was a scathing rebuke of the intent of a board that, at that moment, was a mere twenty-four hours young.

Earlier that morning, when we sat down with the leader, Guv had opened his remarks by addressing her simply as "Suu." It always made me crack up when he called her that. But that was his way. Nobody else would dare approach "the Lady" with such casual familiarity. Suu

Kyi was the Oxford-educated daughter of Aung San, the "father of the nation," a towering military and political leader who was assassinated in 1947, when she was two years old. She was known for exuding a distinct formality. Almost no one in Myanmar called her Suu. Most often she was addressed by her full, formal name, Aung San Suu Kyi...or *Daw* Aung San Suu Kyi, *daw* being a high honorific that falls somewhere between "madam" and "aunt." "The Lady" was about as casual as anyone dared to get.

"Thank you for having us," Guv continued. "We've been friends for more than twenty years. I helped you when you were a political prisoner in your own country."

This was the first meeting of the international advisory board, but the setup seemed off. Instead of the private session that was planned, Daw Suu Kyi had brought in some of her ministers and generals, men we knew she neither liked nor trusted. That was the first sign that something nefarious was up.

"Not only me," the governor continued, motioning to the four other board members who sat beside him at the table. "The rest of us here are also your friends. And we are here to help you with the crisis in Rakhine. But you need to help us too."

The discomfort in the room jumped a few notches right there.

"We need tangible deliverables and success," Guv continued. "You need to *do* something tangible with the Rohingya, and you need to make sure the two Reuters journalists you have arrested get a quick and fair trial, protecting the freedom of the press in Myanmar."

With that, the room remained silent for an uncomfortably long moment. The others seemed to hold their breath. The governor was challenging Suu Kyi and the group she had convened. Any hope she'd had of making this a simple photo op was crushed in that moment.

The two Reuters journalists were Wa Lone and Kyaw Soe Oo. Wa Lone was a friend of mine. He'd been a volunteer translator with a storytelling group that went to schools across Myanmar, performing stories from children's books about tolerance and acceptance. After becoming a journalist, he had joined a couple of our previous delegations, and we had become good friends.

Both Wa Lone and Kyaw Soe Oo had been arrested a couple of months before the international advisory board meeting as they were exposing a massacre and a mass grave of Rohingya in Rakhine State. Their arrests were a setup, staged by Suu Kyi's government for political effect. The charges were outrageous: *treason* under the nation's Official Secrets Act. Ironically, Aung San Suu Kyi would later be charged with the exact same crime.

"Why did you come here, Bill?" Suu Kyi loudly broke the silence. "You are not here as a politician, so don't talk like one."

This was my eighth meeting with Daw Suu Kyi. I had certainly never seen her so upset. But even in her anger, she possessed an air of calm calculation. "We understand the challenges better than you," she declared.

So then why did you ask for this advisory board? I thought to myself.

"These journalists broke the law," she said. "They are traitors, and they will be tried as such."

No doubt Suu Kyi was showing off her grit in front of the other ministers and the generals she had included in the meeting. She was throwing twenty years of friendship aside in a showy display of political dominance. "The West," she said, "needs to stop imposing Muslims on Myanmar."

I was stunned. It was a moment of epiphany for me. The leader in front of me was not who I'd thought she was, and if that was the case, then our whole strategy for making a tangible and positive impact for the Rohingya and for getting Wa Lone and Kyaw Soe Oo freed from jail was hopeless. This international advisory board, I realized, had been established to whitewash the crimes against the Rohingya and quiet the international uproar by using the stature of the board members as a guise of action.

Guv just sat there and took it in. I was surprised by his idleness. He let her throw the punches and did not punch back.

* * *

I TAKE MYANMAR PERSONALLY.

I knew only the basics when I showed up there for the first time in 2012. This former British colony of fifty-four million people, formerly and still sometimes known as Burma, was squeezed between Bangladesh, India, China, Laos, Thailand, and the Indian Ocean and was shaped like a wobbly fan at the bottom of Southeast Asia. Since winning independence in 1948, the country had gone back and forth between military and civilian governments, mostly back, and the military regimes tended to rule with a very harsh hand. But like many newcomers, I was won over immediately by this beautiful but troubled land and its sweet, warm people. And I soon found myself heading back and back and back again.

The high point of that first visit was going with the governor to Aung San Suu Kyi's house on Inya Lake, where she'd spent years under house arrest. The most famous woman in Myanmar, she'd been celebrated around the world for her courage and leadership and was expected to run the country one day. As leader of the National League for Democracy or NLD, the nation's largest civilian party, she had led a boycott of the last election, in 2010, over claims of fraud and corruption by the military. Now another election was scheduled for 2015. There'd be no boycott this time.

"What can we do to help, Suu?" Governor Richardson had asked warmly as he and I sat in her living room over tea and biscuits, gazing out at the water.

"Two things, Bill," she said without hesitation. "Help train the young political activists who are going to stand for the Pyidaungsu Hluttaw," Myanmar's bicameral parliament. "They need to be ready to serve when the time comes. And bring delegations of American investors and social entrepreneurs to Myanmar, especially in the areas of food security and water distribution. We need their investment, and we need their expertise."

"We can do both," Guv assured her.

And we did.

Under the auspices of the Richardson Center, we spent the next three years training 3,500 first-time candidates in two of the key skills of democracy, what it means to run for public office and what it means to serve. Since Myanmar had no real democratic tradition, all this had to be learned from the ground up. And the training wasn't just for members of the NLD or the smaller civilian parties. We also trained the candidates who would be representing the Union Solidarity and Development Party, the political wing of the Myanmar military, some of them still in fatigues or crisp khaki uniforms. We weren't there to pick winners. We were there to teach the process of democracy—and to help everyone understand: democracy is worth it, but democracy takes work.

We brought small teams of elected officials and bright young government staffers from the United States, including the newly elected mayor of South Bend, Indiana (and future Democratic presidential candidate and US transportation secretary), Pete Buttigieg. The trainers loved sharing their passion for democracy—what it means to campaign for office, to represent constituents, to write a budget, to make hard policy choices, and to separate personal interest from the public good. Real-life stuff. We led role-playing exercises. We toured key government venues. These aspiring public servants got an up-close view of what democracy is all about, and they really seemed to soak it up. I know the sessions were inspiring for the visiting trainers too.

Leading our efforts on the ground were Mindy Walker, a dedicated young woman from Wisconsin who was living in Myanmar, and Aye Moe, a local-hire contract employee whose own life nearly epitomized the country's burgeoning democracy. A young teacher and democracy activist, Aye Moe taught classes in inclusion and acceptance and authored children's books on tolerance. Both women were thrilled about the prospects for democracy in Myanmar—and even more thrilled to help propel them. Mindy and Aye Moe made an extraordinary team, often assisted by aspiring journalist Wa Lone.

It was fascinating to watch the budding local politicians confront the practical challenges of self-government. One person would play the president. Someone else was the prime minister. Others grilled them with tough questions. We had seventy-year-old retired generals debating big issues with young rural activists: *Should we give more money to the farmers or more money for education?...What's the best way to spur economic development?...How can we be sure the justice system is fair?*

It was all a little messy...just like democracy.

"What a dichotomy!" Mayor Pete marveled, casting a glance at three middle-aged trainees in military uniform. "Some of them are probably responsible for terrible abuses in the past. And yet here they are, arguing passionately over poor people's rights."

He got it, and that reminded me again: There is no sharp line between good and evil. There is genuine humanity inside all people, whatever bad things they may have done previously. They want to educate kids because they are *their* kids. They want the country's economy to grow because it's *their* country. Taking personal responsibility is important—and Myanmar's former military leaders clearly needed to do some of that. But almost no one is pure evil.

Eventually the International Republican Institute and the National Democratic Institute, the global training arms of the two main US political parties, got into the mix, conducting their own training sessions in Myanmar. From all those efforts, genuine progress was being made.

At the same time all this training was underway, we also brought delegations of Western investors and social entrepreneurs to Myanmar, fulfilling the second half of Aung San Suu Kyi's request. They came because they were curious, because they sought adventure, and because they wanted to share their expertise with a developing nation. Some of them were also scoping out future investment prospects in this resource-rich, technology-poor land. The decades of on-and-off military rule had left many of the country's basic needs woefully unmet.

One group introduced clean-cook stoves, a simple, low-cost alternative to open fires for cooking, a longtime source of lung disease and air pollution. Another group expanded internet use, helping local businesses create their first websites and establishing Myanmar's first popular search engines. A brilliant woman named Cynthia Koenig introduced something called the Waterwheel, a plastic barrel that could be filled with fresh water at the local well, then rolled home like a wheelbarrow. Inexpensive to produce, yet so effective! It was far easier and more efficient than the old water jugs, and it freed women and girls for more productive activities, such as attending school. Soon Cynthia was adding a water filtration system to the rolling barrels. She even inserted a tiny dynamo that could charge cell phones, which were just then arriving in Myanmar.

Such simple ideas...with the genuine capacity to change lives. And gloriously, our preelection efforts really paid off.

All the nation's political parties participated in the vote on November 8, 2015. Turnout was robust. Many first-time candidates ran—and won—and many of them had been trained by our scrappy Richardson Center teams. The National League for Democracy amassed a staggering victory with a supermajority of seats in both houses of the national parliament, putting the government firmly in civilian hands for the first time since General Ne Win's bloody coup d'état on March 2, 1962. Because of a quirk in the national constitution, Aung San Suu Kyi could not assume the title of president. But she was appointed to the newly created office of state counselor, which made her the de facto head of state.

People cheered around the world.

"Welcoming the New Guard," blared the headline in the state-run Global New Light newspaper. The military government conceded without any further fight. "We will respect and obey the decision of the electorate," said spokesman Ye Htut. "We will work peacefully in the transfer. Congratulations...to the chairperson Aung San Suu Kyi and her party for gathering the support of the people."

For Myanmar and its friends around the world, this was a time of tremendous optimism. But there was still a major issue, lying quietly below the surface, that was dangerously unresolved.

The Rohingya.

* * *

A NOMADIC MUSLIM ETHNIC GROUP WHO CAME ORIGINALLY FROM THE
Arakan coast of Southeast Asia, the Rohingya had been in the Rakhine
State of western Burma for more than a thousand years. They were
denied freedom of movement, access to education, and citizenship no
matter how long they'd been in the country, and their legal rights were
as stingy as those under South African apartheid. That was Archbishop
Desmond Tutu's analogy, and he should know. The Rohingya were one
of the most persecuted minorities in the world, according to human
rights groups. Going all the way back to the days of British colonialism,
the Rohingya had been promised a land to call their own. They were still
waiting.

Part of the hostility toward the Rohingya had grown out of disputes
over land, water, and other resources. But it went much deeper than that.
A lot of it was cultural and religious. Myanmar is a heavily Buddhist
nation, with 132 different sects of Buddhists. Aung San Suu Kyi wasn't
speaking only for herself when she snapped at Guv: "The West needs to
stop imposing Muslims on Myanmar."

It had all gotten worse as hundreds of thousands of the Muslim
nomads streamed over the border from Bangladesh, pushing their population in Myanmar well above one million. Then the Myanmar government announced that Rohingya families could have no more than two
children and tried to place limits on Rohingya marriages. Eventually
Rohingya militants attacked the Myanmar Army. In response, the army
and the local police launched a brutal crackdown in mid-2017, sending
730,000 Rohingya fleeing back across the border to Bangladesh. It was
ugly all around. That mass displacement led the International Criminal
Court to probe crimes against humanity and the International Court of
Justice to use the word *genocide*. Of course, the media also dove in.

Some of the best investigative journalism on the Rohingya crisis—or
the Rohingya Genocide—was being done by my good friend Wa Lone.
After volunteering as a translator on our democracy-building campaign,
he'd written a story about our work for the *Myanmar Times* and had

since gone to work as a full-time journalist, covering Myanmar for the global news service Reuters. By then he had excellent sources around the country and a real nose for news. He was digging into reports of a massacre outside the village of Inn Din in Rakhine State when he and a young colleague, Kyaw Soe Oo, were lured to a dinner with police officials, who said they had important information to share. As soon as the young journalists were handed an envelope of documents, they were taken into custody and charged with violating Myanmar's colonial-era Official Secrets Act, which carried a maximum sentence of fourteen years in prison.

11   DASHED HOPES

As we were leaving our intense meeting of Aung San Suu Kyi's international advisory board just before Guv resigned, the question became, *How do we separate ourselves from this farce, make a strong, clear statement, and get safely out of the country?* My mind was racing to design a way out, to choreograph a delicate political dance. My military training had prepared me to evaluate threats and possible scenarios at each turn. This was not my first unexpected extraction.

Steve Ross had a good insight.

"The government controls the media," he said to the governor. "If we tell them you are resigning but hold off on releasing the letter until we are out of the country, then they will spin this before we get out. They will control the narrative, and we will be chasing the news."

That's almost always a losing proposition.

"So we have to get the letter published before them," Guv said, picking up on Steve's thought. "We have to beat them to it. We can't let them appropriate the story." It wasn't so much that the governor was concerned about his reputation being besmirched by Suu Kyi. Her clout as a Nobel Peace Prize winner had already begun to fade once she failed to condemn the genocide within her own country. We all wanted to make sure that truth and justice for the Rohingya was the headline of our story.

"But wait," I jumped in. "If we make this letter public while we're still in Naypyidaw, we still need to get from here to Yangon, where the international flights depart. That gives them plenty of time to detain you, Guv. And I should remind you that if you are arrested, there is no other Governor Richardson out there to get you out."

The truth is that I was feeling trapped. We were in a faraway nation that was still dominated by a brutal military that wasn't exactly known for respecting people's rights. And we had just pissed off the government. It had the upper hand in every scenario. As peaceful and open as I had always found the Myanmar people to be, the government had eyes and ears on everyone, everywhere, and that included us. So the follow-up question had become, *How do we evade suspicion and make it to Yangon International Airport to catch a flight out?* We were trapped in a small cage inside a larger cage.

"The biggest and only advantage we have over them now is that they don't know you have decided to resign," I said. "They know you are upset. They must assume you are thinking of resigning. But they will not pull the trigger before they know for certain. They would rather avoid this altogether. We must maintain this advantage for as long as we can. We have to keep them wondering."

Guv immediately grasped that. "Tomorrow morning," he said, "we are scheduled to depart in helicopters for Rakhine State. Steve, how long is that flight?"

"I think it's about two or two and a half hours," Steve replied.

The lights in my brain started flashing. I could feel the plan formulating right there. *One helicopter will have Myanmar government officials and the advisory board members, and the second helicopter will have the journalists. All of them will be captive and incapable of responding for two and a half hours.*

"That's our window," I said. "We keep them believing that you are sticking with the advisory board agenda until one minute before departure. I will just come out of your room and tell them that you have decided not to join the trip to Rakhine."

"Are we telling them I'm resigning?" Guv asked.

"No. We want them still wondering when they take off. Then we have two and a half hours to get to Yangon, which is a one-hour flight."

"We can use KMT to purchase our domestic tickets to Yangon without them knowing," Steve said. "We can have a departure time thirty minutes after the helicopters take off."

Khin Maung Thein, frequently known as KMT, was an old friend of the governor, a retired military officer in Myanmar and former ambassador to Japan. They'd met when Guv first came to Myanmar twenty-plus years earlier as a young member of the US Congress. Guv was there to plead with the military leader to ease the imprisonment of Daw Suu Kyi. At the time, KMT was a young officer assigned to handle the governor during his visit. As he often did with his handlers, the governor befriended KMT and stayed in touch over the years. When I started traveling to Myanmar on behalf of the governor, I used KMT as my anchor. He and I developed our own friendship. KMT was well known in the ranks of the Myanmar military. A real asset as a friend, he was especially valuable at times like this.

"OK," Guv said, "get KMT to buy our tickets. Don't tell him why. Tell him to also get us cars for pickup. Make sure he knows not to share the information."

"We also need to get our international flight tickets ready," Steve added.

"But as soon as we change our tickets, the Myanmar Foreign Ministry will know," I reminded him. "They have the manifestos. That will blow our ambiguity and will give away our plan. Let's buy departure tickets for five different days, the first one being tomorrow night. That way, if anyone asks why we are purchasing the tickets, I can simply explain that we do not know yet what Guv wants to do, and as staff, I must prepare options for him. That will keep them guessing for a while."

I saw a smile on Guv's face. He was starting to like this plan. At the end of the day, he enjoyed feeling like the central character in a bestselling thriller. Of course, he still thought I was overreacting. In his mind there was no chance in hell that the government of Myanmar would dare detain him.

"What do we do when we get to Yangon?" Guv asked. "How do we get our story out?"

Steve had a suggestion. "We can take day rooms at a hotel downtown and do a couple of one-on-one interviews with leading reporters and have the pieces embargoed until we are wheels up."

The plan was being tightly knit.

"Let's have KMT pick us up when we land in Yangon and take us to the hotel room," I said. "And tell him to book the rooms for a couple of nights. The other side won't know we're planning to leave the country that same evening."

"Remember," Steve cautioned, "they have eyes in the lobbies of the hotels."

"Good point!" Guv said. "We'll do the interviews in my room."

"Even better, Guv," I said, "let's do the interviews in *my* room. We're less likely to be surveilled there. Steve can tell the journalists to meet me at the elevators, not the lobby. That way, the government minders won't be suspicious."

This was all coming together quite nicely, I thought. We would keep the Myanmar government in the dark regarding Guv's resignation. At the last minute, we would pull out of the trip to Rakhine and still not say Guv was resigning. Only when the board and government officials were airborne would we fly to Yangon, get picked up by KMT, have two discreet interviews, and head to the international airport. The interviews and Guv's letter would go public only after we were in the air.

Definitely not an easy feat to execute, but doable!

"Wait!" Steve said. A thought had just hit him. "I don't have a seat in the helicopter tomorrow. They are sending me on an air force transport plane to Rakhine. I'm set to depart *before* you tell them that you aren't going to Rakhine. If I cancel before you do, they will know. And if I don't cancel, I will be flying to Rakhine while you are making the move. Am I going to be in trouble?"

Uh-oh. That felt like a checkmate. Or maybe not.

"Is it a direct flight?" Guv asked. "Can you find out?"

It took Steve a few minutes. Calls, texts, a short wait, then a response. "We are flying through Yangon," Steve said.

"Well, that gives us an out!" Guv told him. "You go ahead as if nothing is off. You board that flight, and just after seven a.m., you tell them you just got a message from me that I am not going to Rakhine and that you should deplane in Yangon, and I will arrange for your pickup. Are you OK with that, Steve? That way, we can meet you in Yangon and leave the country together."

Steve nodded. *Ingenious.*

"But tonight, Guv," I said, "you need to continue as if you are still on the international advisory board. You have to go to the state dinner. Who knows, maybe Suu Kyi will apologize."

The truth was that Steve and I were still hoping there would be a way to rescue our involvement. Steve had lived in Myanmar for several years, and this was my eleventh visit. We had both come to love this country. More than that, the whole premise of fringe diplomacy, my work, and my ability to make a difference, relied on being in the room and being around the table. We had worked so hard to be included on the international advisory board. Resigning now and fleeing the country would erase the last six years of our engagement. The impact we'd had on helping to shape democratic institutions in what had then been seen as a country ripe for democratic reform and the political capital we'd gained there—it would all be lost once we took off. I was really hoping the state dinner would give cooler heads an opportunity to prevail. I was hoping Suu Kyi would do the right thing and reconcile with Guv following her destructive theatrics earlier that day. I was hoping.

"OK," Guv said, "I'll go to the dinner. But don't expect me to reach out to her, and I'm not changing my mind. This advisory board is a sham."

"I know, Guv," I said. "But if she reaches out, keep an open mind."

"Yeah, yeah." He nodded.

* * *

WHEN WE ARRIVED AT THE STATE DINNER, I HAD FAR TOO MUCH ON my mind. Steve and I had spent the remainder of the afternoon putting all the pieces of the plan together and trying, at the same time, to keep an eye on what was happening with the rest of the board. I was hoping that Suu Kyi and Guv would have a quiet moment after she arrived at the formal event. But she walked coolly by, yet another small act of personal defiance. *The Lady does not like to bend!* I could feel myself seething. I imagined Guv felt the same way. *Maybe she'll reach out at the dinner table,* I thought to myself. But they'd had no direct interaction so far.

Guv was seated directly across from Suu Kyi, but the table was very wide. I was standing behind the table, observing. There was no way I could sit at the "kids' table" and eat. I needed to monitor the movements and behaviors of the principals, much as the military minders had done with me.

About halfway through the meal, it finally happened. Suu Kyi looked at Guv. "Bill," she asked, "are we still friends?"

Doesn't she have any sort of emotional intelligence? I thought to myself. *Doesn't she realize that by ignoring the elephant in the room for almost two hours, she just widened the breach between herself and the governor?* Guv had been playing his gentleman's best, waiting for Suu Kyi to reach out.

"Of course we are still friends, Suu," he said earnestly. "But as your friend, I will continue to speak the truth to you. That's what friends do."

Ouch!

The state dinner had devolved into the diplomatic version of a screaming match between these two masters of diplomacy. To say their exchange was undiplomatic would be a vast understatement. I knew it was over between them. Now we had to execute our extraction plan.

In my room that night, I couldn't sleep. In my head I obsessively replayed the events of the past thirty-six hours, trying to make sense of things. Suu Kyi must have known Guv was going to push her on the jailed journalists. That was why she'd changed a private meeting of friends into a formal session with ministers and generals. She'd known she was going to deliver a show of force. Her audience had been the generals. But how had she known? Eventually I dozed off as I continued reviewing the extraction plan in my head.

That next morning, Steve departed for the airport before the rest of us. The plan was in motion. I sat in Guv's room, waiting for the clock to say 6:58.

"The governor decided not to join today's trip to Rakhine," I told the Myanmar chief of protocol when I stepped outside. "After yesterday's events, he needs to take some time. I hope we can join you when you return."

The chief of protocol looked anxious. This was the last thing he wanted to deal with when a helicopter packed with journalists and the members of the international advisory board was just about to take off. I walked back inside. I didn't want to engage in conversation, but I wanted to make sure no one approached the governor's room. All our suitcases were packed and ready to go.

The first step of our plan worked perfectly. The rest of the advisory board and the Myanmar government officials decided they could not hold the helicopters and took off. Within five minutes, KMT's car arrived at the resort. Guv and I jumped in and drove to the Naypyidaw airport.

As Guv and I rushed through the terminal, I received a text from Steve. My flight is delayed. Try to avoid our lounge. I don't want the Myanmar government staff to see you here.

Got it, I texted back. I'll get Guv into the other lounge.

Our flight took off before Steve's did. We were on our way to Yangon. As I breathed a sigh of partial relief, I kept my fingers crossed that Steve's flight would be only slightly delayed.

Just after we touched down in Yangon, Guv elbowed me and motioned out the window. "Look," he said. "Military vehicles. They figured out we were here." That couldn't be good.

Our plane stopped short of the gate. The doors opened, and all the passengers climbed down the stairway to the tarmac.

A military officer approached the two of us. "Governor Richardson, please come this way."

We climbed into a minibus flanked by military vehicles. "Where are we going?" Guv asked.

"You are a VIP," the officer said. "We are taking you to a special lounge."

This was no hospitality gesture. I was sure of that. After figuring out that Guv and I were on that plane, some part of the government must have intervened to control our movement. They couldn't afford to have a pissed-off Governor Richardson running amok in Myanmar.

The bus arrived at a dusty old room that felt more like a holding room than an international VIP lounge. The uniformed officers and armed guards also gave the space an air of hostility. But in typical Myanmar fashion, we were offered sodas and biscuits, a gesture of hospitality despite our being held in a room without a view...or cell service.

"What do you think?" Guv asked.

"Well, I'd say their VIP lounge looks an awful lot like a military holding room," I told him.

We sat there quietly for a while, sipping our sodas and politely nibbling on the snacks that were offered to us. Suddenly the officers turned toward the entrance and snapped to attention. Beyond the door we could hear loud voices speaking in Burmese. Suddenly a charismatic and familiar voice filled the stale room.

"He is with me." Those were the words.

It was KMT to the rescue...and I breathed a big sigh of relief.

He exchanged salutes with a few of the officers, shook some hands, and then approached us. "Welcome to Yangon, Guv," KMT said with a serious face. "They are coming with me," he told the officers.

It was not a request. It was not a question. It was a statement, and no one—not the officers, not the guards, no one—raised any objection. KMT was a rare soul who could walk the tightrope between these two worlds and still garner respect from both sides.

Silently we walked out toward his black SUV, which was waiting by the curb. *Good thing we didn't have checked luggage*, I thought. It was one of Guv's basic rules: Never bring more than a carry-on. You never know when you'll need to move fast. We got into the car. KMT sat with us in the back, and the driver sped away.

"Steve is on a separate transport plane," I said. "Do you have him?"

KMT shrugged at me. "He's in the car behind us."

"What kind of trouble are you up to?" he asked with a smile as soon as we cleared the airport gate.

"I think I pissed off the Lady," Guv said with his own signature menacing smile.

KMT laughed. He was a man of few words.

"The minister of home affairs keeps calling me to ask if I know where you are and what you're planning," KMT said. "I told them I have no clue."

"Good," Guv answered. "Do we have the hotel rooms?"

"All set. We'll be there in ten minutes."

"Hey, KMT," I said. "Around six p.m. today, will you come by the hotel with your car? Guv wants to take you out for dinner."

KMT nodded. He must have figured we had other plans in mind. But the less he knew, the more plausible deniability he had.

My eyes scanned the periphery as we casually strolled into the hotel lobby. I was trying to spot the "minders." Too many possibilities. It could be anyone. We checked in and went to our rooms.

"I scheduled the two interviews forty-five minutes apart," Steve said.

"I'll come by your room in twenty minutes to pick you up," I said to the governor. "And I'll bring you to my room for the interviews. Now's a good time to shower, change for our flight, and pack everything back up."

Steve told the reporters to meet me at the elevator and not to linger in the lobby. "He'll be the one with the black suit, black T-shirt, and buzz-cut hair," he said. That had become one of my rules in life: always wear your own uniform.

The interviews were probing. The reporters were both total pros. We shared Guv's resignation letter with them and reminded them they couldn't publish anything until they got an email from me later that night. When they saw the letter, they understood why. I could see the excitement in their eyes. They knew they had a great story for their editors and their readers. It wasn't often that significant political leaders stood up defiantly to The Lady. By this point, everyone seemed to know she was complicit in the crisis in Rakhine. But as is too often the case in politics, no one had yet shown the guts to out her as an accomplice in gross human rights violations. This was Daw Aung San Suu Kyi, human rights icon and Nobel recipient. That powerful image was about to come tumbling down.

When KMT arrived with his car that evening, we hustled Guv into the back seat. "Just a minute," I said. "We forgot something in the room. Steve, can you come help me?"

He and I went upstairs and grabbed our three carry-ons. "I guess we are not going for dinner," KMT said.

"I'm sorry, my friend," Guv answered. "We have to get to the airport. Our flight leaves in two hours. I didn't want to get you in trouble by telling you beforehand."

KMT smiled. "I guess I'll read about it later?"

It was an intricate dance we were leading with KMT, and he hadn't missed a step.

* * *

My nerves were raw as we approached passport control. None of us said a word. The Foreign Ministry would know we were departing the country as soon as we checked in for our flight. Up to that moment, we'd had the cover of ambiguity: several flight itineraries, multiple hotel rooms booked, and no real sign of us leaving.

"Now we'll find out how efficient the Myanmar government is with information sharing," I whispered to Steve.

We checked in and cleared passport control and were anxiously waiting to board our flight to Tokyo. I drafted my email to the reporters, saying the embargo was off. They were free to release the interviews and the resignation letter. I didn't hit *send*.

"When are you sending it?" Guv asked me. "We can't afford them getting the draw on us."

"I'll send it as soon as the plane accelerates on the runway," I responded. "Think Ben Affleck in *Argo*. I don't want to risk a delayed departure."

Guv laughed. He didn't either.

I needed to time it perfectly. I needed to be absolutely sure we were departing before I pressed *send*. But I also needed to make sure I was still connected to the internet before we were electronically stranded for six hours in the air. If our statement didn't get published first, then the Myanmar government would have six full hours to control the narrative, and our whole extraction plan would have been for nothing.

Sent.

I signaled Guv from my seat with a thumbs-up just as we felt the wheels of the plane lifting off the runway.

* * *

SIX HOURS OF DISCONNECTION. SIX HOURS TO REFLECT. YES, WE GOT out. And so did the story, our version. But this was also a failure. I failed. The democracy-building strategy we'd worked so hard and long for had completely collapsed. Wa Lone and Kyaw Soe Oo were still incarcerated. A mere couple of days earlier, I couldn't have imagined such a thing. The two Pulitzer-winning Reuters reporters would eventually win their freedom in early May 2019. But as I sat on that plane with the time to think about it, I and my mission had failed.

Was Aung San Suu Kyi really that two-faced? Had she really fooled the whole world all these years? She was an icon of peaceful protest. A voice for millions silenced, but only temporarily, by military dictatorship. A beacon of hope that Myanmar could one day welcome a peaceful, democratic government. But now she had proven herself to be something far darker than that, a stubbornly ethnocentric leader who was unwilling to acknowledge the humanity of a group different from her own. In her eyes, the lives of the Muslim Rohingya minority held no value to the Buddhist nation of Myanmar. How had I missed seeing her true self? The truth was that she was human. She was multifaceted. Her blind spots had led her to be complicit in a genocide. The world needed to know. We had publicly promised to help the Rohingya, and they needed to hear us speak up.

Now, in the silence of the flight to Tokyo and with the hindsight of the past two days, my mind was beginning to absorb the many pieces of this. Pieces I had not connected before. Suu Kyi was her father's daughter, the daughter of a military leader deposed and killed in a coup. She lived her life in the shadow of her father's assassination. What a burden to carry! From the time that she was two! She had grown up in a military household. She believed that ruling Myanmar was her destiny, and now was her time. And despite all the democracy training that we and others had done in Myanmar, she was running her own party the only way she knew how, as an autocracy. She was not exactly in cahoots with the military. She despised it. But that did not make her the democratic reformer we wanted her so badly to be. She had an autocratic program of her own that competed with the autocratic program of the military. Suu Kyi was genuinely devoted to peace and reconciliation for all of Myanmar's 132 ethnic groups…as long as they weren't Muslims. She did not believe the Rohingya were equal to the "real" people of Myanmar. How could she hold such a glaring exception? People are complex beings.

"Will you speak against the violent rhetoric toward the Rohingya?" I remembered asking her on that delegation I'd led, six years earlier, at her house by the lake.

"This will be unwise for me to do," she'd answered with a stern look that day. "It would be very unpopular with my people, and we need to first win the elections in three years."

That was all she said. Yet in my mind, I'd completed the sentence for her: *And then we will solve the hatred toward the Rohingya.* That had been my cognitive biases taking control. She'd never said what I wanted to hear!

Thump.

The wheels of the plane touched down in Tokyo. The phones came back to life.

"I told you so," I said to the governor, leaning over and holding up my phone. "Look at this statement from the Ministry of Information. They say you are in contempt of Myanmar law. They would have detained you!"

Yes, I was feeling exonerated. No, I hadn't overreacted with my extraction plan. "But Guv, what do we do now?" I asked, feeling the sadness and disappointment of failure creeping back.

"Little Jewish man," Guv answered, using his favorite playful phrase for me, "when they don't like you in Myanmar, they will like you in Bangladesh! With all this blowing up, we can be very effective in helping the Rohingya refugees on that side of the border. You and Steve should put together a program for us there."

On to Bangladesh!

12 RECIPROCAL ARRANGEMENTS

"Mickey, it's Rob. I've been asked to coordinate a meeting between you and the family of Paul Whelan. Can you do it this week?"

Rob Saale was a former FBI agent who looked and sounded just like Hollywood's idea of an FBI agent. Rugged. Charismatic. Excellent posture and a square jaw. But Rob had something extra: a real knack for connecting with people, especially people who found themselves under duress. And unlike some veteran bureaucrats, he was always ready to take the initiative, even take a risk, when the circumstances called for it. In my experience, Rob was never a prisoner of *That's the way we've always done it.*

He'd been director of the Hostage Recovery Fusion Cell, a newish entity that brought together the FBI, the State Department, the Defense Department, the Treasury Department, and the other federal agencies that were concerned about Americans held hostage or wrongfully imprisoned abroad. A month after the return of Otto Warmbier from North Korea, Rob had called me out of the blue.

"My name is Rob Saale," he said. "I read about you and Governor Richardson and your involvement in Warmbier's release. I wanted to reach out. Together, I'll bet we could find some ways to help people."

Over the course of several conversations, Rob and I became friends. He was proud that the Fusion Cell had taken a "whole-of-government" approach" to the hostage issue, and now he was ready to be even more inclusive. "We are willing to talk and work with anyone, as long as it is ethical and legal, to help get our folks back home," he said to me. "We're trying to take a 'whole-of-society approach.'"

Rob was talking my language. I felt like I had just found someone I'd been looking for, a fringe-diplomacy accomplice on the inside, and we had the perfect case to test our new public-private partnership. Governor Richardson and I had been working hard to find Jeff Woodke, an American aid worker who had gone missing in West Africa and was presumed kidnapped by militants in Niger. I showed Rob the inquiries we were about to send to an African nation's government, knowing that would create some chatter on the continent. "If the FBI turns its covert ears in the right direction," I told Rob, "you guys might pick up some valuable intelligence that could help locate Jeff." Rob agreed to try. While bureau policy prevented him from sharing what might have been discovered, it was a great demonstration to both of us of the value of our collaboration. And we agreed to keep at it.

Rob had a well-focused team working with him. The Fusion Cell's terrific external engagement coordinator, Brooke Neuman, joined with the Richardson Center to host periodic get-togethers in Washington of all the groups, agencies, and individuals trying to free American hostages abroad, a much-needed means of making connections, trading ideas, and coordinating the efforts in and out of government. The group of three dozen or so included Democrats, Republicans, intelligence agents, former politicians, ex-military officers, think-tank brainiacs, business leaders, media figures—anyone we felt might bring something to the table. "Influencer meetings," people started calling these gatherings.

After Rob's retirement from the FBI and Fusion Cell, he set up his own consulting firm and stayed close to the issue. When US Marine veteran Paul Whelan was arrested in Moscow and his family contacted Rob, the former FBI agent suggested bringing Richardson and me into the fold.

"Of course I'll meet," I told Rob that cold February morning in 2019.

* * *

MY FIRST CONVERSATION WITH ELIZABETH WHELAN, PAUL'S SISTER, was over Zoom. Rob and I were in the Washington office of the family's lawyer, Ryan Fayhee. It was not the intimate setting I preferred for a family-member conversation like this one. Around me I could see lawyers, advocates, and others coming in and out—it was certainly less personal than I'd have liked. But Elizabeth's anxious sentiments were completely familiar to me. I could certainly feel her pain.

Paul Whelan had loved being a United States Marine. Born in Canada to British parents and holding US, Irish, and British citizenship, he'd started his career as a sheriff's deputy in the college city of Ann Arbor, Michigan, before joining the US Marine Corps Forces Reserve in 1994. He'd later accepted a job as an IT manager for Kelly Services, the office-staffing company. He took military leave from that position in 2003 to serve as a staff sergeant with Marine Air Control Group 38, where he was an administrative chief during Operation Iraqi Freedom. After leaving the marines, Paul was soon back at Kelly, where he rose quickly through the ranks to senior manager of global security.

Fast forward to December 2018, three months before our Zoom call. Paul Whelan was in Moscow, a city he had visited many times. Now he was there for the wedding of a marine buddy and to show the groom's family around on their first visit to Russia. Three days after Christmas, the forty-eight-year-old corporate security director spent several hours with a longtime Russian friend before returning to room 3324 at Hotel Metropol to dress for the wedding rehearsal dinner. That's when agents from the Russian Federal Security Service burst in and arrested him for espionage. Whelan's Russian friend had supposedly slipped him a USB thumb drive that contained "a list of all the employees at a classified security agency." Instead of returning to Michigan on January 6 as he had planned to, Paul Whelan greeted the New Year from a Russian jail cell, awaiting trial in Moscow City Court and facing the terrifying prospect of decades in a harsh, foreign prison.

US intel officers speculated that Whelan's arrest was most likely a product of the rising tensions between Moscow and Washington. The bilateral bitterness had been exacerbated in recent months by the case of Maria Butina, who'd been arrested in Washington by the FBI and had just pled guilty to acting as an unregistered Russian agent. Was this

Russian tit for tat? It wouldn't be the first time. Butina had been awaiting her sentencing in Washington when Whelan was arrested in Moscow.

His Russian defense attorney, Vladimir Zherebenko, said his client had clearly been set up. The ex-marine had believed his friend's thumb drive contained personal information like "photographs, videos, anything at all, about his previous holiday in Russia." Whelan had had no idea there were any secrets there, if in fact there were.

I'd been following Paul Whelan's detention from afar since the story broke. But Richardson and I did not get involved until Rob Saale and Elizabeth Whelan reached out in February. Though by then I'd had my hand in hostage cases in many nations around the world, I had no experience with the Russians. Fortunately, Guv had been dealing with Russian officials for decades, including some of the nation's current leaders. So we had some contacts and some leads. But we still needed to find a crack in the door that we could push our way through.

* * *

"You know, it's funny," Anatoly Antonov said when Guv, Ambassador Hume, and I finally sat down with him in mid-June. "You raise these concerns with us about Paul Whelan's health and treatment. But you don't care about the terrible health condition and treatment of Konstantin Yaroshenko."

Before taking his current position as Russia's ambassador to the United States, Antonov had been Russia's deputy minister of defense and deputy minister of foreign affairs. Without a doubt, these high-level postings had put him in Vladimir Putin's inner circle and reflected the importance that Putin's government placed on its diplomatic channels with Washington.

Antonov was sharp, direct, and wickedly funny. A sarcastic kind of funny. Delivered with a straight face and a rapid-fire pace. Sometimes it took me a few seconds to catch up. But once I got to know Ambassador Antonov, I would learn to anticipate the jibes and the jokes and actually started looking forward to them. In our first meeting, however, I'd been

War Zone: At the Litani River, southern Lebanon, 1996

Fallen Friend: With Nir Shreibman during our Israel Defense Forces officer course, 1996

True Love: Dating Robin, 2002

We Do: Our wedding day at Brandeis-Bardin Institute in Simi Valley, California, 2002

Proud Parents:
Celebrating with my
mom and dad, Gay
and Baruch Bergman,
Brandeis-Bardin
Institute, 2002

Major Mentors: With Bill Clinton and Rob Malley at the Clinton Global Initiative, 2006
The Clinton Global Initiative

Displaced People: In the Knoungu refugee camp near the Chad-Sudan border, 2005
Richard Levine

Next Generation: Laughing with a young refugee near the Chad-Sudan border, 2005
Richard Levine

Rescue Mission: Flying to Khartoum with Governor Richardson, 2007

Waging Peace: Richardson's Sudan delegation with Darfur rebel leaders, 2007

Common Ground: In Khartoum with Sudanese president Omar al-Bashir, Amjad Atallah, Larry Rossin, and Ken Bacon, 2007

Family Time: With Robin and four-year-old Noa, 2017
DeSilva Studios

Tense Talk: With Guv, Google chairperson Eric Schmidt, Tony Namkung, and Kevin Bleyer in Pyongyang, North Korea, 2013

Cold Comfort: At the mausoleum in Pyongyang with Eric Schmidt and delegation members, 2013

Team Leader: Beside North Korea's Taedong River with Rick Downes and P Willey, 2016

Between Meetings: At Kim Il-sung Square in Pyongyang, 2016

For Otto: With Han Song-ryol, North Korea's vice-minister of foreign affairs, 2016

The Lady: With Daw Aung San Suu Kyi at her home in Yangon, Myanmar, 2012

Rakhine's Burden: With Guv, Daw Aung San Suu Kyi, and KMT in Naypyidaw, Myanmar, 2017

Keep Talking: With Guv and Iranian foreign minister Mohammad Zarif in Doha, Qatar, December 2019

Official Visit: With Vice President Joe Biden and his national security advisor Tony Blinken in Tel Aviv, 2010
Official White House Photo by David Lienemann

Public Servant: In Myanmar with Aye Moe, five years before her arrest, 2015

All Smiles: In Yangon with Guv and Aye Moe, immediately after her release, 2021

Pressing Freedom: Flying home from Myanmar with Danny Fenster, 2021

Takeoff Time: Guv, Ambassador Cameron Hume, Steve Ross, and a US embassy official on the tarmac in Myanmar, 2021

Russian Sit-Down: With Guv, Sergey Lavrov, and Ara Abramyan in Moscow, 2023

Speaking Out: With Guv at the "Bring Them Home" mural in Washington's Georgetown neighborhood, 2022

Square Dealing: With Guv and Cameron Hume in Moscow's Red Square, 2023

Brainstorming: In Moscow with Sergey Lavrov and Sergei Ryabkov, Moscow, September 2023

Crossing Over: At the Russia-Poland border with freshly released American prisoner Taylor Dudley, Steve Menzies, Guv, and Taylor's mother, Shelley, 2023
Jonathan Franks

All Hugs: Celebrating Brittney Griner's release, Phoenix, 2023
Andrew Jenks

Home Again: Brittney Griner and Neda Sharghi, 2023
Andrew Jenks

momentarily taken aback when the ambassador interrupted Governor Richardson's introduction of Ambassador Hume, pointing out a tiny error Guv had made in Hume's bio.

"Don't you read the paper?" Antonov scolded without cracking a smile. "We know everything about you. We listen to you in your homes."

In sitting down with Antonov, Guv and I knew we had our work cut out for us. Our first goal would be to establish a positive channel of communication. That would be an achievement right there. You can't just meet someone like this for the first time and jump straight to your endgame. We weren't going to say, "Nice to see you, Mr. Ambassador...now please release Paul Whelan." We had to ramp up. This was going to take some finesse. Together with Elizabeth Whelan, we'd decided that our first aim with Antonov would be to see if we could get a medical examination for Paul. Outside his prison. A humanitarian, goodwill gesture. Paul had not had a proper medical workup since his arrest.

Given the conditions in many Russian prisons, that seemed vital to all of us, especially his worried family. But we were not quite prepared for Ambassador Antonov's response raising Konstantin Yaroshenko's health. It was almost as if the ambassador had been anticipating our moves and was prepared for them. (Was he listening to us in our homes? *Nah!*) He was clearly a serious, methodical diplomat and thoroughly prepared. I had been expecting him to raise Maria Butina. After all, if Whelan's spying arrest was in retaliation for Butina's spying arrest, wouldn't that be the kind of reciprocity the Russians were known to seek? But by the time we were meeting with Antonov, Butina had already received a relatively short sentence, eighteen months in prison, more than half of which she had already served. She had only a few months to go. They must have figured: *Let her do the rest of her time, then come home. No need to waste a valuable asset like Paul Whelan for something so minor.*

"Mr. Ambassador, can you say a little more about Yaroshenko?" I asked. "As a nongovernmental, humanitarian organization, we are not exclusively focused on American prisoners," I reminded him. "Maybe we can help with Yaroshenko's health issues."

I recognized we had to show genuine concern for the health of the Russian prisoner if we expected the Russian to be concerned for the health of the American. But little did I know how well prepared the Russian ambassador really was! Within minutes, I was holding a stack of letters—official letters on Russian embassy stationery—that the ambassador had sent to various US government agencies, raising concerns about Yaroshenko and requesting immediate action. None of these letters, Antonov told us, had received any response from the Americans.

Yaroshenko, a Russian pilot and alleged drug smuggler, had been arrested in the African nation of Liberia in 2010. While in Liberian custody, it appeared he'd been beaten severely, which had badly damaged his teeth. After Yaroshenko told his Liberian captors he was a friend of Vladimir Putin, they extradited him to New York, where he was found guilty of using planes to smuggle $100 million of cocaine into South America, Africa, Europe, and, perhaps, the United States. By the time Paul Whelan was grabbed in Moscow, the fifty-year-old Russian pilot was halfway through his twenty-year sentence at the US federal prison in Danbury, Connecticut.

I listened closely to the words of the Russian ambassador. Throughout our meeting, he never explicitly said that Whelan's medical treatment was dependent on dental treatment for Yaroshenko. Diplomatic professional that he was, he just left that impression hanging in the air as he kept mentioning the importance of symmetry and reciprocity.

Symmetry and reciprocity, I would grow to understand, are cornerstone principles in the Russian mindset. Exchanges always needed to go both ways.

"This is clearly a test," Hume said to Guv and me as soon as our car pulled away from the Russian embassy on Washington's Wisconsin Avenue. "Antonov wants to see if we have the ability to influence the Trump administration. If we can get Yaroshenko his dental care, we may be in business here."

That made sense to me. "And it's just as important," I said, "that we demonstrate to Antonov that we genuinely care about the well-being of *his* prisoner. Symmetry, reciprocity…and humanity."

Guv agreed.

We would try to help. We just had no idea what our chances of success were. We had very little leverage inside the Trump administration.

* * *

THE FEDERAL BUREAU OF PRISONS IS PART OF THE US JUSTICE Department. So to arrange for a dentist to see Konstantin Yaroshenko at the federal prison in Danbury, we decided, we had a better chance going through Justice than through the White House. And since all this had ramifications for the health and safety of a former US Marine held prisoner in Russia, we figured we might as well aim high.

In early August we were able to meet with Attorney General William Barr. Richardson and Barr had worked together when Richardson was a member of Congress and Barr was an assistant attorney general in the George H. W. Bush administration. That was back in the days when Democratic congressmen and Republican Justice Department officials actually talked to each other. So the initial conversation between the two of them sounded like the conversation between a couple of aged classmates at a high school reunion trying to remember how they had known each other way back when.

"I remember we did something together when you were in Congress," Barr started.

"Yeah, you're right, but for the life of me, I can't remember what it was," Guv responded. "But I *think* it was positive."

Both of them laughed at that.

Bonding achieved.

Guv explained to Barr what we were trying to do, emphasizing that this wasn't a straight-up exchange, but that we had good reason to believe that the Russians would reciprocate if we could get a dentist in to see Yaroshenko.

"My foundation will pay the dentist's bill," Guv assured the AG.

It was clear that Attorney General Barr had no affection for the convicted Russian drug smuggler. Nor was there much sympathy for Yaroshenko's oral-health concerns. But Barr immediately grasped what Guv was trying to achieve, and he sounded inclined to be helpful if that might ease the suffering of an American prisoner in Russia who also happened to be a marine veteran. Barr instructed his staffer David Burns to coordinate with the Bureau of Prisons.

"Make sure there's no good reason why the Russian prisoner can't be seen by a dentist," the attorney general said.

Wow! That went better than I expected!

This was my first meeting with Attorney General Barr, a Trump cabinet member I was supposed to dislike because of his political outlook. I know I shouldn't have been surprised at this. But when we finally met in person, I was reminded again how most people, even our rivals, are human beings first, not nearly as awful as we are made to believe. We might see the world differently. We might vehemently disagree on certain policies. Yet people are people, and most of them are complex beings. Good (and evil) exists in each of us. I'd known for a long time how true that was about our "sworn external enemies." I'd been finding the humanity inside dictators and despots for years. Now I was confronting the same exact principle closer to home...with someone who often lined up on a different side from me.

Attorney General Barr and his team delivered. Within a week of our meeting at Justice Department headquarters in Washington, a dentist visited Konstantin Yaroshenko at the federal prison in Connecticut, providing the Russian with the checkup he needed and some basic dental care. And in a reciprocal act less than two weeks later—whether that was how it was labeled or not—Paul Whelan was taken from his Moscow prison cell and driven to a Western-style medical center, where he was seen by a doctor and received his first thorough examination since his arrest.

We were onto something here! I could feel it! We had proof of concept! The next question was obvious: How far could we push this new momentum?

We made sure to express our gratitude to Ambassador Antonov for facilitating Paul Whelan's medical care. Antonov reciprocated by expressing his gratitude for our role in arranging the dental visit for Yaroshenko and for the humanitarian concern we had displayed. Governor Richardson immediately suggested a follow-up, which I passed on to the ambassador: perhaps the governor and I could travel to Moscow and meet with his longtime friend, Foreign Minister Sergey Lavrov, to discuss some issues of bilateral concern—humanitarian efforts including the issue of prisoners—and just catch up on the good old days they'd spent together as key members of their nations' diplomatic corps.

Lavrov and Richardson had served together at the United Nations. Each had been representing his government as ambassador. *Frenemies*, I believe, is the word. Rivals by nationality but friendly in their personal capacities. I had heard plenty of stories over the years from Guv about his encounters with Lavrov. Being the longest-serving diplomat on the face of the planet, the veteran Russian diplomat was clearly good at his job, loyal to his government, sophisticated, smart, and possessed of a keen sense of political smell. Later, when I met him, I would see all of that in person. But for the time being, our request for a meeting was politely denied.

"Governor Richardson is always welcome to visit Russia, but unfortunately, the foreign minister's schedule is packed, and he is unable to meet at this time." That was the email reply I received from Igor, an officer at the Russian embassy. Igor was my point of contact with the Russians. I liked Igor a lot.

It was a start, but the time for a visit to Moscow was not ripe yet, at least not on the Russian side. Ambassador Antonov followed up on Yaroshenko's dental visit and then contacted us with his findings. "The dentist confirmed that Yaroshenko needs some implants," Antonov told us the next time we met. "His teeth are dying, and he is in pain."

As it happened, Whelan's medical exam in Russia also revealed that he was in need of a nonemergency medical procedure, something the ex-marine very much did not wish to experience at the hands of the Russian prison's medical staff. But if we could arrange for him to have the procedure done in one of Moscow's more Western medical centers, he'd be deeply relieved, his sister told us.

So we went at it again. Symmetry and reciprocity. This time I had confidence that we could pull it off. After all, it worked the first time— didn't it?—and both sides were pleased. Why on earth couldn't we replicate that success?

Guv and I went back to the attorney general's office in early November. We asked for permission to pay for Yaroshenko's dental implants, knowing that otherwise they would not be provided. We also made clear what we believed would be the reciprocal act by the Russians, explaining why it was so important to Whelan. Barr agreed…in principle. But he said his team needed to review the bureaucratic procedures with the federal Bureau of Prisons.

The follow-up was not as smooth this time.

Barr's aide David Burns kept telling me he was doing his best to push the dental procedure through. I believe he was trying. But he reminded me that the Bureau of Prisons has strong autonomy, and central Justice can't just issue orders. That's what David said, anyway.

"But doesn't the Bureau of Prisons understand what's at stake here?" I implored.

I did not get a clear answer. While Paul Whelan's medical procedure was not an emergency, it could have turned into an emergency any day. And if it turned into an emergency, no one would ask for his consent, and Paul would be dragged into the prison clinic for the procedure, a prospect that absolutely terrified him. And *that* terrified his sister. She knew Paul was strong, but his days and nights in a Russian prison were taking its toll on him.

As time passed, my frustration grew. How could we, the United States of America, not provide much-needed medical attention to a prisoner in our custody? Even more so when it would help one of our fellow Americans in prison in Russia!

Over the next few weeks, I made sure to meet frequently with Igor at the Russian embassy. Reassuring him that we were still working on Yaroshenko's dental implants. Getting reassured that the reciprocity we had discussed regarding Whelan was still intact.

But time was not on our side. These were the early days of COVID-19. The world was just learning about the gravity of the deadly pandemic. Soon it became clear we had lost our window for getting authorization from Justice for Yaroshenko's dental implants, as COVID shut down all nonessential health care in US prisons.

But then the inevitable occurred. In early February, Paul Whelan's nonemergency medical procedure became urgent. He was taken into the prison clinic he desperately wanted to avoid. Without his consent, the medical procedure was performed on him. Thank God it went well, and Paul recovered. But still, I couldn't get over the fact that this entire part of the drama could have been avoided with such simple action by our own government.

* * *

THE PANDEMIC HIT HARD. EVERYWHERE. THE WORLD WAS ON LOCK-down. *I* was on lockdown. And it was killing my spirit. Meetings and negotiations went from in person to Zoom, text, and phone calls. Far less effective for someone who draws so much from interpersonal inter-actions. Nuances were lost. Nonverbal communications were lost. Like so many other Americans forced to work from home, I found myself working out of a backyard shed, which I converted into a backyard office. Substituting text for in-person negotiations meant I had to break down complicated concepts into a million basic questions. It didn't help that once in receipt of my texts and emails, many of my counterparts resorted to their mother tongues, which meant that our negotiations were also being conducted via Google Translate, which is brilliant and maddening, both at once. At least I had emoji. Believe it or not, I found those expres-sive little figures very useful in conveying emotions and tone. Often, they were all I had.

Winston Churchill supposedly said, "Never let a good crisis go to waste." Well, that's how we approached the pandemic. With COVID raging around the world, especially in the world's prisons, we figured there could still be an opportunity to stage some mutual humanitarian gestures to relieve this special burden on prisoners' health.

With that in mind, Guv, Hume, and I went back into the Russian embassy in mid-May wearing the highest-quality protective masks we could find, hoping we could make progress on the Whelan case. "Look," Guv said to Ambassador Antonov, "we've had success with mutual medical gestures. This pandemic is a major problem. It will be terrible for both sides if one of our nationals dies in the custody of the other. Let's go right to the endgame. Can't we find a way to get Paul Whelan home as a humanitarian gesture in the midst of this global pandemic?"

The Russians, as always, were prepared. "I believe we have already demonstrated to you," the Russian ambassador answered, "humanitarian gestures will be reciprocated."

Guv wanted to make sure he was hearing the ambassador correctly. "Are you saying that if we get Yaroshenko released as a medical gesture, you will do the same for Whelan?" he prodded.

"I am saying that humanitarian gestures tend to be reciprocated."

Always the professional diplomat, that's how Antonov responded. He chose his words carefully, and he stuck with them. He would get no more specific than that. He made *us* say it. And when we did, he used his silence and his gentle nod as his signal of agreement. Only now, when everyone was wearing face masks, it was even harder to read the non-verbal cues. But that's what we had, and I couldn't help but hear the nodding and the silence as a yes. Not in words, of course...but still. The Russians would agree to reciprocal humanitarian releases at this time of health emergency: Konstantin Yaroshenko for Paul Whelan.

I certainly liked the way that...not sounded...*looked.*

I rushed this information to Roger Carstens, President Trump's newly appointed special envoy on hostage affairs. A top-of-his-class

West Point and Naval War College graduate and retired army special forces officer, he'd fought in Iraq, been a civilian advisor in Afghanistan and served in the State Department's Bureau of Democracy, Human Rights, and Labor. I did not know Roger well, not yet, but he seemed as if he could become a valuable ally on the side. I got him up to speed as well as I could: "We have an arrangement with the Russians. If the US agrees to release Konstantin Yaroshenko as a medical humanitarian gesture due to the pandemic, the Russians will reciprocate and release Paul Whelan for the same reason."

Yaroshenko's conviction was only tangentially connected to America, and he had already completed half his long sentence. "Why should US taxpayers need to finance his well-being in the middle of a global pandemic?" I asked the Trump administration envoy. "Send him home and save an innocent American."

I gave the pitch everything I had.

I knew that Roger was not the decision maker, but I liked him and I was beginning to trust him and I wanted to convey my passion and my best arguments for him to use. Roger took careful notes. He was going to pass along the information to his administration colleagues.

The humanitarian prisoner swap seemed like a no-brainer to me, but top officials in the Trump administration weren't interested. Not in this swap. Not now, if ever. And that is where a good idea died.

What a missed opportunity!

So close and yet so far!

How big a missed opportunity would become clear only later on, as US-Russian relations grew more and more complicated and Paul Whelan got stuck in Russia with no obvious way out. For now, the former US Marine accused of espionage in Russia remained in his Moscow jail cell awaiting trial while Konstantin Yaroshenko remained behind bars in Connecticut, serving out the balance of his drug-smuggling sentence...with little prospect that either man would be seeing his loved ones back home anytime soon.

* * *

THAT WAS NEITHER THE FIRST NOR THE LAST TIME WE USED THE
global pandemic as an argument for bringing a wrongfully detained
American back home. As COVID ravaged communities around the
globe, we employed the health crisis to create urgency and as a catch-
all vehicle for humanitarian gestures. When captors hold political prisoners, they do so because they believe it provides them an advantage
of some sort. Leverage. But the risk of having political prisoners die in
your custody—while they're your responsibility—changes the risk calculation. Suddenly finding a way to get rid of those very same prisoners,
while also saving face, seemed like a less risky proposition to some governments. With the pandemic offering such a tempting off-ramp, we had
to give it a try.

That was our logic when Guv and I flew into Caracas, Venezuela, to
meet with President Nicolás Maduro. Maduro was holding eight American prisoners we were trying to get back: six oil executives known as
"the Citgo Six"—Tomeu Vadell, Alirio and Jose Luis Zambrano, Jorge
Toledo, Gustavo Cárdenas, and Jose Pereira—and two former US Army
Green Berets, Luke Denman and Airan Berry.

The US and Venezuelan governments had no diplomatic relationship.
They didn't communicate with each other at all, unless you count the
occasional sharply worded public statement or hostile social media post.
When you can't or won't talk with the other government, how can you
possibly expect to get your people out? Needless to say, the US government hadn't made progress on bringing the eight incarcerated Americans
home.

Guv did have a history of engagement with Venezuela, starting with
former president Hugo Chávez. He knew Nicolás Maduro, the current president, quite well. We used that familiarity to open the door.
The proposition was similar to the one we'd used with the Russians. We
raised the pandemic again: with COVID raging and no vaccine in sight,
they could make a humanitarian gesture by releasing the Americans.
And boy, we came close!

Assisting us on this dicey mission to Venezuela was Steve Menzies, a public-spirited American businessman who provided no fewer than three private aircraft for us to use. One was his own jet. The two others he chartered for us—one to take us in and out of Caracas and the other for backup medical evacuation, in case we were able to free some or all of the Americans. Steve also made sure we had a medical team on standby in Puerto Rico. A successful entrepreneur, he founded Applied Underwriters in 1994 and grew the company into a global risk-service giant, helping governments, businesses, and individual clients manage risk through insurance, reinsurance, and investments. Now he was sharing his organizational savvy and strategic expertise with those of us in the fringe-diplomacy world.

Steve and I had first met a couple of months earlier when he flew from the West Coast to northern Virginia on a cold early-spring afternoon. Since the pandemic was spreading around us, we sat outside in my backyard, six feet apart, while Robin and Noa watched through the windows and policed our every move. It was really cold, and I felt horrible that this was how I was hosting this generous businessman who had flown in just to learn how he might be helpful. But that was the pandemic.

Also joining our mission to Caracas was Rodrigo Aguilar, a Mexican American friend of the governor who served as our special advisor. Familiar with the culture, language, and leaders of Venezuela, Rodrigo offered insightful perspectives that helped us navigate the nation's deeply suspicious government.

We were the only guests in our hotel, which was opened just for us. We were tested and retested for the coronavirus every day. Even at mealtimes, we weren't allowed to leave our rooms. We had to call a special cook the hotel had hired since the regular kitchen was closed. It was all very surreal, unlike anything I'd ever been part of. In retrospect, it was an extremely risky mission. Pandemic raging, no vaccines, a government that had proven already it was willing to jail Americans on the thinnest of pretexts. Robin was furious with me for going. So furious it reignited some of the depression symptoms she had worked so hard to overcome in recent years. Our two decades of marriage had been punctuated by mental-health battles, episodes of deep depression, and bouts of suicidality. But this was by far the most severe crisis between us. She believed the mission was reckless. I believed I had to go. It really almost destroyed our family, which is the most important part of my life.

When Guv, Rodrigo, and I left our hotel rooms to conduct meetings with the Venezuelan leaders, we were all wearing N95 masks, ski goggles, and face shields. We could barely see what or who was in front of us. I believe the Venezuelan officials genuinely appreciated our presence at a time like this and what it represented. Just by being there, we proved how seriously we took the mission. We got some strong indications that we were about to succeed, returning home with some, if not all, of the imprisoned Americans. But just as we were heading into our final meeting with President Maduro, a US Navy ship sailed extremely close to Venezuelan territorial waters, an act that the president interpreted as an unwarranted provocation.

"Under the circumstances," the agitated leader said to Governor Richardson, "because of the American provocation, I cannot hand over these prisoners to you."

It was a serious disappointment, returning home empty handed. But that mission did mark an improvement in the prospects for the long-awaited release of some of the Americans. Unfortunately, it would take another couple of years before that happened, a couple of years of unwarranted incarceration. And even less fortunately, it would not include all of them.

13 ACADEMIC FREEDOM

"Your proposal for a global prisoner exchange?" I said to the Iranian foreign minister, Mohammad Zarif, trying to strike just the right tone, frank but not disrespectful. "It was dead on arrival with Trump. You are misreading how the president thinks."

"Really?"

I couldn't tell if the foreign minister was surprised—or just saddened—to hear me say that.

We were in his well-appointed suite at the Millennium Hilton, just across First Avenue from the United Nations. The 2019 session of the General Assembly was already underway. That September morning, I'd gone to see the foreign minister along with Governor Richardson and an old friend of the governor's, former congressman Jim Slattery. The two veteran American politicians, one from New Mexico, one from Kansas, had started in Congress together three and a half decades earlier, when they were both in their midthirties. For years Slattery had traveled in and out of Iran and engaged with Iranians, promoting academic, faith-based, and business exchanges and getting to know many Iranian officials, including Zarif.

So why was *I* delivering the tough news to the foreign minister of Iran?

The governor and I had been working hard for the release of Xiyue Wang, a PhD candidate in the Princeton University history department, who'd been arrested while studying Farsi and doing archival research at an institute in northern Tehran. We'd been working hard...and getting nowhere. The Chinese-born graduate student, who was an American citizen, was charged with espionage and had been held for almost three years in Iran's notorious Evin Prison, with seven more to go. No way was Xiyue Wang a spy! He had a legal visa from the Iranians and a grant from Princeton's Sharmin and Bijan Mossavar-Rahmani Center for Iran and Persian Gulf Studies. His dissertation, which was supervised by renowned historian Stephen Kotkin, focused on the nineteenth- and early-twentieth-century Qajar dynasty. "Everything he did was normal," Kotkin said. Xiyue Wang was an apolitical husband, dad, and history nerd whose son was barely three when Wang was taken into custody, 6,157 miles from their home in New Jersey.

The evidence seemed clear to me: the budding historian was just the latest unlucky pawn in the forty-plus years of hostility between the United States and Iran.

Guv and I had been pushing some of the usual buttons to get him out. We tried to get the US government to make Wang's case a top priority. Not much traction there. The Trump administration had no interest in communicating directly or indirectly with the Iranian regime. Any such communication would violate the "maximum pressure" strategy, which was the cornerstone of the administration's Iran policy. We had a couple of small-group conversations with Gholamali Khoshroo and Majid Takht-Ravanchi, respectively the outgoing and incoming Iranian ambassadors to the United Nations. Polite talk but no obvious progress. We even attempted to persuade the Chinese government and some corporations to lend a hand, thinking Iran might be quicker to do a favor for Beijing than for Washington. For the Chinese, that could have been a way to embarrass the Trump administration by helping to save an American citizen, which the Americans had so far failed to do. But nothing doing there. The only real flash of hope came that April, when Foreign Minister Zarif made a sweeping proposal that went far beyond Xiyue Wang, floating the idea of a global prisoner exchange. The minister proposed to free almost *all* of Iran's foreign prisoners if the US and several other nations would release the Iranian citizens *they* were holding behind bars. The Iranian motivation was obvious. There were more Iranians imprisoned in the United States than Americans locked up in Iran. So in order to make the numbers work, the Iranians wanted to increase the scope of the deal.

"Exchange them, all these people that are in prison inside the United States," Zarif said in a speech at the Asia Society in New York. "We believe their charges are phony. The United States believes charges against these people in Iran are phony. Fine. Let's not discuss that. Let's have an exchange. I'm ready to do it. And I have the authority to do it."

That would have been a giant leap forward...*for everyone*. But the timing of the Iranian proposal could hardly have been any worse: just as the Trump administration was pulling the United States out of the Obama-era Iran nuclear deal and imposing its maximum-pressure sanctions against the regime. There was absolutely no appetite in the White House for making any kind of accommodation for the government of Iran.

The Trump administration didn't even respond to the global exchange proposal. Silence was all it sent back to Tehran.

* * *

IN THE PAINSTAKING BUSINESS OF FRINGE DIPLOMACY, PATIENCE ISN'T just a virtue. Sometimes it's a necessity, for us and for the loving families we are trying so urgently to help. So it was with the case of Xiyue Wang. His wife, Hua Qu, first emailed the Richardson Center on March 5, 2018, asking for our help. Her husband had been in Iranian custody for seventeen months by then, and the US government didn't seem to be doing much about it. She was referred to us by Diane Foley, a good friend of ours and one of the great heroes of wrongfully detained Americans and hostages around the world. Diane had a tragic story of her own. She was a family nurse practitioner in New Hampshire whose life had been changed forever in 2012 when her son, photojournalist Jim Foley, was kidnapped and held hostage while covering the Syrian Civil War. The young journalist was brutally beheaded in August 2014, making him the first American citizen killed by the Islamic State of Iraq and Syria. It was an unspeakably horrible outcome. Diane and her family put their immense anger and grief to meaningful use, creating the James W. Foley Legacy Foundation to, as they put it, "advocate for freedom for all U.S. nationals wrongfully detained or held hostage abroad, to ensure government accountability to prioritize their safe return and to educate and protect journalists and international travelers."

Heartfelt, vital work.

In Xiyue Wang's case, the Foley Foundation was supporting Hua Qu and the couple's young son, Shaofan, even before Guv and I were asked to step in. We began, as we always do, by learning everything we could about the case. We needed to do our own due diligence, making sure the grad student really was being held unjustly. There was zero doubt this time.

After getting nowhere with the Trump administration and Beijing, we were eager to cultivate the new Iranian ambassador to the United Nations, Majid Takht-Ravanchi. Guv knew him a bit. We hoped Ravanchi would help us arrange a trip to Iran to visit Xiyue Wang in prison and step up our efforts on his behalf. The maximum-pressure campaign in Washington wasn't making any of this easier. But finally Ambassador Ravanchi agreed to meet for dinner.

Governor Richardson called John Bolton, the president's national security advisor, to give him a heads-up. Even though we hadn't gotten much encouragement so far from the US administration, we wanted to keep US officials fully in the loop. We'd surely need them later. Guv actually had a good relationship with the hawkish Bolton, whose hard-line views included a strong inclination for regime change in Iran. Bolton had followed Richardson as UN ambassador, and the two veteran diplomats had known each other for decades.

"Look, John," Guv said. "I have a relationship with the Iranian ambassador here. He's invited me for dinner. I'm going to raise the subject of the American prisoners. We've been working with the family of Xiyue Wang."

Bolton said he had no problem with any of that. "Have the meeting," he said. "Explore what can be done." Clearly there was a basic trust between the two old hands. It was impressive hearing them interact.

We had our dinner at the Brook, the governor's club in midtown Manhattan. There were five of us: Ambassador Ravanchi, his aide Nabi Sonboli, and our consultant, former Ambassador Cameron Hume, along with the governor and me. That elegant dinner was a perfect chance for us to dive a little deeper into the issue of American prisoners in Iran and to build a personal rapport with the ambassador and his aide. We discussed Xiyue Wang's case, of course, but also brought up the imprisonment of a forty-seven-year-old US Navy veteran from California named Michael White. He'd been arrested in July 2018 while visiting his Iranian girlfriend. Apparently the navy vet had posted a photo on Instagram showing the two of them holding hands, which must have caught the attention of Iranian authorities. He was promptly hauled off to jail. We weren't officially on that case, but we'd been following it closely, and we'd been alarmed by reports that White's health was deteriorating badly in prison.

Cameron also mentioned Robert Levinson, a former FBI agent who had disappeared on Kish Island, Iran, allegedly while on a mission for the Central Intelligence Agency in 2007. There were reports that Levinson had been tortured and killed. But exactly what had happened to him remained one of the unsolved mysteries of US-Iranian relations, a deeply painful one for his family and former colleagues. By this point Levinson was presumed dead, but no one really knew for sure.

As the evening wore on and the conversation wandered, I brought up something else, a humanitarian issue that I thought might pique the interest of Ambassador Ravanchi. I'd heard that as the tougher US sanctions took hold, Iran was having trouble importing certain lifesaving medications. Drug imports were not supposed to be blocked under the new rules, but the meds weren't arriving in Iran as they had before.

"What if we could help Iran get cancer medicine for children?" I asked Ambassador Ravanchi. "Is that something that might be valuable?"

The ambassador lit up immediately. Who could be against cancer medicine for children?

"Of course, we are interested in the prisoners," I made clear to the ambassador. "But we'd also like to work on cancer drugs for children. I think that's something we could help with." He thought that sounded like an excellent idea.

"Let me do some homework," the ambassador said. He promised that Nabi would get back to us with a list of needed medications, and we could take it from there. As for the prisoners, he added, "I will bring that up to the foreign minister and see what the foreign minister says."

Progress...at last.

One added bonus to our dinner conversation that night: It reminded the Iranians that we at the Richardson Center were private citizens, independent of the US government. We could still engage with officials from Tehran, even if their relations with the Trump administration were strained or downright hostile. Dealing with us was also a good way for them to prepare for the next administration, whoever's it might be.

They seemed to get that without our even saying it.

* * *

NABI CIRCLED BACK WITHIN A FEW DAYS. HE HAD A LIST OF pediatric-cancer medications that were in especially short supply. We got right on it. We consulted with Peter Kucik, a good friend and a former official with the US Treasury Department's Office of Foreign Assets Control, an expert on the arcane topic of import-export regulations under sanctioned regimes. Peter had traveled with me to Cuba. I trusted him fully. He gave us valuable advice about the many intricacies of sending pharmaceuticals to a sanctioned nation like Iran and how to stay on the right side of the law. We also met with Sarah Levinson Moriarty, who wasn't only the daughter of the missing Robert Levinson. She had also worked in the pharmaceutical industry and had some good leads on drug companies that might be willing to donate pediatric-cancer medications if that could help bring American prisoners home.

"This is really coming together," I told Nabi and Guv.

We met with representatives of the drug industry's leading manufacturers and prepared a white paper that US officials wanted before they would grant a specialized license for the cancer-drug exports. All this stuff was complicated, but we pressed diligently ahead. I think the Iranians appreciated the effort, and I had no discomfort making it. To me this was a genuine humanitarian cause...which might have other benefits if we were lucky.

Eventually, despite our best intentions, the bureaucratic hurdles proved too difficult for us to deliver on the pediatric-cancer medicine. While pharmaceuticals were exempt from the American sanctions against Iran, all financial transactions were sanctioned. And even if the drugs were donated, there would still be some financial transactions. That scared the banks and the pharmaceutical companies, who feared the US Treasury Department would come after them for violating the sanctions, which could kill their businesses.

Yet the genuine effort, while it lasted, gave us a perfect reason to engage frequently with the Iranians. I was up at the Iranian mission every week or so. Being carefully screened by security. Leaving my phone outside. Being logged, ID'd—and photographed, I'm sure—by an alphabet soup of US intelligence agencies keeping a constant eye on this little patch of Iran. These visits did take some getting used to, I have to admit. I wasn't just an American. I had been born and raised and had served with the military in Israel, Iran's sworn enemy.

This is sovereign Iranian territory, I kept reminding myself. *And I am wandering the halls.* Meanwhile, US-Iranian relations were growing more tense by the day, every time the Iranian regime put out another anti-American comment or President Trump took aim at Iran in another barrage of tweets.

"Navigating this terrain," I reminded Guv, "really does take some diplomatic ingenuity."

He just laughed and shrugged, as if to say, *Second nature.*

You want to know how bitter the feelings on both sides had grown? I saw one example right up close. While we were pushing for the release of the American prisoners and working on the cancer drugs for kids, Ambassador Ravanchi was battling stomach cancer. His condition deteriorated so badly he needed to be hospitalized. When Foreign Minister Zarif arrived in New York for the 2019 United Nations General Assembly, he wanted to visit the ambassador at the hospital about an hour north of the city.

Technically, the hospital was outside the zone where Iranian officials were allowed to travel. The foreign minister requested a waiver. The Trump administration said no.

"Maximum pressure" at work.

From what I heard, the foreign minister was furious—understandably so, I thought. He considered the refusal a personal affront. At Nabi's request, I agreed to make inquiries. "This is no risk to national security," I said to one official in the US State Department. "It's a bedside visit from the ambassador's boss. Is this really where we want to draw the line with the Iranians? Just on a human level, do we really want to make our stand here? Let's do the right thing."

US officials wouldn't budge. And they didn't budge a few weeks later when Ambassador Ravanchi's medical condition worsened even more and a couple of his grown children applied for a visa to travel from Iran and visit their cancer-stricken father. Though he would ultimately pull through, for a time there, his family really thought he was about to die. The answer was the same.

Maximum pressure.

No.

* * *

IT ISN'T EASY FOR AMERICAN CIVILIANS TO GET PRIVATE TIME WITH the foreign minister of Iran. When we finally got the meeting with Mohammad Zarif, thanks to our efforts with Ambassador Ravanchi, our engagement with the mission, and a firm push by Guv's old House friend Jim Slattery, we wanted to make the most of it. Zarif had floated the global exchange proposal, hadn't he? Even though the idea had gone nowhere, it did suggest the foreign minister was open to fresh ideas.

An old-school diplomat and foreign-policy thinker, Zarif was totally charming, as Guv had assured me he would be. Gracious. Calm. Unflappable. Before becoming foreign minister, he'd been Iran's chief nuclear negotiator and the country's United Nations representative. His English was flawless, better than mine. "Honestly," he said to the governor that morning at the Hilton across from the UN, "I don't understand it. We offer the global exchange, and Trump just rejects it. No explanation. Just rejects it. Doesn't he want to bring Americans home?"

That's where I jumped in, telling the Iranian foreign minister I thought he was misunderstanding the American president. When he asked what I meant by that, I tried to explain.

"Well," I said, "it's true that Donald Trump wants to bring back Americans. I think it's a personal passion of his. But he also doesn't want to appear as if he's *giving* anything in return. That's why your global exchange is dead on arrival from Trump's perspective."

At that, Zarif's tone of voice turned even more serious. "So I guess we're at a dead end here."

"Um, not necessarily," I offered.

He seemed to perk up at that. At the very least, he didn't stand up to leave.

"We just need to approach prisoner exchanges in a different way," I said. "I understand that a global exchange is your ultimate objective. You'd like to resolve all the cases everywhere," a goal that Guv and I and everyone else connected to the Richardson Center certainly shared. "But considering what we know about Donald Trump, maybe we should start with one by one, then find some ways to ignite the positive momentum from there. We just need to identify the right prisoners to start with—in Iran and the United States—and set it up the right way."

The foreign minister didn't answer immediately, but I could tell he was intrigued. "So let's talk about how we might proceed," Guv jumped in. "We have two cases in mind. Let's figure out what it would take to do those two cases specifically. Try and get those done...and then keep going."

"Tell me," Zarif said earnestly.

Right then is when I was certain this was a breakthrough conversation. The Iranian foreign minister was seeing something he hadn't seen before. He saw that if we were going to get something done here, it would not be wrapped in a single grandiose bargain. As I told him, "It needs to be something small. It needs to be very carefully choreographed. And it needs to be done in such a way that your government gets what it wants but Trump has deniability about whether he gave up something in return."

One by one was the only way to go, I said—two by two at most.

Guv and I had decided earlier to broach two cases, those of the two current prisoners we had mentioned to Ambassador Ravanchi: the Princeton history student Xiyue Wang and Michael White, the navy veteran with the Iranian girlfriend. Wang was the only one of the two whose case we were officially working on at that time, but they were both thoroughly worthy cases.

Foreign Minister Zarif seemed open to the incremental approach. But just as we had addressed the peculiarities of getting Trump's sign-off, he alluded to the internal politics of Iran when he said, "Three approvals need to be given before we can proceed." He said *he* had to want to make the deal. The Islamic Revolutionary Guard Corps, Iran's military elite, had to want to make the deal. And Supreme Leader Ali Khamenei had to want it too. That sounded like a lot of people to get on the same page in Iran, but I knew the foreign minister's political skills. If he was behind it, I liked our chances. A lot.

* * *

FOREIGN MINISTER ZARIF GOT RIGHT BACK TO US WITH AN INITIAL decision: the Iranians were open to a prisoner exchange, and they'd like to start with Xiyue Wang. *Yes!* They had also identified the imprisoned Iranian citizen they hoped to trade for the American graduate student.

His name: Masoud Soleimani.

A respected scientist and stem-cell researcher in Iran, in October 2018 Soleimani had boarded a flight from Tehran to the United States, where he was a visiting scholar at the prestigious Mayo Clinic in Minnesota. He was returning to complete his research on treating stroke patients. The Iranian scientist was arrested as soon as his flight landed in Chicago. He and two of his former students were accused of conspiring to export biological materials from the US to Iran without authorization. Apparently the US sanctions had made those biological materials hugely expensive in Iran. The crime carried a sentence of up to twenty years in prison. He was being held at a federal detention center south of Atlanta.

The proposed trade—Wang for Soleimani—had a certain symmetry to it. An academic for an academic, each accused of crimes connected to his research. The Iranians liked symmetry, I was discovering. Now it was up to Guv and me to help open a dialogue with the Trump administration and see if a deal like this could be made at such a dicey time.

I couldn't say for sure what our prospects were, but at least we had a path to follow now.

One challenge was obvious right away: When Wang had been arrested, in August 2016, Barack Obama was president and the campaign between Hillary Clinton and Donald Trump was just coming into focus. But by the time we got involved, Trump had moved into the White House. That might be good. It might be bad. But it was definitely different. It wasn't just that Obama had signed the nuclear deal and Trump had walked away from it. On almost every level, Trump maintained a tougher stance toward Tehran.

So could we get the Trump administration, reluctant as it was to negotiate with Tehran, to agree to such a high-profile deal? That was the question ahead.

* * *

GOVERNMENTS, EVEN VERY LARGE GOVERNMENTS, ARE MADE UP OF people. So when it comes to persuading governments to do things, it always matters which people are in which jobs. In September 2019, just as we were meeting with Mohammad Zarif at the Hilton across from the UN, Robert O'Brien was replacing John Bolton as Donald Trump's national security advisor. It is fair to say that O'Brien was a notch or two less hard-line than Bolton had been, even though they both worked for the same president. O'Brien was a charming man with natural charisma, tall and silver-haired with piercing blue eyes. And it couldn't hurt that he was the former special presidential envoy for hostage affairs at the State Department. He certainly had a feel for this sort of thing. In those days, O'Brien had been a regular at the periodic meetings Guv and I hosted for a couple of dozen people who worked in the field, seeking creative solutions for hostage and wrongful-detention cases around the world.

And so we began shuttling between the Iranians and the Americans. Feeling the two sides out. Advancing the idea of Wang for Soleimani. Once we were focused on those two names, things actually moved pretty quickly. It wasn't long before we felt as if we had the outlines of a deal. A one-for-one swap, an academic for an academic, perhaps with the assistance of Switzerland, a country whose diplomats represented the American interests in Iran, even at tense times. It wasn't long before we had a detailed plan—or thought we did.

In early October, Guv and I went to the Trump White House to meet with the leadership of the president's National Security Council. It was a strange feeling stepping into *that* West Wing, certainly different from visiting under previous presidents. The first thing I noticed was all the blown-up photos in gold frames on the walls, action shots of President Trump getting off a helicopter, celebrating at the inaugural ball, and engaged in other presidential activities.

Ironically, the White House was more accessible to us under Trump than it had been under previous, Democratic presidencies. Sounds counterintuitive, I know. But despite the fact that our work was thoroughly apolitical, my boss was a well-known Democratic politician and diplomat. So why was access easier during a *Republican* presidency? Exactly for that reason! Richardson was a known Democrat! If he and I tried something crazy and failed, the Republicans in the White House had easy deniability. *Crazy Democrats*, they could say. But if we failed when a Democrat was in office, the public linkage could be a political liability.

Our initial meeting with Trump's National Security Council included Chris Miller, who would later become acting secretary of defense, and two other top aides, Victoria Coates and Rob Greenway. The meeting was very friendly and positive. Our presentation was well received. Of course they expressed skepticism and suspicion about the Iranians. But we weren't rejected outright, not at this initial meeting, anyway. As Chris Miller escorted us out, he said he thought our plan could very well succeed and we should continue working out the details, though he added that the White House still needed to do more homework before giving us the green light. They'd be in touch, Miller said.

My main contact with the National Security Council was a young officer I'll call Darren. Darren and I were able to develop a solid and genuine relationship. I could call him when I needed to. He was open and available.

A week passed. No word from the White House. Guv and I were waiting for the formal go-ahead. Meanwhile, the Iranians were eager to move forward. After ten days, I reached out to Darren. "I know that when people have bad news, they tend to go silent," I said. "Can we meet?"

Darren said sure. We went to a coffee shop near the White House.

"Yes, we have an issue," Darren said as soon as he sat down. "While our team is supportive of the Wang-for-Soleimani formula, the Department of Justice is against it. We can't proceed."

Our straightforward deal was being sidelined by Justice? *Damn!* "Let me ask you this," I said. "Do we know what their main objection is?"

"We can't really ask them," Darren said. "There are constraints on our discussion."

"Would it be OK for Richardson and me to try to meet with someone at Justice and see if we can figure it out?"

"Do your thing," Darren said with a smile. "But this conversation never happened."

14 DOUBLE CROSS

THE PRIMARY MISSION OF THE UNITED STATES DEPARTMENT OF Justice is to uphold the rule of law—finding, prosecuting, and punishing those who violate it. This means sending felons to prison, not making deals with other government agencies to let the criminals out prematurely. So the department's skepticism about an international prisoner exchange wasn't hard to understand.

Governor Richardson and I have a very different mission, and sometimes the two conflict. We are committed to bringing innocent Americans home. Unfortunately, that can require releasing convicted criminals in return. Though these international prisoner swaps can seem unsavory, they can also be the moral, just, and patriotic thing to do. It's a clash of values, tough choices with right on both sides. Navigating that tension—and making the case when we need to—is part of what makes our work so interesting and part of what makes it so hard.

The Xiyue Wang case was a perfect example, which was why Guv, Cameron Hume, and I had to weigh our options carefully as we navigated our next moves. As always, we wanted to understand the Justice Department's specific objections and see how we might answer them. Maybe there was a creative way to reduce the costs and help us get a deal.

It was certainly worth a try. And why not start at the top?

Dropping Richardson's name, I reached out to Attorney General Bill Barr. We had met with Barr a couple of months earlier in our efforts to free Paul Whelan from Russia. The attorney general had been surprisingly open and encouraging, which made me optimistic this time. But Barr wasn't available to see us now. Too bad. Still, two of the top people on the department's national security team, John Demers and David Burns, agreed to meet with Cameron, Congressman Slattery, and me. When we all sat down together at Justice headquarters in Washington in early November, Demers and Burns seemed like true professionals. They clearly took the prisoner issue seriously. And we didn't hold back. We got straight into the thick of it.

"We understand that Justice is objecting to the Wang-for-Soleimani deal," I said. "We want to understand what your objections are. Maybe we can find a way to mitigate them."

Demers and Burns were just as direct with us. "We have two major problems," Demers said. "First, we can't set a precedent of tarmac exchanges, trading innocent Americans for foreign criminals. That looks terrible, and it makes other countries think we are ready to trade." I nodded, letting him continue. "And second, there can be no outside intervention in the American judicial process. Soleimani's trial hasn't even begun yet."

Cameron spoke up first. "Two very valid points," he said. "What if we can find a way to structure a deal so that both those issues are addressed? Give us a few days. Hopefully, we can figure something out."

They agreed to listen.

"What about a plea bargain?" Congressman Slattery asked when the three of us shared our meeting notes with Guv. "Soleimani would admit he'd committed a crime and plead guilty, then be deported back to Iran as part of his sentence. Plea deals happen in federal court all the time."

That made sense to us. Would it make sense to Justice? The idea was certainly worth a try.

And what about the Justice Department's other objection? That would be harder. How could we skip a tarmac exchange? When two nations exchange prisoners, it's usually done simultaneously at a neutral location, often an airport, at which point each of the freed prisoners is immediately flown home. Yes, just like in the Tom Hanks movie *Bridge of Spies*. And that was exactly what the Justice Department wanted to avoid. But there's a good reason most prisoner swaps are done that way:

Neither side trusts the other not to cheat. So the swap has to happen all at once in a location neither side controls. Thus the tarmac exchange.

"But what if we could get away without a tarmac exchange this time?" I suggested. "Cheating only makes sense if the exchange is a one-time deal." In other words, cheating is beneficial only if you never need to repeat the action or deal with the other side in the future. Cheat once, and you will never be trusted again. But Wang and Soleimani were hardly the only prisoners on the US-Iran agenda. There was also the imprisoned Michael White and whoever hoped to be sent home after him. Foreign Minister Zarif had made that clear. If this exchange succeeded, there could certainly be more to come, a benefit to both sides. If the US could be confident that the Iranians wouldn't cheat—and vice versa—who really needed a tarmac exchange?

"Does that open the door to a staggered release?" I asked, meaning one side going first, followed by the other. As we batted that around among ourselves, everyone agreed that it might.

Here's what we came up with: First, Soleimani would plead guilty in return for a sentence of time served and immediate deportation. At the same time, the Iranians would promise that twenty-four to forty-eight hours later, Xiyue Wang would be released from Iran for whatever excuse they chose to use. That way, we could satisfy both of the Justice Department's stipulations: no interference with the American judicial process and no international tarmac exchange.

It wasn't ideal, but you know what? It just might succeed!

Congressman Slattery swung into action. Within days he was in contact with the office of BJay Pak, the US attorney prosecuting Soleimani in Atlanta. To our surprise, one of Pak's assistants told Slattery that the federal prosecutors wanted to secure a plea bargain in the case, but that this approach had been rejected at Justice headquarters in Washington. This was an opening for us. Though the prosecutors had been turned down before, we were always looking for the slightest crack in any shut door. Maybe the team in Atlanta would like to ask again? At the very least, it meant we'd have an ally in the local US attorney's office when we pushed the idea of a plea deal with central Justice. The prosecutors in Atlanta agreed to float the idea again. Now it was up to us to make sure it wasn't rejected a second time.

We'd have to go back to Demers and Burns at Justice. But first we wanted to check in with the Iranians. If our guilty-plea-with-immediate-deportation approach gained approval in Washington, would they accept that we'd lived up to our part of the deal and release the Princeton student as they'd promised to? These two nations deeply distrusted each other. Had we constructed an arrangement that both of them would feel committed to? We were about to find out.

I went back to New York to share all this with Nabi Sonboli, my contact at the Iranian mission. I was really starting to think of him as a friend. All that work on the children's cancer drugs had been bonding, despite falling short on delivery. It had been time well spent. Now I had to see if we could get a formal sign-off for the prisoner swap on the Iranian side.

Nabi wasn't the decision maker, of course. He was a mission staffer. But he could convey the message to his superiors in Tehran. When we met, I explained the arrangement, and he forwarded it and got a reply a few days later.

"We have a deal," he said.

* * *

THE IRANIANS WERE ON BOARD NOW, BUT WE STILL HAD TO TAKE ALL this back to Demers and Burns at the Justice Department. This meeting had to be handled even more deftly than the last one. We needed to convey the plan without suggesting any interference from the outside. We knew that Justice was supersensitive about that.

I started gently as Cameron Hume and Congressman Slattery sat beside me. "We have an idea," I said.

I could tell we had their attention. I continued carefully. "We understand that in a few days, you might get a proposed plea bargain from your prosecutors in Atlanta. Obviously we cannot tell you what to do or suggest anything that would interfere in your internal process. But we would like you to have a piece of data in mind as you consider the plea bargain." I took a breath, stalling for time. But I couldn't gauge any early reaction. I pressed on. "The life of an innocent American, Xiyue Wang, can be saved if you accept the plea in this case. This plea will not be attached to a prisoner exchange. No official quid pro quo. But we are telling you that we can get Wang released immediately afterward—*on our own*—if the plea and deportation of Soleimani are executed as proposed."

Demers and Burns took notes the whole time I was talking. They asked a few questions to make sure they understood what we were saying. I tried not to say anything that might spook them or be taken as interference in the department's internal operations.

"And," I added, "there will be no tarmac exchange. Given the incentives on both sides, we have concluded that won't be necessary."

I could feel the relief in the room. We didn't get a direct answer immediately. We didn't expect one. But I felt good about the meeting. We had come up with a way to avoid the two objections the Justice officials had raised with us, and they understood the approach we had devised. So would they and the department agree? Hopefully, we would have that answer soon, one way or the other.

Meanwhile, Robert O'Brien and his colleagues on the White House National Security Council had warmed to the deal, as long as they could maintain that the two prisoners were not actually being *traded*, that Wang was simply being freed *after* Soleimani pleaded guilty and was sent home. "Sequence, not causation," as one White House official described the relationship between the two cases.

"Exactly," Guv said.

After that exchange, I could feel the wheels of justice begin to turn. We didn't get any official notice. But in mid-November, Congressman Slattery heard that the plea bargain proposed by the prosecutors in Atlanta had been formally approved by central Justice. A court date was set. December 11. That morning Soleimani would appear in court. He'd plead guilty and would promptly be deported to Iran.

Exactly as we imagined it. Right according to plan.

I was ecstatic. But I still wanted to be doubly sure the Iranians would live up to *their* part of the deal. It would be tragic, not to mention deeply embarrassing, if we finally corralled the US government only to have the Iranians renege at the last minute.

The Iranians wouldn't screw us…*would they?* We couldn't let that happen, and we had less than three weeks until the court date in Atlanta to make sure it didn't. So many things could still go wrong.

Guv, Cameron Hume, Congressman Slattery, and I all worked to keep all the pieces together. Multiple meetings with Iranian ambassador Ravanchi, who was back at the mission now after his cancer battle. Multiple exchanges with the White House National Security team. Making sure nothing had changed at Justice or at State. If anyone in the mix started messing with the deal even a little, there was an excellent chance the whole thing would fall apart. It was that delicate.

With Soleimani expected at the federal courthouse in Atlanta on the morning of December 11, we assumed he'd be shipped out of the country that afternoon or maybe the day after. The Iranians agreed to release Wang on December 14. That gave us all a little breathing room in case something got delayed, but not so much that we would lose the bilateral momentum. It was a careful balance, like everything else in fringe diplomacy.

We still needed a nation in the middle that could communicate with both sides. So we turned to our excellent partners the Qataris. The Qataris were the perfect intermediaries, always willing to be helpful when it came to getting prisoners released. They would fly Xiyue Wang out of Iran and back to Hamad International Airport in Qatar, where we would meet him and bring him home. Not a tarmac exchange. Just a connection and a delivery. With that, I finally began to feel confident enough in our plan to bring Hua Qu, Wang's wife, up to speed on everything. We hadn't wanted to do that prematurely, before we were confident the trade-that-wasn't-a-trade was likely to go through. What if we failed?

Guv and I met with Hua and debriefed her on what was about to happen. She was thrilled, eager to join us at Hamad Airport when the Qataris flew her husband from Tehran and the carefully orchestrated *nonexchange* occurred. We were eager to have her there. I knew her husband would be.

I knew I'd be arriving from Bangladesh, where I was scheduled to lead an investment delegation that week, part of our work to help the Rohingya refugees. This was all coming together beautifully…or so I thought. Then something came flying at us from our blind side, just when we expected it least.

* * *

"SOMETHING IS OFF," I EMAILED GUV.

It was 2:00 a.m. in Dhaka, Bangladesh's capital city, where I had just landed. "Soleimani's lawyer told Slattery he hasn't been allowed to communicate with his client for twenty-four hours," I said. "This isn't normal."

"What do you think is happening?" Guv emailed back.

"I'm not sure."

The Soleimani court date was still four days away. But something was certainly happening.

"I bet they are moving ahead without us, Mickey," Guv said.

Guv always had a gut intuition about these things—about the way people in government and politics are quick to shove their supposed allies aside and grab credit when they think they can. And he was exactly right. Again. Within minutes, I received a long and beautiful note from Hua, though it contained one odd phrase.

My dear Mickey, after 48 hours of numbness, I am slowly recovering from loss of words. Laying down with Shao on the flight to Frankfurt, I finally find peace high above in the air. Richardson Center together with Congressman Slattery paved the way for this exceptional swap! Although it eventually played out differently than expected, all is beautiful, and your tremendous efforts are eventually translated into such classic victory of humanity and diplomacy. You sent us a Christmas miracle.

A beautiful, heartfelt note!

But "played out differently than expected"? What exactly did Hua mean? We'd soon find out.

At the same time Hua was thanking us so profusely for making all this happen, high-ranking officials in the Trump administration were rushing in with their own backroom deal. Kicking over the furniture was more what it felt like to me. At their insistence, we had constructed this delicate piece of fringe diplomacy, only to have the State Department swoop in at the eleventh hour, dropping their previous demands, changing everything around, and keeping us as far away as possible.

If an American was going to be released from an Iranian prison, they wanted all the credit, it seemed. People in politics and government care a lot about credit, I have learned.

At the last minute, the State Department's special representative for Iran, Brian Hook, had pushed through a direct prisoner swap. Wang for Soleimani. Let me repeat that. A *direct prisoner swap!* Just what his colleagues in the Justice Department and the White House had insisted was impossible and adamantly refused to do. And Hook would be the US official standing there, with cameras nearby, no doubt. They'd already arranged with the Swiss ambassador in Tehran to help with a tarmac exchange. *A tarmac exchange!* In Switzerland. Now we knew why the attorney had been unable to see his Iranian client. Soleimani was already being flown in secret from Atlanta to Zurich. He didn't admit guilt. He didn't enter a plea. He wasn't sentenced to deportation or anything else. They just pulled him out of the federal lockup in Georgia and put him on a plane—criminal case be damned.

They sure could have saved us all a lot of trouble if they'd agreed to all that from the start.

I was furious. I was ecstatic. I was confused. I felt relieved. I felt betrayed. I honestly felt all those emotions mixed together, which meant I couldn't tell how I felt, other than rattled. I was excited for Hua that her husband was being freed from unjust Iranian custody. I felt angry that the deal that we had worked so hard for, the deal that without our work would not have even been considered, was getting executed without us. That the people in the State Department had not even had the decency to give us a heads-up. I was in Bangladesh. There was nothing I could do about any of it but seethe.

I sent Hua a congratulatory note. I focused on the genuine happiness I felt for her, her husband, and their son. I also called my friend Darren at the National Security Council to express my congratulations…and my frustration. Darren understood both parts, exactly where I was coming from.

For the next five days, as I was leading the investment delegation in Bangladesh, I kept reflecting on what had happened. How had I not anticipated Brian Hook's late-hour maneuver and bald credit grab? Had it been inevitable? How could I reconcile my conflicting emotions at having Wang released and at the people who'd made it happen being pushed completely out of the deal?

Hook had violated both of the iron principles the Justice Department had insisted on. Soleimani left the United States an innocent man after costarring in a classic tarmac exchange. Exactly what the people at central Justice had insisted they could not abide.

Trying to give them the benefit of the doubt, I told myself that it was possible Hook and his White House colleagues genuinely believed that the Iranians would not live up to their part of the deal. That once Soleimani was deported, they'd cheat and keep Wang in prison. I saw no evidence of a planned double cross, and I strongly suspect they didn't either. To me, this really was a breach of trust. The Iranians weren't the double-crossers here. How could I keep working with government officials who had pulled something like this? Could I?

Well, I had to. I knew I did. The story wasn't over yet. We still had Michael White to bring home.

* * *

As I wrapped up my Bangladesh investment mission, I met up with Governor Richardson in Doha, the fast-growing capital of Qatar on the Persian Gulf. Just where we had planned to go before the US government reshuffled the deck. We went anyway because we had a meeting scheduled with Iranian foreign minister Zarif. We figured we might as well toast the Wang-Soleimani release and plan for what we hoped would be the next one, getting Michael White safely home to America.

Zarif was all smiles when we met in his lavish suite. He congratulated us and said that when the Swiss ambassador reached out to him with a deal that was different from the one we had all agreed to, he'd had no choice but to accept it. The Swiss ambassador had been speaking on behalf of the US government, the ones holding Soleimani. Zarif said he too couldn't understand why Washington had changed course at the end like that or why the Trump administration had decided to squeeze us out of the deal after we had put it all together. We didn't belabor the issue. We took some photos and discussed some options for the release of Michael White.

Guv and I knew that going forward, we'd have to navigate differently with the Trump administration. We needed a formula to get Michael White home that didn't rely so heavily on official channels in Washington. That was a tall order. But after a lot of discussion and looking hard at the world's large web of political prisoners, we found a path. It involved an Iranian prisoner held in a third country. Guv and I decided to give it a try, and we were making progress…until the Trump administration found a way to botch our efforts again.

I don't believe the obstruction was purposeful this time. It was more a matter of failing to think things through. But it did make me wonder: *What's up with these people?* On January 3, 2020, the US military targeted and killed Qasem Soleimani (no close relation to Wang-swap prisoner Masoud Soleimani). Qasem Soleimani was the commander of the Quds Force and one of the main leaders of the Iranian Revolutionary

Guards. Some Western analysts considered him the right-hand man of Supreme Leader Ali Khamenei and the second-most-powerful person in Iran. The assassination was a huge blow to their country, practically and emotionally.

Nabi, my counterpart at the Iranian mission, was furious and distraught. And he expressed his anger to me. I listened. I told him I didn't believe violence ever solves problems in the long term. But I could feel Nabi's genuine pain. I also knew that after this high-level assassination, no progress would be made anytime soon on getting Michael White home. Feelings in Iran were too raw. So I listened to Nabi. I didn't push him, and I didn't ask for progress. But all our efforts came to a halt. At least for the moment, we were stalled.

* * *

MY TWITTER FEED SUDDENLY EXPLODED. IN *FARSI*. I DO NOT SPEAK Farsi. I don't read the language either. But I got the message loud and clear. The image of my face with a superimposed target wasn't hard to understand. Using Google Translate, I teased out what was happening. I was trending in Iranian social media…and not in a good way.

Following the killing of Qasem Soleimani, one of the pictures we had taken in Doha—of Governor Richardson, Minister Zarif, and me—had made it into a tweet. My face was circled, and the text, directed at Minister Zarif, read something like this: "Why were you, Zarif, meeting with an Israeli security agent two weeks before Soleimani's assassination?"

Crap!

I had gone wildly viral on the social platforms of Iran. Tweeted, retweeted, shared, and commented on. People were getting madder by the moment. Soon the posts included calls for violent retribution against me. By name. With my home address attached. This was no joke.

I have to admit I was worried. I had a wife at home! And a daughter! I was puzzled too. My name had never been mentioned when that picture appeared on the TV screen during a Richardson interview with Wolf Blitzer on CNN. I was the unnamed staffer standing with Governor

Richardson and Minister Zarif, both of whom were far more famous than I was. But someone must have recognized me, someone with a vivid imagination and a sharp agenda. And now I was being fingered as an Israeli spy with some sort of connection to the assassination of a high-ranking leader of Iran's Revolutionary Guards.

Suddenly, my lifelong anonymity didn't seem so bad.

I don't believe I was the real target of the tweet. I was collateral damage. The primary aim, as far as I could figure, was to attack and delegitimize Minister Zarif, insinuating that he was complicit in Soleimani's killing. That preposterous claim was propped up by the assertion that the foreign minister was associating with me, a supposed *Israeli* security agent involved in the killing.

There was a link attached to the "Target Mickey" tweet, supposed "proof" that I was an Israeli security agent. Of course, the claims were false, and the so-called evidence made no sense, as with most conspiracy theories. It was a twenty-year-old article from the *Jewish Journal of Greater Los Angeles*, recounting my experience as a soldier in the Israel Defense Forces. And what did that prove? That before moving to the United States nearly two decades earlier, I'd been a young man in Israel? Anyone who googled my name could find many references to my military service, more than twenty Google pages' worth, before reaching this particular article. I never hid my military service, any more than I hid my Israeli upbringing. It was out there for anyone to find. And of course, Israel has universal military service. So my chances of having been in the Israeli army were extremely high.

With a little digging, I figured out that the initial tweet did not, in fact, come from Iran. It had been launched through a fake account established by Israeli cyberintelligence. *Israel!* Certainly whoever had written this had to know how bogus their own "evidence" was. Their apparent objective: to harm Minister Zarif, an Iranian official who was able to engage positively with the United States. I, again, was just collateral. An immigrant to America, caught between Israel and its sworn enemy, Iran. Once the tweet went viral, the original account was mysteriously deleted.

Yet thanks to the way things fly across the internet, the tweet and its many variations very much lived on and on and on.

Beyond the threat to me and my family, this digital hit job from Israeli cyberintelligence did have an immediate, practical impact. It hurt my ability to engage and negotiate with my Iranian counterparts. It also embarrassed and hurt Zarif, the real point, I suppose. I felt bad about that, though I hadn't caused it and I had no power to make it any better. But I had to stop all my communications with the Iranians for now. To do anything different would only have fueled the damaging and dangerous misinformation.

We still needed to free Michael White from his Iranian prison cell and bring him safely home to America. Thankfully, Cameron Hume was able to step into the void. It took longer than it should have, another six months. All that time, the US Navy veteran languished in Iranian custody, as his health continued to deteriorate. Like Wang, White had been sentenced to ten years. His purported offense: "insulting the country's top leader and posting a private photograph publicly"—the hand-holding photo with his Iranian girlfriend.

I was still involved, but I remained in the background. Through Richardson and Hume, we continued to explore possible pathways for getting White home. I made several trips with my colleagues from Washington to New York, where I had to wait outside the Iranian mission while they were inside negotiating. I hated that, but I understood.

Before long, we came to realize that getting White home would require yet another direct exchange of prisoners between Iran and the United States. We also learned who the Iranians were interested in getting in return. But we certainly didn't want a repeat of what the Trump administration had pulled with Wang. We needed a fresh plan.

Jonathan Franks represented Michael White's mother. He was the one who had brought the navy veteran's case to our attention and introduced us to the family. By then, we were officially involved. A creative, dynamic, and unique personality, relentless in his pursuits and deeply committed to the cause, Jon had worked with us on several cases in the past, making a name for himself as a brilliant tactician who knew how to get attention and force action on behalf of wrongly imprisoned Americans. Michael White was no exception.

On March 19, 2020, White was transferred from Iran's dangerous Vakilabad Prison to Swiss custody on a medical furlough after he developed COVID-19 symptoms. By that time, we had a pretty good sense of the swap it would take to bring Michael home. We knew from the Iranians that the Americans were simply not willing to negotiate over White. Not directly and not through the Swiss, the usual intermediary. We also knew that the White House would simply not listen to our urging. Not after Wang. They'd demonstrated that very clearly. We had to come up with a creative way of motivating this administration to make a deal.

Jon Franks did not disappoint. Since Michael White's COVID was not yet public, Jon suggested that the White family issue a public statement confirming Michael's diagnosis as a way to increase the urgency for getting him home. "That in itself probably isn't enough to move the White House," I warned Jon.

"Well, wait...," Jon said excitedly. "What if we inserted a line in the family statement, insinuating that Richardson is close to making a deal? Wouldn't that get the White House in a frenzy? The last thing they would want is a Richardson-brokered deal."

I had to smile at that. Very smart! We could use their own vanity against them.

We spent a few hours drafting the statement and running the idea by Guv. He approved. The statement from White's mother revealed her son's COVID diagnosis, then thanked Governor Bill Richardson and his team for making such significant progress in negotiating Michael's release.

There is no way for me to know for sure. But from where we stood, it sure seemed to work like a charm. Within forty-eight hours, we learned from our Iranian counterparts that indirect negotiations with the Trump administration had begun.

It wasn't until early June that the two governments arranged a second prisoner swap. In exchange for White's freedom, the United States granted an early release to an Iranian American physician, Matteo Taerri, also known as Majid Taheri, who had served sixteen months in prison for violating US sanctions against Iran and US banking laws. Taheri flew home to Iran, and Michael White flew home to California.

Unconventional? Sure it was. But also highly effective.

PART IV
NOTHING'S
EVER
QUITE
AS IT
SEEMS

15 STRIKE TWO

How big a missed opportunity was the potential Whelan-for-Yaroshenko swap? Even bigger than we realized.

Soon Paul Whelan wasn't the only former US Marine to find himself behind bars in Moscow. It happened again in August 2019, nine months after Whelan's arrest. This time, it was a twenty-eight-year-old marine veteran from Texas named Trevor Reed. He'd enlisted as an infantryman in the first term of the Obama administration. He won a prestigious appointment as a marine presidential guard, protecting Vice President Joe Biden at Camp David. After being honorably discharged in 2016, Trevor enrolled at the University of North Texas, where he was majoring in international relations and taking Russian-language courses. He came to Moscow to spend time with his Russian girlfriend, Lina Tsybulnik. The two had been dating for three years after meeting online.

The trouble started with a cocktail. Then another cocktail. And then a couple more.

Trevor and Lina were at an office party at the law firm where she worked as an associate attorney. He drank quite a bit that night. Enough that his girlfriend and her friends decided they'd better take him outside. They were in a nearby Moscow park when the police arrived. The officers said they would take the intoxicated American to the police station so he could sober up, telling his attorney girlfriend she should collect him in a few hours. But as the officers drove off with Reed, they claimed later, he tried to grab the steering wheel, causing the police car to swerve wildly, and also assaulted the driver and his partner. Reed was charged under part 2 of article 318 of Russia's Criminal Code: violence committed against Russian officials.

That official story would slowly unravel. The factual evidence would show that at the very least, the police officers exaggerated how out of control the drunk American was. But for now, two ex-marines, a generation apart, Paul Whelan and Trevor Reed, were sitting in Moscow jail cells. And neither one of them was going anywhere anytime soon.

* * *

PAUL WHELAN WAS THE FIRST OF THE TWO TO STAND TRIAL.

His lawyer argued to the Moscow court that there was no proof the American security director had known what was on the thumb drive his Russian friend had handed to him. During the short, closed-door trial, Whelan insisted he was innocent, describing himself as a victim of "greasy, slimy Russian politics, nothing more, nothing less." That may not have gone over so well with Russian officials. He was quickly found guilty of receiving state secrets and sentenced for the crime of espionage.

Sixteen years in a harsh Russian prison.

"Whelan, do you understand the sentence?" the judge asked in Russian.

The fifty-year-old ex-marine stared blankly ahead. "Nothing is translated, Your Honor," he protested, as an interpreter scurried over to explain his fate. He was soon transported to high-security Lefortovo Prison, famous for torture and mass executions during Joseph Stalin's Great Purge of the late 1930s.

The following month, it was Trevor Reed's turn to face justice, Russian style.

During his trial in Moscow's Golovinsky District Court, the police officers testified about the marine's drunken behavior, saying he had been aggressive and violent toward them. Trevor's girlfriend, Lina, also testified. She didn't deny her boyfriend had had too much to drink. But she said she'd been following the police car, and she directly contradicted the officers' claim that the vehicle swerved dangerously on the way to the station. She would certainly have seen that, she said. At the trial, there was a curious absence of video from the security cameras in the police vehicle and police station. The Russian prosecutors said the footage had been mistakenly erased. Trevor's lawyers also brought out testimony that while he was in custody, the Moscow police had questioned him intently about his US military career. What did that have to do with the charges against him? But none of that seemed to matter. It certainly didn't persuade the judges hearing the case. On July 30, Trevor Reed was convicted just as swiftly as Paul Whelan had been—and his punishment was almost as severe. For that one drunken evening, the young American was sentenced to nine years in a Russian penal colony in Mordoviya, about three hundred miles east of Moscow, a Soviet-era labor camp for political prisoners with a long reputation as one of Russia's toughest lockups.

When the judge read the verdict, Lina burst into tears. "Are you serious?" she blurted out as police quickly escorted her from the courtroom. "This is the image of Russia?!"

Afterward the young ex-marine told the reporters who had covered his trial, "I think anyone who has eyes and ears and who has been in this courtroom knows that I'm not guilty." His father, Joey Reed, added, "I don't know at what level this was pushed. But somewhere someone in the government has pushed for Trevor to not leave Russia. It's obvious. There's no way that anyone, Russian or American, should ever have been convicted of this nothing."

And that is about where things stood—with two former US military men in Russian prisons and little immediate cause for optimism— through the summer and fall of 2020 and the US presidential election and the final, tumultuous months of the Trump administration.

All we could hope for was that the new president would arrive at the White House ready to take a fresh look at the cases of Americans unfairly incarcerated around the world…and get more involved.

* * *

WE GAVE PRESIDENT BIDEN A COUPLE OF MONTHS TO GET SETTLED IN the White House. A new administration always means lots of new appointees finding their way into lots of new positions, learning about lots of difficult issues. But as winter gave way to the spring of 2021, the presidents of the United States and Russia, Joe Biden and Vladimir Putin, were set to meet face-to-face in Geneva, Switzerland, in June.

"Isn't the upcoming summit a great catalyst for the issue of the prisoners?" I mentioned to Guv over the phone. "The last thing President Biden would want to hear in front of Putin is a question from a reporter about Whelan and Reed. It would be to the benefit of both these leaders to have those cases resolved before the summit."

Guv agreed. "Why don't you and Cameron go see Antonov and ask if the Russians would be interested?" he said. "Maybe we can revive something."

Ambassador Antonov was not available, we were told. But my friend Igor and the Russian deputy chief of mission received Cameron Hume and me at the embassy in early May.

"Feels like it's been ages," I started as the two Russian diplomats led us into an ornate conferment room.

"The pandemic," Igor grumbled.

"But Richardson asked us to come in and share some thoughts with you and see what you think," I said.

Cameron jumped in. "Last time we met, we discussed the reciprocal release of Konstantin Yaroshenko and Paul Whelan. I'm sorry it didn't work. We tried. But now, well, now we have another American, Trevor Reed, in your custody. We would like to explore what can be done to bring both of them home."

"What do you have in mind?" Igor asked.

"As you know, we do not negotiate on behalf of the US government. We are here on behalf of the two families." I always needed to make that clear. "But it occurred to us that with the presidential summit coming up next month, both presidents might benefit from reciprocal humanitarian releases. That would remove a contentious issue from the agenda and set a positive momentum for the meeting. The global pandemic gives everyone a great reason to do this."

"We have demonstrated before that reciprocity is key to success," Igor said, repeating the Russians' usual mantra. I was relieved to hear that. We were still on the same wavelength.

"So," Cameron continued, "what would reciprocity look like if we were talking both Whelan and Reed?"

"Of course, I am not authorized to make any promises," the Russian responded. "But between us, I would think that a humanitarian release of Konstantin Yaroshenko and Viktor Bout would be reciprocated by the release of Paul Whelan and Trevor Reed."

Bout.

That was a name we hadn't discussed before, but I knew exactly who he was. Lately I had become quite an expert on well-connected Russians doing time in US prisons. I had to be.

A former Soviet military translator, Bout had purchased a fleet of old military cargo planes after the collapse of the Soviet Union and started an airfreight business, which he always insisted was legitimate. But according to human rights groups, he was soon selling arms all over Africa—in Angola, Sierra Leone, Liberia, and the Democratic Republic of the Congo—in violation of United Nations embargos. Though he acknowledged frequent trips to Afghanistan in the 1990s, he denied supplying arms to al-Qaeda or the Taliban. And some of his business was clearly legitimate. Bout's companies provided airfreight services to the French government, the United Nations, and the United States military, flying supplies into Iraq after the 2003 invasion. His cargo over the years included fresh flowers, frozen chicken, French soldiers, UN peacekeepers, and African heads of state. In the 2005 movie *Lord of War*, Nicolas Cage's lead character is based on the swashbuckling Bout.

The US government had been trying to prosecute the Russian airfreight operator or arms trafficker (take your pick) since the early 2000s, even while contracting with his companies. It wasn't until 2008 that undercover agents from the Drug Enforcement Administration, posing as arms buyers for Colombia's Revolutionary Armed Forces of Colombia (FARC) rebels, were able to build a case. Bout was arrested in Bangkok that year by the Royal Thai Police, based on an Interpol Red Notice from the United

States accusing him of providing material support to a designated foreign terrorist organization. Over loud protests from Moscow, Bout was extradited from Thailand to New York City. By the time he got to trial in Manhattan federal court, the charges had expanded to include conspiring to kill Americans, conspiring to acquire an antiaircraft missile, illegally purchasing aircraft, wire fraud, and money laundering.

Had federal prosecutors reached too far?

The judge in his case said almost as much. After Bout was convicted in late 2011, Judge Shira Scheindlin gave him the shortest sentence allowed under the federal guidelines—twenty-five years, which he began serving at the federal penitentiary near Marion, Illinois. She didn't call Viktor Bout a model global citizen. But she did point out that he wasn't being convicted for a lifetime of questionable activities—just for this one DEA sting. And she added, "There is no evidence that Bout would have committed the crimes for which he was convicted had it not been for the sting operation."

Only one thing was sure: his conviction and prison term greatly pleased American prosecutors and deeply angered the Russians.

So when the two Russian diplomats brought up Viktor Bout as the second Russian prisoner to be included in a two-for-two COVID swap, Cameron and I were not surprised. In fact, we'd anticipated it, and Cameron's response was brilliant. He laughed out loud. Not mocking our counterparts. Not insulting them. Just giving what appeared as a nervous laugh. "I don't think that would work," Cameron said, quickly collecting himself. "We want to find the formula to resolve this, but I don't think we can get the White House on board with a release of Viktor Bout."

"If you want us to take this to the White House, we will," I added. "But please, trust us. We will not win with Bout. Give us someone we can win with."

The Russians did not appear surprised by our response. They did not get upset. They did not stand up and walk out of the room. They were prepared too. They already had another name in mind.

Roman Seleznev.

Seleznev was a young Russian computer hacker also known by his online name, Track2. Seleznev was a digital genius—no doubt about that—and he didn't think small. He'd been arrested in 2014 at a vacation resort in the Indian Ocean island nation of Maldives, then handed over to the US Secret Service. The allegation: that he'd hacked into computers to steal credit card data, ripping off banks and other Western financial institutions for more than $169 million. After a federal jury in Washington State found him guilty of bank fraud, wire fraud, and other bad acts, he was sentenced to twenty-seven years in an American prison. He also happened to be the son of Valery Seleznev, a prominent member of the State Duma, the lower house of the Russian assembly, which meant his family had friends way up in the Kremlin.

Seleznev was a name we were much more comfortable with. We were finally getting somewhere!

* * *

THIS TIME, WE DIDN'T JUST RUN THE INFORMATION TO THE WHITE House. We wanted to get the concept fully cooked before bringing it to our new colleagues in government.

We were dealing now with people we knew, familiar faces from the Democratic side of the foreign-policy establishment. Well-credentialed professionals the governor, Cameron, and I had interacted with over the years, now holding down top administration posts. Veteran government officials all. Secretary of State Antony Blinken, who'd been deputy national security advisor and deputy secretary of state in the Obama administration and, before that, Democratic staff director of the Senate Foreign Relations Committee. I knew Tony well. I had been introduced to him fourteen years before by Rob Malley. We played soccer together at a league at the Washington Jewish Community Center. I loved Tony. A true mensch with a huge, pure heart. One of the best humans and friends I could imagine. In fact, in 2010, when then–vice president Biden was on his way to visit Israel, Tony called me from the plane. He'd learned that I was in Israel visiting my dad on his deathbed. He invited me to join Biden and him for a chat at the vice president's suite. I did. When I came back home to Ra'anana, I showed my dad the pictures of me with Biden and Tony. My dad could no longer speak, as cancer had completely consumed his body, but his eyes opened wide, as if to say, *You've got to be kidding me!* My dad passed away six hours later. It was my last moment with him, and I am forever grateful to Tony, and to Biden, for that honor.

Tony's top deputy, Wendy Sherman, had served in the State Department under both Hillary Clinton and John Kerry and been lead US negotiator on the Iran nuclear deal. She had also run the Center for Public Leadership at the Harvard Kennedy School. With just as shiny a résumé, Jake Sullivan, the new president's national security advisor, had been deputy assistant to President Obama, national security advisor to Vice President Biden, deputy chief of staff to Secretary of State Clinton and a visiting professor at Yale Law School. Jake's deputy, Jonathan Finer, was a former foreign and national correspondent for the *Washington Post*, who'd covered the war in Iraq before leaving journalism to become a White House fellow, a speechwriter for Vice President Joe Biden, and chief of staff to Secretary of State John Kerry. Still in place from the final year of the Trump administration was Roger Carstens, the special envoy for hostage affairs. During the transition from Trump to Biden, I and five other colleagues in the "hostage sphere" coauthored a memo to Jake Sullivan, asking the new administration not to replace Roger. The families trusted and appreciated him and our international issues needed continuity. Roger was always responsive to us and genuinely seemed to care. And now, we hoped, with a new administration in place, maybe he'd get more traction than he had been able to before. We were relieved when Roger was asked to stay on.

If we were going to accomplish anything over the next four years, we needed good working relationships with all these people. We didn't have to agree with them about everything. That seemed unlikely. But we were eager to collaborate and get Americans home.

I liked the lineup in the new administration. I liked the timing of the latest release proposition we'd gotten from the Russians, just before Biden and Putin were set to meet. I certainly liked the substance of it, a two-for-two deal that would free both Paul and Trevor. As far as I was concerned, that would be getting off on the right foot! If a quick prisoner release could be executed before Putin and Biden even sat down together in Geneva in June, wouldn't that build confidence and goodwill for the years to come? It would certainly say to the world (and the suffering families I cared most about), *Look, we can negotiate productively even though we have strong disagreements on a range of other thorny issues.*

* * *

With Guv's guidance, we built a script. A detailed logistical plan for how this series of reciprocal humanitarian gestures could play out. The US government would release Konstantin Yaroshenko quietly. Representing the Richardson Center, we would fly him to Moscow and hold him there for a couple of days, until the Russians released both Whelan and Reed to us. We would fly the two back home, and two days later, the US government would release Roman Seleznev. Not a swap. Not an exchange. Reciprocal humanitarian releases due to the pandemic. This would be executed a week before the presidential summit and would nicely set up the two presidents for a very good meeting.

By mid-May, Guv was on the phone with Deputy Secretary Sherman. He told her about the indirect two-for-two opportunity we had cooked up. I handled the follow-up, sharing the details with Roger Carstens a couple of days later.

"Thank you for this," Roger said. "We've got it from here."

Over the next week, I prodded Roger for updates. He assured me that he and his colleagues in the administration were making progress, but he said he couldn't share any details. I understood that. This was classified information. I didn't have a security clearance. They needed to do what they needed to do. For the time being, the new team at the White House made clear, they didn't need any further assistance from us.

As the days kept passing, I realized the clock was running out on us.

The summit was approaching, and it didn't look as if we would be able to execute all this in time. I was still hoping that the sides were negotiating based on the formula we'd worked out, but we still weren't hearing anything from our own government.

My Russian colleague Igor, on the other hand, was much more open with me. To the best of his knowledge, he said, the two governments had made no progress on the proposed prisoner exchange.

Disappointing, to say the least. But maybe Igor wasn't read in on the details. Maybe.

Unfortunately, as we soon discovered, our two-for-two, COVID-fueled, presummit exchange just kind of sat there as the agenda for Geneva was assembled around it. There were no negotiations at all on the prisoner topic, not that we could detect. No proposals sent back and forth. No serious conversations of any sort. At least not according to the Russians and whatever else we could pick up on the margins.

Maybe the idea got a glancing mention when the two sides arrived in Switzerland, I'm not sure—but certainly no more than that. With no one on the inside pushing the idea on behalf of the prisoners or their families, the notion of an early-term prisoner release—Whelan and Reed for Yaroshenko and Seleznev—didn't move forward at all.

So frustrating!

As I was learning quickly, the new crowd could be just as maddeningly distracted as the old crowd when handed a promising opportunity… shiny résumés and all. To be fair, the people I was putting my high hopes in had just assumed power in a government that was broken from the inside and ally relations that were broken from the outside. They had to spend much of these first few months resetting procedures and stabilizing relations with allies. In a reaction to the previous four years, they needed to have proper decision-making processes. Establish principles for the way they would govern. All these things were worthwhile. All took time. But for us and the families we were trying to help, this was excruciating. For these families, every day was the day they might hear their loved one had been hurt or killed. That sense of urgency is not always understood by those working in government, as they spend their days balancing the demands of competing interest groups and the concerns of national security.

So frustrating!

It was the second time we could have brought Paul Whelan home, and again the opportunity was squandered. First by the Trump White House. Now by the Biden team. And with every proposition we failed to deliver on, we lost some credibility with our Russian counterparts, which made the next effort just a little harder.

If that stung more than it should have, it was because we'd achieved so much with our unique brand of fringe diplomacy, and with a new administration, I'd had expectations for even more.

And it was not our only effort that was getting stalled. By this time, COVID-19 vaccines were readily available. The number of detained Americans we were trying to help in Venezuela had grown to nine with the arrest of Matthew Heath, a US Navy veteran who had been kidnapped from Colombia. We were worried sick about any of them contracting the virus. So we came up with a fresh proposal: President Nicolás Maduro's wife, Cilia, had two nephews doing time in a Florida prison for drug trafficking. If we could get them vaccinated in prison, would the Venezuelan government allow us to fly into Caracas and vaccinate the American detainees?

Some perfect fringe-diplomacy reciprocity.

We forwarded the idea to the Department of Justice. I took it directly to Roger Carstens. Vaccinating prisoners was already a stated policy of the Biden administration, but federal prison officials were still working their way slowly through a long backlog. So we asked to accelerate the nephews' vaccinations so we could protect our Americans in Venezuela.

We got nowhere. I was not sure why. But in this dicey business of ours, we couldn't afford hurt feelings. We had to keep moving ahead.

16 GETTING DANNY

"We're asking you to delay your trip," Wendy Sherman said to us on the phone that day...and not for the first time.

Wendy was the number two person in Joe Biden's State Department, the deputy secretary of state, just below the secretary, Antony Blinken. A veteran diplomat who'd been the chief nuclear negotiator with North Korea and Iran, the under secretary for political affairs under Hillary Clinton, and an in-demand Democratic policy wonk for decades. Guv and Wendy had known each other for years.

"Again?" Guv shot back. "And why should we wait...*now?*"

"We have the ASEAN Summit a week from now," she said, meaning the annual meeting of the Association of Southeast Asian Nations, set to open October 26, 2021, in Brunei. "We don't want the junta in Myanmar to use your visit to try and create legitimacy. We're pushing everybody else to isolate them. We'd hate to see that undermined."

The governor let out a sigh. For months, Wendy and her colleagues at State had been asking us to delay this mission. We were set and ready to go. Everything was all lined up, not an easy task in a pariah nation like Myanmar. Now the deputy secretary was calling a week before we were supposed to leave.

It might appear simple to delay or move trips like this one. What's another week, right? But in reality, rescheduling a mission is extremely complicated. At the time, there were no commercial flights in or out of Myanmar. We had to fly commercial to Qatar or Tokyo, then charter a small plane for the six-and-a-half-hour flight, each way, in and out of Myanmar. We had to get tested for COVID and coordinate those tests with our departure times. We had to arrange hotels, cars, and landing-and-departure permits. And those were just the logistics. We also had to figure out how to explain to our hosts why we kept delaying our visit.

Unlike major governments, we don't have teams of people for logistics, finance, and advance. The Richardson Center at that point was Governor Richardson and I and two experienced consultants: Steve Ross, our Myanmar expert, and Ambassador Cameron Hume, the former US ambassador to Sudan, Algeria, South Africa, and Indonesia. Years after I got to meet Ambassador Hume on my first mission with Guv to Sudan, we had enlisted him as an advisor to the center. It was hard to imagine doing what we did without them. We had an extremely limited budget, and we had to raise the money ourselves. Every time we needed to delay or move a mission, I needed to handle all the details. This wasn't the time or place to remind Wendy Sherman of that reality, but we knew it all too well.

"Wendy," Guv said, "at your request, we'll delay the trip for one more week. But don't ask us again. We've got an American citizen, an American *journalist*, at Insein Prison. His family is desperate. He's been in custody almost *five months* now. He did nothing wrong. We can't delay this anymore." When the deputy secretary didn't try to interrupt him, Guv pressed on. "And when we go," he said, "I need you to be positive about the trip. I can't have you saying, 'Oh, this is ill-advised.'"

That was a sore spot with the governor. I'm sure Wendy knew exactly what he was alluding to. Seven years earlier, she had been working for Hillary Clinton while the governor and I were on our way to North Korea to free Kenneth Bae. The State Department hadn't wanted us to go. When we went anyway, Wendy had put out a statement calling the trip "ill-advised," which undercut our ability to bring the American citizen home.

"Wendy," the governor emphasized now, "I would like you to be positive this time."

She said she would be. The three of us hashed out some language, a short comment the State Department would release when the media started asking about our next mission: "We're aware of the governor's trip. It's a private, humanitarian visit. We wish him the best." Not exactly a standing ovation. Just some benign language that wouldn't make things ten times harder for us.

Then Wendy added, almost in passing, "And Governor, I need to insist again that when you go and visit them, you do not raise Danny Fenster in the meetings."

"I will not proactively raise him," he assured Wendy.

Wait, what did Guv just agree to? That we wouldn't mention Danny Fenster? Isn't Danny's case the entire reason we're going to Myanmar?

We'd been working day and night trying to get over there so we could sit down with General Min Aung Hlaing, the hard-line leader of the new military government, and try our best to negotiate Danny's release. We'd already been delayed by the State Department two, three, four— honestly, I'd lost count of how many times it had asked us to postpone our trip. And now, when we were finally getting there, it was asking us not to raise the American prisoner we had come to rescue? Does this seem counterintuitive? Maybe. But the request by Deputy Secretary Sherman was not a surprise. It was not that Wendy or anyone else at the Department of State did not want to see Danny Fenster come home. Quite the opposite. They very much wanted the young journalist to be freed. I cannot be sure exactly what calculations were being made inside those State Department meetings, but I had to assume they were led by two thoughts. First, department officials were trying to work with third-country nationals, mainly Japanese, to help get Fenster released, trusting these people when they claimed that progress was being made. And second, Wendy and her team were probably worried that if we asked the military government leader for Fenster, the general would ask for something in return from the United States government, something the State Department almost certainly would not be willing to give. And that could be a problem.

Of course, I knew I'd be the one placing the next call to Danny's brother, telling him, "Bryan, yeah, we're finally leaving for Myanmar, but you should probably know: the State Department doesn't want us to raise Danny."

It was my job to design the call so that Bryan, and therefore the Fenster family, could provide us with sufficient space to try to bring Danny home, if we could make that happen.

* * *

DANNY FENSTER WAS AN AMERICAN JOURNALIST WHO'D COMMITTED the worst imaginable crime in Myanmar. He'd somehow managed to offend the nation's new military regime.

Exactly how he'd done this wasn't entirely clear. A thirty-seven-year-old American expat, Danny came originally from suburban Detroit. He'd been a reporter for the bilingual news agency Myanmar Now and then managing editor of the magazine *Frontier Myanmar*. On May 24, 2021, less than four months after the generals removed the nation's civilian government in a coup, Danny was stopped for questioning at Yangon International Airport just as he was about to fly home to Michigan for a surprise visit with his parents, who'd been missing him while he was living abroad.

Danny had the permit he needed to leave the country. He had his ticket and a seat on the plane. None of that mattered. He was taken into custody instead. From what the authorities told him, someone had noticed his name on the website of Myanmar Now, a banned organization, though he hadn't worked there for nearly a year. Now he was under arrest.

He immediately texted his wife, Juliana: Hey, I'm being detained. Let my parents know and contact the embassy. So word of Danny's arrest reached Michigan and the US State Department without delay. Within hours, I received a Facebook Messenger text from an old friend I had gone to summer camp with twenty years earlier, the same camp where I met Robin. Sara Jasper Epstein was her name. "Hi Mickey," Sara wrote, "I'm in a FB group of lawyer moms and someone is seeking help regarding her relative, a journalist, who is being detained in Myanmar. I know you've worked on matters similar to this in the past and thought perhaps you could help."

Four hours later, I was on the phone with Danny's brother, Bryan.

"Danny was made to disappear," Bryan said in that first call with me, the fear and anguish plain in his voice. "Myanmar's a scary country these days. We have no idea what to do. We need to save his life! Can you please help us?"

Of course.

Bryan had good cause for alarm. The recent news from Myanmar was horrifying. The military government forces were said to have carried out mass killings and used torture against protesters, lawyers, health workers, and political opponents. Crimes against humanity, critics in the West were calling these assaults. The reported targets also included journalists.

Right away, I called a few friends in Myanmar to get an accurate read on what was happening on the ground, people (including our old friend KMT) I'd known from our democracy-building campaign there and from our efforts to free two Reuters journalists who were being held by the previous, civilian government. These people would certainly know. Soon after seizing power, the generals had issued a command to all journalists to stop using words like *coup*, *regime*, and *junta* to describe the military takeover. When many reporters ignored the order, the military government took a more comprehensive stand against free expression, arresting nearly a hundred journalists, outlawing dozens of news sites, and cutting off mobile data service. Though Danny wasn't the only journalist to be targeted in those early months of the new regime, he did appear to be the only American.

I immediately began sending out feelers to the military government. Sooner or later, I had to assume, Guv and I would be traveling to Myanmar, sitting down with General Min Aung Hlaing or one of his ministers and trying to work something out. But maybe we could find an easier way. Maybe a few quick calls with the right people could bring Danny swiftly home. It was certainly worth a try. I knew from past missions how important it was to get moving quickly. In cases like this one, there is often an early window before the government digs in. Who knows? Maybe Danny's arrest hadn't been ordered by the top generals. It could have been an on-the-spot decision by some low-level airport guard. Sometimes it was possible to resolve a case like this one right at the start and avoid a lot of trouble for everyone.

With that in mind, I reached out, indirectly, to Myanmar's foreign ministry and the State Administration Council, the official governing body the generals had established after the coup. "This is probably just a misunderstanding," I said, giving my counterpart a face-saving way out for his colleagues in government. "Let's try and resolve it before things go too far."

Speaking of far, I didn't get far at all with these indirect attempts. Not at first. But at least the military government now knew that the Richardson Center was working with the Fenster family, that we were paying attention to Danny's imprisonment, and that we were eager to advance the American journalist's release.

"So what about Ari Ben-Menashe?" Guv asked me. "Maybe he can help."

A well-connected, Iran-born Israeli Canadian lobbyist living in Montreal, Ari had a lot of bases covered. He had been hired by Myanmar's military leaders to represent their government's interests in Washington. I took that as an encouraging sign. The generals wouldn't have hired a big-time lobbyist (at a reported fee of $2 million) if they didn't care how they were being perceived in the West...would they? By then, the Biden administration had already begun imposing sanctions on the generals in the State Administrative Council. Danny's arrest certainly wasn't making the military government look any better in America. The media coverage had been universally negative. Maybe Ari and the generals would like to counteract that perception problem by helping to advance Danny's release.

Ari offered to try, as Guv and I began exploring the complicated logistics of flying to Myanmar and getting an audience with someone who had the power to order Danny's release—a very short list, I was sure. By mid-June, it was clear the early window I'd been hoping for was already closed. Danny remained in custody. The government in Myanmar was dug in. This could take a while.

From the start, we'd been in regular touch with the US State Department, letting American officials know we were on the case and keeping them informed about our efforts. It would be hugely helpful, I knew, if the Biden administration took Danny's arrest seriously, as a real issue between the two countries. We got some initial encouragement from Roger Carstens. As special envoy, Roger was turning out to be a gifted communicator and a strong champion for the families. He and I were developing a real trust. We had to.

Roger assured us that the US government was laser focused on Danny's case and making quiet efforts on his behalf, the details of which he was not yet prepared to share. What the hostage envoy needed from us, he said, was patience, admittedly not something Guv liked to exercise. Not when an American citizen was being held unjustly in a prison cell 7,800 miles from home. Not when the American's family was so desperate for help.

In early July, I traded Signal messages and then a phone call with the US ambassador to Myanmar, Thomas Vajda, a career Foreign Service officer, who expressed support for our efforts and promised to do what he could to help. By then, Ari Ben-Menashe, the lobbyist repping the Myanmar generals in Washington, seemed to have disappeared. He hadn't made any progress with the generals that I could detect. It soon became clear that the Ari thread had gotten too thin to follow.

I stayed in touch with Ambassador Vajda, who told the Fensters that a friendly Japanese businessman was working behind the scenes to facilitate Danny's release. Great. But when we pressed for details, the ambassador said he couldn't share anything more. And then nothing seemed to happen with that at all.

The US government had never recognized the military government in Myanmar as legitimate and thus had had no direct contact with the new regime since it had assumed power in February of that year. So Ambassador Vajda, despite his best intentions, was not allowed to engage directly with Danny's captors. He had to use intermediaries. That was a real problem.

Since the military had ousted Aung San Suu Kyi, the senior general had ruled with an iron fist, imprisoning the former head of state, hundreds of parliamentarians, and more than a hundred local journalists. He'd also locked up Aye Moe, the former Richardson Center contract employee who, along with Mindy Walker, had helped run our democracy-building campaign. Aye Moe had become a close and loved friend of mine over the years, and the news of her arrest in May triggered old trauma from Wa Lone's previous detention. Aye Moe was a very special person, intelligent, driven, loyal, and a real force for change. To me, she always embodied the great potential of Myanmar and its people.

This, again, was very personal for me.

* * *

By early August, Danny had been in custody in Myanmar for two and a half months. We hadn't heard anything specific from Washington for weeks. The Fensters were growing more alarmed by the day, especially when they learned that Danny had been moved to Myanmar's notorious Insein Prison, the hellhole where the Reuters journalists and, way back when, even Aung San Suu Kyi had been held. Now Danny's name could be added to the cursed roster of inmates, a list no one could possibly want to join.

We had no direct contact with Danny, so we never really knew how he was doing. He was allowed a few short calls with his family and a handful of meetings with his attorneys. It was only through them that Danny learned the nebulous charges against him, which included incitement, "disseminating information that could be harmful to the military," and violating a colonial-era statute called the Unlawful Associations Act. Such offenses could easily carry more than a decade in prison. What they all added up to, really, was...*journalist who may have written stories the military government did not enjoy.* There really didn't seem to be any more to his alleged criminality, and Danny still didn't have a trial date.

Guv and I knew we needed a crafty strategy for this one, a fringe-diplomacy bank shot that would give us the right kind of access to the generals, something they cared about that might also allow us to bring up Danny Fenster. A direct approach—simply demanding that they "release the political prisoner"—that was never going to work. They would just ignore us. We'd never get in the door. We needed something creative and tangible. That's what fringe diplomacy is all about. So we asked ourselves: *How does all this look from the generals' point of view? What can we help with that might leave them open to the "humanitarian gesture" of releasing the American journalist?* We didn't expect the military government to admit it had done anything wrong. Just to release Danny!

Then it hit us. An idea. COVID vaccines.

By the fall of 2021, the world was a couple of years into the deadly coronavirus pandemic. The first vaccines had been released to the US public that August. But rollout was far slower in some other parts of the world, especially isolated countries with poor trade relations, like Myanmar. Myanmar was a vaccine desert. Could we help General Min Aung Hlaing get COVID vaccines? Wouldn't he see that as a way to help his own people?

It was worth a try. Through a back channel, we floated the idea with the military government. And we got a bite.

On August 13, Governor Richardson received a call from the Myanmar Foreign Ministry. An official there said they might be willing to meet with us if we wanted to come to Myanmar…and discuss COVID vaccines. Finally an opening. Once we got in the room with the generals, I knew Guv or I could find a way to bring up Danny's plight.

We immediately updated Wendy Sherman, who seemed to appreciate being kept in the loop, though she may have been dubious about our ability to procure the vaccine. We also offered to brief State Department counselor Derek Chollet, though without explanation, he canceled the scheduled call with us. A week later, Guv spoke with Kurt Campbell, the

Indo-Pacific coordinator at the White House National Security Council. We weren't going behind anybody's back. And we could certainly use their collaboration. Kurt made one helpful suggestion: "Talk to Peter Sands." That was a good idea. A British-born banker, Peter was now executive director of the Global Fund to Fight AIDS, Tuberculosis and Malaria, a major player in the international public health field. Lately he'd been working with the Pandemic Preparedness Partnership, advising the leaders of the world's large industrial democracies on the coronavirus pandemic. He could definitely be helpful getting COVID vaccines into Myanmar.

We got busy figuring out the details of all that.

"I have the honor to express my best wishes to Your Excellency," said the invitation letter from Myanmar's foreign minister. "We are now addressing challenges posed by the third wave of COVID-19 pandemic across the country....In this regard, I wish to invite you to visit Myanmar to discuss with me on matters related to our efforts in prevention, control and treatment against the Pandemic."

The invitation arrived on August 31, and we shared it immediately with our contacts at the State Department, the US embassy in Yangon, and the White House National Security Council. But three hours after the invitation from Myanmar arrived, the State Department suddenly reversed course. I received a call from Roger Carstens saying he had a message for us from Wendy Sherman: "Please hold off on going to Myanmar. We have a good indication that Fenster will be released next week."

Wow! What great news...if true. So was it true? We hadn't heard any rumbles of an imminent release from our sources in Myanmar. But I was certainly ready to be surprised. When I pressed Roger for details, though, he clammed up entirely. "All you need to do is keep quiet," he emphasized. "Let the process play out."

And that's what we did. We stayed quiet, and we waited.

That same day, Peter Sands, the British banker turned pandemic consultant, canceled the scheduled call with the governor. Later that day,

I had an exchange of Signal texts with Gwen Cardno, the deputy chief of mission in Yangon, who said cryptically, "I have to ask that you trust our experience. We know what we are doing." After that, I suspended all communication with the embassy staff in Myanmar.

The next day, something happened that I didn't understand. Wendy Sherman went on Twitter and publicly blasted the military government in Myanmar. "U.S. citizen and journalist Danny Fenster marked his 100th day detained in Burma," she tweeted. "Danny's unjust detention is a reminder of the military junta's crackdown on journalists and press freedom in Burma. We will continue to work for his release until we #BringDannyHome."

It wasn't so much that her sentiment was wrong, but her timing was puzzling. Only a day before, the State Department had asked us to lie low and let the process play out while we waited for the next hearing. And now, before that same hearing, this tweet was doing the opposite. I sent an email to Roger asking for clarification. He did not respond. And, apparently, Danny had to pay the price. Three days later, on September 5, he was back in court, having his pretrial detention extended for another fourteen days. Clearly the State Department's read on the situation was very different from ours—deeply flawed, I thought. When I finally reached Roger, he had no real explanation. He just urged us to wait another two weeks, until Danny's next court hearing, before we said or did anything. This was getting difficult to digest. We couldn't just hold. We had an invitation in hand. We could either accept or decline. And with every delay in our response to the military government, we risked that it would withdraw the invitation. If State's analysis was wrong, we could lose the single best chance we had of getting Danny home.

I got in touch with the government in Myanmar and scheduled our trip for the end of September. Guv and I figured that we had to respond to their invitation. By scheduling the visit for the end of the month, we could let State's strategy play out without infringing on it.

I wasn't completely surprised when the State Department kept asking us to delay…and kept declining to offer much of a reason. It was just *Please wait.* Late September turned into early October, just as early October would turn into late October. When Danny returned to court on October 6, he was ordered held for another fourteen days. There was no doubt in my mind that our analysis was right. We had to press ahead, despite the resistance from the State Department.

Sensing fresh opposition, Guv figured we'd better try to broaden support for our humanitarian mission. So he met with US Senator Robert Menendez, United Nations Secretary-General António Guterres, and the US ambassador to the United Nations, Linda Thomas-Greenfield. He got good receptions all around. We wanted to round up as much support as we could.

Realizing we would soon be leaving for Myanmar, others at the State Department started calling, urging us to "decouple"—that was the word—decouple our humanitarian vaccine efforts from the Danny Fenster case. On October 14, Wendy Sherman called Guv with the same message. Decouple. When Guv pressed for details of her reasoning, she offered to have a team of State Department officials brief the Richardson Center team on exporting COVID vaccines. We said sure, we'd be happy to have a briefing, which turned out to be a lackluster meeting hardly worth the drive to the department's headquarters in Washington's Foggy Bottom.

We set a new date for our trip to Myanmar. October 25. But on October 19, six days before we were set to leave, we got that call from Wendy Sherman: "We're asking you to delay your trip."

"Again?" Guv asked.

On October 18, for "humanitarian reasons," the Myanmar government announced that 5,636 prisoners were being pardoned in time for the Thadingyut Festival. The pardon proved that the government was "committed to peace and democracy," the officials said. Danny Fenster's name wasn't on the list.

Now that Guv had extracted a promise from Wendy to be positive about our trip, we agreed to the State Department's request that we hold off for one more week. But that was it. It was time to make the call to Danny's brother, Bryan. "We are finally heading to Myanmar," I told him. "But you should know that the State Department has asked us not to raise Danny's case while there."

I paused.

In planning for this call, I'd anticipated two possible reactions from Bryan. He could tell me that the Fenster family wanted us to raise Danny's case regardless of the State Department's wishes. That would give us a clear mandate. After all, we were working on behalf of the family, not the government.

Bryan didn't say that. Instead, I got the second reaction I'd anticipated.

"Hmmmm…" Bryan slowly gathered his thoughts. "I guess if they ask you not to raise Danny's case, they know what they are doing."

I did not argue. I was prepared.

I let the silence sit for a few seconds. "OK," I said. "Understood."

The last thing I ever want to do is to add to the pressure on a family member in a situation like this one. These families are often put in an impossible position, asked to make decisions based on partial or wrong information. Decisions that might save or doom a loved one. It is unbearable. I was not going to add to that. "But you know, Bryan," I said in a lighter tone, "if we have the opportunity to bring Danny home, we will not leave him there…"

I could hear Bryan laughing on the other end of the call. "No, if you can bring him home, please do not leave him behind." I laughed too. Now we had just enough space for our mission.

17 SECOND CHANCE

THERE'S A CERTAIN SMELL IN THE AIR IN MYANMAR. A COMBINATION of natural freshness, incense, and the slightest hint of burned wood. It has always reminded me of my childhood days in Nigeria. But by now, I had learned to appreciate the uniqueness of Myanmar's fresh but pungent air.

Guv, Ambassador Cameron Hume, Steve Ross, and I spent two full days, November 1 and 2, in Naypyidaw, Myanmar's modern but eerily quiet capital city. It was certainly strange to be back after our "escape" the last time. Leaving Myanmar in secrecy a couple of years earlier, I had been convinced I would never be allowed to return. Life is full of curves and surprises, isn't it? As Guv often reminded me, "There is always the next round." I had to admit, despite the dire circumstances, I was happy to get a next round in Myanmar. I had failed in my last mission. I was prepared to deploy the lessons I had learned from that failure.

In Naypyidaw, we met with some of the government's top ministers, hashing out the details of delivering COVID vaccines. The ministers were definitely engaged. It was clear that the military government wanted our trip to be successful. Since we had almost no collaboration from the US government or Peter Sands's Global Fund when it came to the vaccines, our own Steve Ross spent many hours interacting directly with humanitarian agencies on the ground in Myanmar. Over the years, I had learned that the humanitarian officers in the field know and understand best what the gaps are and how they can be overcome. Because of Steve's work, our meetings were positive and productive. And there had been no mention of Danny...yet. We wanted to make sure our hosts knew that we were not faking our intention to help on the humanitarian issues we had been invited to address. We were genuinely there to be useful, regardless of any opportunity to discuss or free Danny Fenster.

Everything we'd done till now had been deliberate—and it had worked. It was the strategy that got us the audience we were hoping most for, with General Min Aung Hlaing, the commander in chief of Defence Services and chairman of the State Administrative Council. As the leader of the military government and now the head of state, he had the one vote that really mattered.

Getting the audience with the general was step one. But once we sat down with him, we had to have a plan that would give us the best chance of getting both Danny Fenster and Aye Moe released.

For starters, we'd learned our lesson from our unsuccessful encounter a couple of years earlier with Daw San Aung Suu Kyi. We were definitely not going to raise the issue of the prisoners in front of others. Not ministers. Not staff. No one. This was for the leader's ears only. It was to be addressed only in a one-on-one meeting between Guv and the general. So the plan was to wait until the end of the formal meeting and then for Guv to ask the general for five minutes of his time, one-on-one.

Next we had to come up with the best way for Guv to establish a personal connection in those five minutes. Something to create sufficient emotional leverage to ask for the humanitarian gesture we had in mind. That's the space where emotional intelligence is king. Not national interest. Not policy logic. Those are irrelevant.

Emotional intelligence.

Most leaders Guv and I sat down with were extroverts, charismatic men with hard-driving personalities and a confident sense of command. Not General Min Aung Hlaing. I had spent time studying him. Asking my contacts about him. Not about his positions, but about his personality, the way he saw the world. Our old friend KMT had been a couple of years ahead of the leader in the military academy. KMT had great insights. General Min Aung Hlaing was quiet, he said. An introvert. He had an unusually soft voice that hardly projected at all. Not your typical head-of-military-turned-head-of-state personality. That seemed like an important point to me. An unusual personality for the position he was in. How did that factor into the way he saw himself? Was it a source of insecurity? Did it drive him to overcompensate in other ways?

Those were all good questions.

Face-to-face, we figured, General Min Aung Hlaing would come off as shy, quiet, and hard to engage. Not a great match for Guv's oversize personality. But would the general have a chip on his shoulder now that he was leading the country? A desire to show how tough he was? A need to prove everyone else wrong? We could only hope not.

In anticipation of Guv's one-on-one with the general, I handwrote four bullet points. I knew that Guv liked to leave papers or documents behind with his counterparts. They could end up anywhere. So I wrote very carefully:

- You know, I meet a lot of leaders. You are a different kind of leader. You have quiet leadership. Not loud. I like it.
- I want to be helpful. You know I get criticized for coming to see you. I don't mind it because I am a friend of Myanmar and the Myanmar people.
- There is something you can do that can really help me with my critics. If you can give me Danny Fenster, to take home. If you can. Not a condition. I will not mention it.
- Another personal thing, if you can. There is a young woman, Aye Moe. She used to work for me when I did training for women in Myanmar. She is detained in Insein Prison. Would you consider including her in the amnesty?

I gave Guv an old picture of him and Aye Moe from a previous visit and wrote her name and location on the back so the general could find her easily, if he chose to release her.

These points were not for Guv to read off a piece of paper. They were to trigger his conversation and add his own unique flavor to the delivery. Guv knew to evaluate how each point was received before deciding

216

whether he should go to the next one. If our initial approach was a miss, he knew he might need to bail before reaching the requests. But if he felt our approach was working and he was on a roll, he would go for everything.

* * *

I found General Min Aung Hlaing just as tough to read as I had expected, as Cameron, Steve, the governor, and I were ushered into the grand meeting room at the palace. The ministers we'd met with previously were all in the room. We reviewed our discussions in front of the general, including the conclusions and next tangible steps. The general just nodded and listened and offered a couple of indecipherable vocalizations. He was stiff, almost taciturn. Was he supportive? Was he not? Hard to say. Even his body language revealed nothing. I couldn't assess where we stood with him and therefore whether we had a shot at getting Danny Fenster or Aye Moe.

That's when Guv made his move.

"General," he said, interrupting my concluding thoughts about humanitarian issues. "Can you and I spend a short time alone?"

"Of course," the senior general replied, motioning to a small room off to the side.

Cameron, Steve, and I chatted with the ministers while we waited for Guv and the general. But I couldn't really focus on our conversation. I was too anxious to find out about the one-on-one. Five minutes turned into ten, and ten turned into twenty. Was that a good sign? I sure hoped it was. Past experiences had taught me to keep my expectations in check. No reason to ride the emotional roller coaster. But the mind can't always control the heart. And my heart was thumping hard.

After a long forty-five minutes, which felt more like two hours to me, Guv emerged from the room and walked toward the exit. Without stopping, he motioned to the three of us to walk with him. We said our quick goodbyes to the ministers and joined him. No words were exchanged among us. Not here. That had to wait until we could talk privately. Guv asked me to ride with him in the first car while Cameron and Steve rode in the car behind us.

"So how did it go?" I asked once the door was shut.

"Well," Guv responded hesitantly, "I think it went well."

I wanted details.

"I spoke to him about his leadership style," Guv said. "Then the meeting became really personal. We talked about family. We talked about leadership. He took his glasses off. It was personal, and it was positive." This sounded encouraging. "After the second point, where I expressed my solidarity with the people of Myanmar," Guv continued, "I felt it was going well. So I asked him about Danny. The general knew about him, of course. He asked me if Danny was a big deal in the United States. I told him, 'Danny's release will be a big story,' but that's not why I want you to release him.' I told him, 'I want you to release Danny as a gesture to me.'"

"And…?" I could hardly wait to hear the rest.

"He looked at me," Guv said, "and he told me that he would release Danny. He said it just like that. 'I will release Danny for you.' He said he would do it here, in Naypyidaw, but that it would take him some time. I told him, 'We have our plane one more day,' but he said that wasn't possible. He couldn't do it that quickly. He asked if I would come back to see him in a week or two, when Danny was ready to be released. Of course, I told him I would."

Wow!

That was fantastic and exciting news.

"Guv?" I asked, almost afraid to hear the answer. "What about Aye Moe?"

"Well, I was on a roll," he said, "so I went for it. The general asked me who she was and what she was charged with. I told him she'd probably just agitated his police in a demonstration, but that she was a teacher and a good kid." *And?* "He took the picture and told me she would be at our hotel in Yangon by noon tomorrow."

I could not believe how beautifully that had gone! I was on an instant high. I knew Guv did not fully appreciate how close I was to Aye Moe and how personal this was for me.

"But Mickey," Guv cautioned, "remember, this is not over until we have Danny and Aye Moe. And the general did insist that we *not* share this with anyone. Not anyone. So we need to plan what we do tomorrow when we meet the US ambassador in Yangon. We can't let anyone spoil this by accident."

Early the next morning, we flew from Naypyidaw to Yangon, where the United States embassy is. The plan was to meet with Ambassador Vajda in the afternoon and brief him about our visit. Meanwhile, we checked in to our rooms, and I remained in close contact with the chief of protocol for the Myanmar Foreign Ministry. Time moved excruciatingly slowly as I waited anxiously for noon, when Aye Moe was supposedly being brought to our hotel. We sat in Guv's suite and ordered lunch to the room. I added several extra dishes to the order, hoping that Aye Moe would be able to eat with us. That was Guv's idea, and I liked it. "Order everything on the menu," he said, "I bet she hasn't had a decent meal in five months."

At five minutes to noon, my phone buzzed. Your special delivery is here, read the text from the chief of protocol. We will bring it to your room. My heart was racing. *What if they show up with the wrong woman? Am I really going to see Aye Moe free?*

I said to Guv, "I'm going to step outside to the hallway to make sure they have brought the right person." Guv motioned in agreement. I stepped outside and stood by the door.

The next two minutes felt like forever. Finally I heard the elevator doors open, far down the hallway. I saw three uniformed men walking with the chief of protocol. A young woman was walking next to them.

Was it her?

Within seconds, they were close enough, and I caught sight of Aye Moe's familiar face. Her eyes widened as she saw me, and she immediately looked down. I did the same. We were both doing whatever we could to avoid smiling and crying. Both of us knew: with any eye contact, we could both lose it.

"Is this the woman you requested?" the chief of protocol asked me.

"Yes, it is," I answered as calmly as I could. "Can I take her into the governor's room?" I was trying to assess for certain: Was this a visit or a release?

"She is free," the chief of protocol said.

Such sweet words!

I thanked him and opened the door for Aye Moe. We walked silently into the foyer. As soon as the door closed behind us, we embraced. Both of us broke down crying. We held each other for a long time.

"Mickey," Aye Moe said through her tears, "until I saw you, I had no idea what was happening. No one told me. I was so scared."

I hugged her tighter. "Am I free?" she asked me. I nodded. I was not able to speak.

I led Aye Moe into the main room of the suite, where she was greeted by Guv, and I introduced her to Steve and Cameron. "Why are you crying?" Guv asked jokingly. I shook my head slightly and smiled. She ate just a little, leaving most of what we had ordered for her. We had only a short time to talk before we needed to leave for the US embassy.

"Did you make any promises in return for my release?" Aye Moe asked Guv. She sounded genuinely concerned.

"No, there are no conditions to your release," Guv told her, "but do me a favor, OK? Don't go out protesting for a while. Just stay low for now."

* * *

AFTER A PRODUCTIVE DISCUSSION AT THE EMBASSY THAT AFTERNOON about vaccines and humanitarian issues, Ambassador Vajda asked the governor, "So, what about Danny Fenster?"

How about that? After pushing us so hard before the mission not to bring up Danny's name, now the ambassador was asking us about the imprisoned American journalist.

"You asked us *not* to raise Danny Fenster," Guv shot back without hesitation, the line we'd rehearsed the night before.

"But did you raise Danny?" Ambassador Vajda leaned in.

"You asked us not to raise Danny Fenster," Guv repeated. Vajda got the message, and we walked into a larger meeting that the ambassador gracefully hosted for us with other foreign ambassadors and some human rights leaders to discuss the humanitarian outcome of our visit.

We had to protect our secret. We could not risk a leak that might spoil Danny's promised release.

That next day, six hours before wheels up, I got a call from Ambassador Vajda. "We have reassessed," he said. "We would like Governor Richardson to raise Fenster." Wendy Sherman and Derek Chollet were behind the new instructions, the ambassador said.

That was interesting. Our meetings with the Myanmar military government had concluded the day before. The ambassador knew that. So what was that about? Were they nervous that when we were asked about Danny upon our return, we would respond with Guv's answer to the ambassador, that "the State Department asked us not to raise Danny Fenster"? Probably.

But there was no point in starting an argument. "Thank you, I will inform the governor," I responded to Ambassador Vajda. Who knew? Maybe that would help us when we came back to pick up Danny.

Then it happened again. Another reversal by the State Department. Call it diplomatic whiplash. While we were in the air on our flight from Myanmar to Qatar, I got a text from Ambassador Vajda. "I spoke too soon," he wrote. Now the State Department was asking us again not to bring up Danny Fenster.

I did not respond.

I texted Danny's brother while we were still in the air: Bryan, we are on our way back. Can we talk on Monday to debrief? Bryan didn't respond. That was unusual.

"What do you think is happening?" Guv asked me.

"My bet is that he is upset with us."

"Why would he be?"

"Well," I said, "we're getting blasted on social media by human rights activists for our visit." I'd read a mean tweet from Phil Robertson, deputy director of the Asia Division at Human Rights Watch: "Did zilch, zero nothing for human rights in #Myanmar while giving a propaganda win to #Burma's nasty, rights abusing military junta. Pathetic."

We would learn later that the State Department staff had told the Fensters that our visit to Myanmar was a "setback" for Danny.

True, State didn't know what we already knew, that we now had a promise for Danny's release. And not knowing that, it was easy for it to conclude that we had failed to help Danny. In full self-preservation mode, it made sense, I guess, for State to point out our supposed failure, hoping to mask its own inability for the past six months to get Danny released. But blaming us for some supposed setback was premature, unnecessary, and certainly unfair.

"What should we do?" Guv asked. "You want to go to Detroit and explain to the Fensters what's happening?"

"Nah," Cameron interjected. "What's the point? If we are right about this, then seven days from now, when we get Danny, none of this will matter." It took just a moment for everyone to realize that Cameron was absolutely right.

"While every fiber in me wants to fly to Detroit and explain this to the Fensters," I admitted, "if I have a bad encounter with them and they take us off the case, we will have no mandate to go back and pick up Danny. Let's stomach the punches for now."

Guv agreed.

And the punches kept coming. Especially after Danny Fenster's trial suddenly concluded on November 12 with a conviction on all charges. This was also his official sentencing. The court showed no mercy. Eleven years of hard labor at Insein Prison. A shocking sentence for practicing journalism!

We were blamed on social media by almost everyone with a keyboard who was even vaguely familiar with the case.

All we could do was remind ourselves: the grander the offense, the grander the punishment...the greater the gesture of the release is. That's a rule of thumb in political imprisonment.

The senior general had told us it would take a week for Danny to be tried and sentenced. So none of this came as a surprise to us, even though we were out on this limb all alone. Once Danny was sentenced, he would be pardoned by the leader of the military government.

That's what the general had promised. And now we waited. I sure hoped he'd keep his word!

* * *

The Signal text flashed on my phone on November 9: I got instructions from my Minister regarding the sensitive issue. Please kindly confirm that the governor can come back to Myanmar on Monday 15 November.

I lit up. This was for real. We were going to collect Danny Fenster. I quickly updated Guv and started working the timeline backward.

After months of painstaking preparations, now we had to fly into action at lightning speed. If we were to be in Naypyidaw for a release on November 15, we had to be in Qatar early on November 14, which meant that we had to depart the US the night of November 12. We had only three days to get this together, to find a new charter flight, to sign a contract, to wire payments, to secure landing-and-departure permits, to book the commercial flights to Qatar and back and get hotels, cars, and everything else we needed.

But wait. How could I book a return flight for Danny when I didn't have a copy of his passport? I didn't even know his full name or date of birth. And I couldn't ask his family, since they didn't know we were going back to get him.

I decided to ask my counterpart at the military government in Myanmar. Could he send a scan of Danny's passport? In addition to providing me the information I needed, that would also serve as further evidence that the government in Myanmar was preparing for Danny's release. I asked. And…a passport copy arrived right away.

But that wasn't all. We also needed to put Danny on a commercial flight from Qatar to New York, and we hadn't taken COVID tests. We would have only four hours on the tarmac in Doha between flights, and I couldn't ask the US embassy in Qatar for help, since the US government didn't know about our extraction mission.

After brainstorming with Guv, we concluded that we would have to rely on our Qatari partners, who'd been strong supportors of the work of the Richardson Center for the past couple of years. "Once we are airborne from Myanmar," I told Guv, "I will call Abdulaziz from the plane and tell him that we will need an ambulance in six hours on the tarmac for a COVID and wellness check. That should work, right?"

I knew it would. Abdulaziz Al Thani was my point of contact at the Qatari Embassy in Washington, a genuine partner who had become a good friend. I had no doubt we could count on him. When we needed something, even in a rush, Abdulaziz delivered.

We were barely able to find a plane. Only one aircraft was available to make such a long trip on such short notice with pilots willing to do the round trip with a brief rest period in between. The owner was Lebanese.

There it was: a Lebanese-owned plane, with a Lebanese crew, flying a former Israeli officer to an anti-Muslim country to rescue a Jewish American journalist. You can't make this stuff up!

Relieved that we found a plane, I rushed through the paperwork and the coordination with the officials in Myanmar.

Before takeoff, we still had two more surprises waiting for us. First, the plane did not have an internet connection. Not a big deal for an ordinary mission. But if we didn't have connectivity on this plane, how could we warn the Qataris that we were coming and ask for the COVID test? How could we handle communications midmission? We had no choice. We paid to install an entire new internet system on the small jet, certainly the most expensive fee I have ever paid for Wi-Fi.

Even more complicated was the second surprise. Twenty-four hours before takeoff, the owner of the jet asked the operator, "Why is there a fifth person on the flight manifesto for the return flight?"

"It's a prisoner they are rescuing," the operator naively responded.

The owner flipped out. He imagined us taking his plane on a violent extraction mission, guns blazing. He demanded a letter from the State Department saying the mission was legitimate. That was an issue. How could we possibly get a letter from the State Department when they weren't even *aware* of the mission? I understood the plane owner's anxiety. So I offered a signed affidavit that no weapons were involved, that the release had been authorized by the Myanmar government, and that I would provide a release letter in English before the prisoner ever boarded the plane.

Thank God, that satisfied the owner!

* * *

WE HAD A FOLLOW-UP MEETING SCHEDULED IN NAYPYIDAW WITH General Min Aung Hlaing. Our main objective was to not say or do anything that might risk or sabotage the release. No need for any last-minute complications. No need to raise new issues or float new ideas. Just go through the motions. Keep everything simple. Get it done. Yet despite all the planning, it still wasn't clear to us how and where Danny was going to be transferred into our custody. Toward the end of the meeting with the general, Guv asked him straight out, "So, how do you want to do this? Will you bring him here in front of cameras?"

"Oh, no," the general said in his now-familiar whisper. "That would not be dignified. The prisoner will be waiting for you at the airport."

His answer gave me pause. There was a side to the military leader that I had not fully appreciated until that moment. He was a very religious man. A devout Buddhist. How did that fit with the actions he had been responsible for in Myanmar since the violent takeover of the government in February? Good question. My answer, the answer I had learned over the years, was very simple. People are complicated beings. There is no pure good or pure evil. Reality and life are lived in the gray. All shades of gray. Good and evil exist in all of us, and different parts play out in unique circumstances.

* * *

DANNY ARRIVED AT THE AIRPORT IN NAYPYIDAW SHORTLY AFTER WE left the meeting with General Min Aung Hlaing. As our leased private jet refueled at the gate, we waited nervously for what we hoped would be a straightforward transfer. Every second we waited felt like an hour. *Please, don't let anything go wrong.* We didn't have to wait for long.

A door opened. A group of uniformed security forces walked in. A disheveled Danny Fenster, still handcuffed and shackled, was immediately behind them, looking thoroughly dazed and confused. His beard was scraggly. His hair was a mess. He was wearing open sandals and loose-fitting prison clothes. He didn't look anything like the groomed young professional I'd seen in his photographs. This could be a homeless man on any American street corner. But the smile on Danny's face was unmistakable. I could see he was trying to regain his bearings. Once the cuffs and shackles were off, he hesitated for a moment before he started walking toward us, as if he wasn't sure that any of this was real. Governor Richardson stepped forward and opened his arms toward Danny for a hug.

It was a long, hard dream come true...for all of us.

As quickly as I could, I walked Danny toward the jet, while Guv, Cameron, and Steve said their goodbyes to our hosts.

I had my phone out. I dialed the number I most wanted to call: that of Danny's brother, Bryan, who was at home in Michigan, waiting with Danny's parents and other relatives.

I said as calmly as I could manage, "Bryan, I'm giving the phone to Danny now. Danny, talk to your brother. Let him know you're OK. But just for a few seconds. We've got to get to the plane. We really need to get you out of here."

"Mickey, I need to ask you a question," Danny said to me after we made it onto the plane. He sounded nervous. "I'm sorry, I just—who is that guy?"

"You mean Governor Richardson?"

"That's what I thought," Danny said, nodding slowly. "But I was told last week that he's the reason I got that sentence!"

"Well, you were told a lot of things that were not true," I said to Danny. "But it doesn't matter. You're going home."

18 VALUABLE ALLIES

I WAS ESPECIALLY WORRIED ABOUT TREVOR REED.

By late fall of 2021, Trevor feared he had contracted either COVID or tuberculosis at the Russian prison, something that was making it painful for him to breathe. He'd been coughing up blood for months and had also suffered a broken rib, which can happen when your coughing gets too violent. After he refused to work in a labor camp, he was placed in solitary confinement. Because he'd been learning the Russian language, he understood a lot of what the guards were saying about "the American marine." As he grew increasingly desperate, he went on a hunger strike and then a second one, losing a total of forty-five pounds, and he hadn't been a big guy to start with. Trevor was taken to a hospital at one point, but he said he wasn't given any medical treatment there and was sent back to solitary confinement. He was then brought to some kind of psychiatric facility, which he described as a true hellhole: Feces on the floor. Blood on the walls. An opening in the floor instead of a toilet. He shared a cell with a dozen other prisoners, many of whom seemed to be drugged. He had truly hit bottom. I feared for his life, and I know his family did too.

This was getting desperate.

We needed to create a fresh sense of urgency with our colleagues at the Biden White House. In early January, Guv and I met in the West Wing with Jake Sullivan, the president's national security advisor. The meeting was friendly and open, as I'd hoped it would be. We discussed several pending cases, those of detainees we were trying to help around the world, and we talked about a large debate that was underway in the White House. It involved the whole concept of prisoner exchanges. Were they a legitimate technique? Did they open fresh vulnerabilities and put other Americans at risk? "Those are serious questions," Jake said.

"They are serious questions," I agreed. "Unfortunately, some of these cases can be resolved only with prisoner exchanges. Not all the cases, but some of them. There's just no other way. Previous administrations have done them. Democrats. Republicans. No one likes them, but these swaps are sometimes necessary. The only questions are, How long will you take to accept that? and How many Americans will be hurt by the time you do?"

We were down to the tough stuff here, but we needed to discuss it openly. We had to.

"It's not savory," Guv added. "But it is the right and patriotic thing to do."

Both Guv and I noticed that when Jake referred to Russia, he sounded pessimistic and alarmed. I took that to mean things were about to get much worse there.

That turned out to be true. By January, tensions were escalating sharply on the Russia-Ukraine front and, therefore, on the US-Russia front. While a Russian invasion didn't yet seem like a foregone conclusion, it sure seemed likely to most analysts. And we didn't want to let this crisis, as bad as it could be, go to waste, blinding us to the opportunities to do some good inside the chaos.

This time, it was a Russian who made the first move. Guv was approached by a British American businessman, Ian Brownlow. Though Ian lived in New Mexico, he was reaching out on behalf of Ara Abramyan.

Ara was a wealthy Armenian Russian entrepreneur and a United Nations goodwill ambassador, who had residences in both the Armenian capital of Yerevan and a tony suburb of Moscow, where he *seemed* to have close ties to people at the highest levels of the Kremlin, including Russian president Vladimir Putin. You have to say "seemed to." In that part of the world, you never quite know. People claim connections they don't have. They deny connections they do have. But before meeting Ara, we checked him out as thoroughly as we were able to. He seemed to be the real deal. At the moment, he was also the *only* deal, a potential conduit to the decision makers in the Russian foreign ministry, the intelligence services, and other parts of the government.

Little did I know how much time I would end up spending with Ara. How much I would learn to appreciate his smarts and courage. How close we would become as friends and how much we would be able to achieve together when it came to bringing American prisoners home. For now, though, Ara's message to Governor Richardson, when they met for the first time in California, was surprising: *Come to Moscow. My friends want to meet with you and discuss the prisoners.*

"You know I don't work for the American government, right?" Guv clarified. "And you know that my main interest is getting these Americans home, right?"

Ara said he did.

While Ara rarely said a word in English and spoke through his trusted friend and colleague Vitaly Pruss, he clearly understood English very well. Vitaly was a Belarussian American Jewish businessman. I would also grow to know and love him. Wickedly smart and deeply knowledgeable about the Russian culture and mindset, Vitaly had known Ara for decades. They were friends, business partners, brothers. They trusted each other fully.

Guv called me after his first meeting with Ara.

"Mickey, I think this is the real thing," he said. "We have an opening to go into Russia next month and meet with the leadership to discuss how to bring Whelan and Reed home. Let's talk logistics."

I was excited. We'd been waiting for this opportunity for a long time. At the same time, the logistics were going to be enormously complicated. How would we travel to Moscow? How would we get our visas? Was it safe there now? How would we coordinate with the White House? What if we were able to get Reed and/or Whelan released—how would we fly them out? Where would the plane come from? Would Robin kill me for going to Russia at such a volatile time?

US sanctions on Russia were already piling up. That complicated things tremendously. But these challenges were my favorite kind. We had an opportunity, a million and one obstacles, and a very short window of time.

I secretly loved the pressure and the adrenaline. I got straight to work!

* * *

"TELL TREVOR THAT FRED SAID, 'OORAH!'"

With that quick sign-off, Fred Smith gave me the final approval for using his plane to fly to Moscow.

It was only two days earlier that I had approached the founder and CEO of FedEx, after Guv instructed me to put together a mission to Russia and gave me very little time to do it. I had met and worked with Fred during our engagement with North Korea. He wasn't only a titan of corporate America. He was also a deeply patriotic American and, like Trevor Reed, a proud veteran of the United States Marine Corps. (Thus the marine battle cry sign-off.) In fact, over the years, Fred and his family had become close to the families of two legendary navy aviators with one of the great stories from the Korean War.

Jesse Brown was recognized as the first Black navy aviator. Tom Hudner was his wingman. While they were flying a mission in an especially dangerous sector of North Korea, Brown's plane was hit and crashed in the snowy mountains. Hudner crash-landed his own plane next to Brown's in an effort to rescue his friend. Sadly, Brown was already dead inside the rubble of the cockpit, and Hudner was taken as a prisoner of war.

Fred and his family were so close to the families of those two American heroes that Fred made it his personal mission to find and repatriate Brown's remains, vowing to bring the barrier-busting aviator back home. The powerful story of Jesse Brown and Tom Hudner is at the center of the movie *Devotion*, financed by Fred and produced by his daughters,

Molly and Rachel. In 2019 I took Fred with me to meet the North Koreans, and together we worked to repatriate Jesse Brown. Fred was everything I'd expected and more. Sharp. Compassionate. An amazing family man.

Now, three years later, when I had to figure out how we could get into Moscow to try to bring Trevor Reed and Paul Whelan home, I suggested to Governor Richardson that I try Fred. "Beyond his usual generosity, he is a marine," I reminded the governor.

"Do it," Guv said.

As you can imagine, that's not an easy phone call: *I know this is a strange and big ask, but is there any chance we can use one of your planes to fly into Russia in a few days?*

Fred didn't hesitate. He just asked a couple of questions and double-checked the plane's schedule. Then, with that full-throated "oorah," he passed me on to his team to coordinate the flight passages, landing-and-departure permits, and other details with the Russians.

* * *

"So how do we approach the White House on this?" I asked Guv.

Of course, he had an opinion.

"Let's see if we can get a meeting with them the day we depart. But you and Cameron should get together with Josh Geltzer beforehand to brief him." The counterterrorism lead at the National Security Council, Geltzer had been working closely with Jonathan Finer on the Griner case. "Make sure you are clear with him: *We do not work for the government. We work for the families. But we want to inform and coordinate with the government.*"

Yes, I'd heard that speech before. "And Mickey...," Guv continued, seamlessly assuming his bossy tone, "don't be weak. OK? Don't be weak. We don't need the White House to publicly endorse our mission, but we do at least want them to be neutral and benign about it."

I had my instructions, Guv style.

Cameron and I got on a call with Josh Geltzer, special assistant to the president and special advisor to the homeland security advisor on countering domestic violent extremism. Also on the call was Eric Green, a special assistant to the president and senior director for Russia and Central Asia. They have a lot of titles at the White House. Both men were at the National Security Council.

The two White House aides expressed an immediate concern... about the same issue that Guv had brought up. They wanted to make sure we—and the Russians—were clear that we weren't representing the US government. I assured them there was no confusion on that point. That was the whole premise of our work, that we *didn't* represent the government.

We did want to get a sense from that call of what actions might be acceptable to the White House, in case the Russians expressed openness to a prisoner deal. We knew Josh and Eric would never give us a commitment. They couldn't. But it sure would be helpful to have a better understanding of what was doable. Both Cameron and I felt like we got that from the call.

The right kind of exchange *might* be acceptable. It would all depend on which of *their* people the Russians wanted back.

"And Josh," I said shortly before we wrapped up the call, "we are aiming to go quietly. But if our mission leaks and you guys are asked about it, can you please just make a benign and neutral statement?"

Josh paused. "I can send you some language," I pressed on. "But something like, *Governor Richardson is on a private humanitarian mission. He informed us of his mission. We wish him the best.*"

Josh Geltzer was quiet. Naturally, the White House doesn't like to be fed talking points. But we just wanted to make it as easy for them as possible.

"Thanks, Mickey," Josh finally responded, his way of saying goodbye. "I can't make any commitment, but we will work something out."

* * *

CAMERON AND I HELD ONE LAST CALL WITH JOSH GELTZER AND ERIC Green on the day of our departure. Guv joined the call this time. He wanted to make sure everything was clear. It was.

We had two other important conversations before we left, with the parents of Trevor Reed and the sister of Paul Whelan. They needed to know what we were thinking. We needed to know that they were on board. As everyone kept reminding me, we *worked for them.*

The Washington strategist Jon Franks, who was helping the Reed family, arranged the call with Trevor's parents. Having worked with Jon on cases in Iran and Mexico, we knew how savvy and thorough he was, and we trusted him.

"Paula, Joey," I said when we got the parents on the phone. "We are heading out to Moscow. The chances of us being able to bring Trevor home on this mission are slim. We don't want you to go on an emotional roller coaster. But we also don't want you to be caught by surprise if our trip hits the news."

Paula was crying. Grateful tears. For the first time in a long time, she said, someone was actually taking a physical step to try to bring Trevor home. Both Joey and Paula were moved by our willingness to go into Moscow in the current environment to try to help their son.

"It will only matter if it works," I mumbled.

I could feel their pain through the phone. It was overwhelming.

My call with Elizabeth Whelan was similar. I explained the backdrop to our mission and what we were hoping to achieve. As I had with the Reeds, I asked Elizabeth not to talk about our mission publicly. And if it leaked and anyone was asked, they should simply say, "We have asked the Richardson Center to help us. We are aware of the mission, and we hope it is successful."

No more, no less.

Everyone agreed.

19 GUV'S GRENADE

"WHO IN THE LORD'S NAME DOES PUTIN THINK GIVES HIM THE RIGHT to declare new so-called *countries* on territory that belongs to his neighbors?"

President Biden went on television on February 22, two hours before we were set to depart for Moscow. At that moment, war in Ukraine seemed not just inevitable but also imminent. We just didn't know *exactly* when Russian troops would storm across the border.

Was this trip too crazy? Should we cancel? Guv, Cameron, and I were sitting in Guv's hotel room in Washington, ready to leave. "This is what we *do*," Guv declared, channeling what all of us were thinking. "Maybe we can do some good here."

"Well, the president's speech won't make the Russians too happy," Hume added.

I had copies of Whelan and Reed's passports with me, just in case.

It was time to go.

We arrived the next day at Vnukovo International Airport southwest of Moscow, one of four major airports that serve the sprawling Russian capital. We could feel it even before we stepped off Fred Smith's plane: Russia was on the verge of war with Ukraine, a former Soviet satellite that had been an independent nation since 1991. The insults were flying in both directions. Putin claimed that Ukraine was in the grip of corrupt neo-Nazis and its people needed rescuing. Ukrainian president Volodymyr Zelenskyy called that preposterous and vowed to defend his country's independence at all costs. Since November, thousands of Russian troops had been assembling along the 1,426-mile border the two nations shared. In January, the US had given Ukraine $200 million in military aid with promises of much more to come as needed. As Putin prepared the Russian people for this "special military operation," as he called it, Biden had a stern warning for his counterpart in Moscow: "Russia will be held accountable if it invades."

Ara, Vitaly, and Ian had taken care of our visas and accommodations, dealing with the various bureaucracies on the Russian side. A huge favor. Now the three of them were waiting for us before we even had our papers checked. I was relieved to have them there as we approached passport and customs control. I knew how tricky the Russians could make it for visiting Americans.

The traffic from the airport wasn't bad. The lobby of the Ritz-Carlton near Red Square was buzzing with activity, as was the square itself. Some sort of a festival was going on, as if this were just another day for the Russian people. I'm not sure anyone really believed that, but there was little outward indication that at five o'clock the next morning, we would be waking up to Putin's declaration that Russian troops had moved into Ukraine in the "special operation" that he'd been promising.

We were painfully aware of the precarious timing. Guv was already thinking about how we were going to get out of there. "Should we change our departure time, leave earlier than we planned to?" he asked Cameron and me when we met up in the lobby. We always left some extra time for the unexpected. But now Guv was worried that because of the troop movement, air traffic could be shut down at any minute and we'd be stuck in the Russian capital.

"No," I told him. "Our departure permits are set and approved. If we start applying for changes, that might raise the attention of the authorities. They could decide to start messing with us."

Fred Smith's pilots, who were with us in the lobby, emphatically concurred. "Better to leave it alone," one of them said. "But let's make sure we aren't late."

As nongovernmental actors, we were used to private missions. But given where we were and *when* we were there, this was going to be more under the radar than usual. Though we'd be meeting with high-level Russian officials, none of those meetings would be formal. We would never meet in a government official's office or enter a government building. The meetings were never on anyone's official schedule. There would be no paper trail confirming that any of this had happened at all.

Nothing on the books. Nothing at the Kremlin. Just people talking, across a large, international divide.

So how did we meet? Simple: we met in restaurants, hotel lobbies, and the private homes of nonofficials. Ara had us for a lunch or dinner at his estate outside Moscow. His friends, from in and out of government, joined at Ara's invitation. The stage had been deftly set for our direct and intimate exchanges with the Russian leadership.

No record. No fingerprints. Deniability all around. And these were major people.

One meeting was with Russian foreign minister Sergey Lavrov, Guv's old friend and sparring partner from their days at the United Nations. And yes, just as in their diplomatic days, the meeting was friendly. Very. And then it was less friendly. Then friendly again. Back and forth.

The two old friends had a language both of them understood, and I don't mean English or Russian. Cautious, diplomatic jujitsu. Lavrov more than Guv. But at the same time, the discussion was clear and direct.

"Bill," Lavrov said at one point, "do you work for the government?"

"You know I don't, Sergey," Guv answered immediately.

"So why do you think your counterpart in these discussions should work for our government?"

I jumped at that opportunity. I didn't wait for Guv's answer. "Understood," I said. "So who should we be working through?"

Lavrov, a cigarette dangling from his lips, motioned with his head toward Ara. That made perfect sense to me. The team from the Richardson Center, a nongovernmental entity, should be working with a nongovernmental counterpart, exchanging messages with the Russian leadership.

Symmetry. Always symmetry.

It was also reassuring that Ara would be our counterpart. It wasn't just that Ara was focused and helpful. His connections were impeccable. And he was the kind of guy who delivered. So far at least, everything he'd said he would do, he had done. Guv and I nodded to each other. We could work with Ara. Very well.

As our meetings and conversations went on, it became clear the Russians were prepared for two options. One was a two-for-two exchange: Whelan and Reed for Yaroshenko and Bout. Yes, the Russians were back to Viktor Bout. The opportunity to get our two Americans for Yaroshenko and Roman Seleznev had passed. The other option was that we would focus on medical concerns and do a one-for-one trade: Reed for Yaroshenko. Our Russian counterparts also made clear to us that no, we would not be flying home this time with either of the American prisoners. Guv was pushing for that so hard that it caused some awkward moments in our discussions.

But no, it wasn't going to happen.

That was disappointing, but at least we seemed to have two tangible options on the table, considerably more than we'd had when we arrived.

It was certainly a surreal time to be in Moscow. We were disconnected from the news back home. We had no reliable reports of what was happening in Ukraine on the first day of the Russian "special operation." Red Square was alive as if nothing at all special were taking place.

But none of that mattered. We were focused on one thing, and one thing only: bringing our American prisoners home.

* * *

WE SAT IN SILENCE ON FRED SMITH'S JET. THE INSIDE LIGHTS WERE off as we waited for the engines to roar, our signal that we'd been approved for takeoff. Vitaly and Ian were on the plane with us. We didn't like the idea of Ara's guys flying commercially at a time like this. It just didn't seem safe. When we boarded, our crew had told us that airspace in and around Russia was shutting down quickly. A cyberattack had paralyzed the Russian air traffic control systems. Clearly the war with Ukraine had ramped up rapidly and wasn't being fought only on the ground. The crew also informed us that we had to change our flight path. In order to exit Russian airspace as quickly as possible, we'd be heading straight north.

The cabin remained quiet, even after we finally accelerated and were in the air. In fact, very little was said until we saw on the video monitors that we had crossed out of Russian airspace. I was sure no one was listening to us…but *still*. Only then did I use the jet's Wi-Fi to send two quick messages. The first was to Robin: Left Russian airspace. The second was to Josh Geltzer and Eric Green at the White House.

Wheels up. Productive meetings. Let's debrief soonest.

I love the quiet hours in the air after a mission. It is a time of reflection, a rare time for me. Replaying conversations and experiences in my head. Questioning the results. Trying to gain insights I might have missed. Wishing I'd said things I didn't or hadn't said things I did. My mind was racing even harder since this was my first visit to Russia. I was trying to articulate for myself how the Russians see the world around them and their role in it. After all, not a single person I'd met and spoken with over the past thirty-six hours was evil, though in some ways we clearly had different understandings of the world. Again, empathy, not sympathy. Not justifying any of it. Just trying to understand: Why were the Russians acting the way they were acting? I replayed in my head our conversations with Ara and his Russian friends. I thought about something that hadn't struck me at the time.

Several times, Ara's friends had mentioned World War II. I'd expected Cold War talk. But World War II? It was mostly in passing, but there were clearly some unresolved emotions there. The Russians repeatedly mentioned that they had sacrificed twenty-eight million of their citizens in that war. Twenty-eight million! That we, "the West," would not have been able to defeat the Nazis and win that war without the Russians' sacrifice and courage. From my reading of history, they were probably right about that. But the opposite was true too. They couldn't have done it without *us*. Still, it clearly bothered the Russians that when "the West" celebrated the victory, it celebrated D-Day or the landing in Normandy or the Western liberation of the concentration camps, never the Russian triumphs.

I had never really thought about that. They did sacrifice. They did play a key role in the Allied victory. We don't dwell on that part. And all these decades later, it still bothered them. As my museum tour in Pyongyang had helped me grasp the North Korean mindset and lingering feeling of loss, so did this emotional mismatch help me understand some ancient emotions many Russians still felt.

As I thought about it, I came to believe that this might help explain why Vladimir Putin seemed to have such an iron grip on his people. He understood that narrative, and he played to it. He had learned to ease some of the frustrations about current conditions at home in Russia by focusing public anger toward the Americans and the West.

Politically brilliant!

As we passed over Sweden on our long flight to Washington, I played back in my head President Biden's speech from two days earlier. He had known his words would be heard around the world. But he was really addressing a domestic American audience in the role of a strong wartime president. I wondered what would have happened if Biden had started his speech in a different way: *Let me first address the people of Russia. Eighty years ago, we fought shoulder to shoulder, you and us, to defeat Nazi Germany. We could not have won that war without you. You could not have won without us. And we both paid a great price. You lost twenty-eight million of your people. Let's not make a huge mistake now. Let's come together, as we did before, to resolve our differences.*

And after that start, Biden could have gone back to the consequences of a Russian invasion of Ukraine. Would that have mattered? I don't know. But a part of me thought that at the very least, it would have put a dent in the anti-American narrative among Russians. At least on an emotional level. And I do not think it would have cost Biden, or the United States, anything.

I dozed off, waking just as the wheels touched down.

* * *

WE ARRIVED IN WASHINGTON WITH TWO OPTIONS IN HAND. TWO FOR two or one for one. Of course, I preferred two for two. I had learned over the years, and even more so over the previous year of negotiations with the Russians, that these deals don't tend to get better over time. Had President Trump accepted the Yaroshenko-for-Whelan exchange in 2019, Paul Whelan would have been home by now…and we'd have gotten him back in an easier swap than we were likely to make now. And maybe, just maybe, Trevor Reed wouldn't even have been taken. That part's hard to prove. But it is certainly possible that Putin decided to up the ante and grab another American—another marine!—only *after* the Trump administration refused to negotiate over Whelan.

Unfortunately, the decision—two for two or one for one—wasn't up to me at all. I had helped to get the offers. We had delivered them home. At that point, I'm not sure anyone in the White House *cared* what my opinion was.

After returning from Russia, Guv and I conveyed the information we had and shared a few insights we had gathered along the way. Some questions were asked. We answered them. We were thanked and sent on our way. The decision about which deal to make, if any, was entirely in the hands of the president of the United States…once his team put the options in front of him.

That's how government works.

That part was hard. It always is. Waiting. Wondering. Not knowing if anything was really being put in front of the president. Not hearing back. Getting heartfelt inquiries from the Reed and Whelan families and having nothing to say.

After a few days, I prodded Josh Geltzer for an update. "Nothing yet," I was told. I wasn't the only one who wanted to know. The *Russians* also wanted to know, and they were asking me why this was taking so long. The Reed and Whelan families certainly wanted to know.

At the suggestion of Jon Franks, Paula and Joey Reed demonstrated outside a military base near their home in Texas on the day that President Biden was visiting there. Jon alerted the media, hoping the TV cameras would get shots of the Reeds standing outside the main gate, holding signs in the pouring rain, as the president's motorcade whizzed past them. It seemed like a long shot at best. But it worked like a charm. The images were gut wrenching. The anxious parents. The president's car. The pleading signs. The pouring rain. And the media helped too, putting Trevor's picture on the screen and reminding viewers that Paula and Joey's son, a Marine Corps veteran who was once part of Vice President Biden's security detail at Camp David, was still being held in a Russian prison after getting drunk one night in Moscow.

Within minutes, the president called. He promised he would invite the Reeds to the White House.

While we did not share with Paula and Joey the details of the deal the Russians had conveyed to us, they knew we had something. As parents, they desperately wanted to make sure the president did everything he could to bring their son home. We knew and they knew: the best way to make that happen was for them to meet the naturally empathetic Joe Biden.

When this happened, Trevor Reed would no longer just be a prisoner a long way from Texas. He would be Paula and Joey's son.

But a week passed after the phone call. No invitation from the White House. Another week passed. Still nothing. Over those same two weeks, we received no update from Josh or Eric or any other indication of any imminent decision by the president. The Russians were losing patience—and, we knew, losing trust in our ability to deliver anything.

I had another call with Josh Geltzer. It got heated.

"He is the president," Josh said to me, firmly. "He needs time to digest."

I was deeply frustrated. It seemed like such an easy decision to me, the easiest presidential decision ever. Yet no decision was being made. I felt emotionally hijacked. I reacted with my emotions before my logical brain kicked in. There was no excuse for my angry eruption.

"Well," I thundered, "if he needs that much time to digest, maybe he shouldn't be president."

That did not go over well with Josh. Understandably. I violated a basic rule of emotional intelligence: get angry with purpose—and at no other time. That was how I felt. But that didn't mean that's what I should have said.

Jon Franks called me on a Sunday. "Mickey," he said excitedly, "I have another idea. I want to fly the Reeds to Washington. This week. I want them to demonstrate outside the White House. I'll plant a question with one of the reporters at the press briefing, get 'em to ask the president why he doesn't keep his word about meeting the parents of a veteran held in Russia."

The small demonstration in the Texas rain had gotten them some attention. This might work—and on a bigger stage. "That's a great idea, Jon."

Jon and I discussed a couple of options. Then Jon made it happen. By Tuesday, Paula and Joey Reed were outside the White House, demonstrating again. At the end of the president's press briefing, CNN White House correspondent Kaitlan Collins asked the president why he wouldn't meet with Trevor Reed's parents, who were demonstrating outside the gate. The president seemed caught by surprise.

Forty-five minutes later, Paula and Joey were sitting in the Oval Office with the president of the United States.

"We asked him," Joey said to me as soon as they came out of the White House.

"We begged him to call Richardson about the proposed deal," Paula said. "The president was noncommittal."

The Reeds pressed. They asked the president when he thought he might be able to decide. He promised them an answer in fifteen days.

We reset our mental timers and started counting down the days.

Fifteen more days of patience from the Russians. Fifteen more days of excruciating anxiety for Paula and Joey Reed. Fifteen more days for all of us.

As the timer was ticking down, Guv was losing his patience. A couple of days before we hit fifteen, he called Jake Sullivan's office at the White House. Jake was not available, his assistant said. Guv asked the assistant to please take a message, and Guv sure left one. He told the assistant to let Jake know: Governor Richardson was calling the Russians to inform them that the deal was off because the White House was refusing to make it.

"Then," the governor added, "I will tell the Reed and Whelan families everything. Everything."

I didn't hear about the call from the governor. I heard about it from a colleague at the National Security Council. Guv rattled the West Wing, for sure. I was surprised Guv hadn't discussed this with me beforehand. He had probably known I'd try to talk him out of it. I probably would have. When Guv gets a strong gut instinct, he follows it. And as much as I wanted to always be right, Guv often schooled me on how things really work and what can be expected to provoke swift action.

"Throw a grenade into a stale process," Guv liked to say. "Take a chance. What do we have to lose? Nothing is happening."

I already knew what he would have told me if I had spoken up.

I wish those sorts of pressure tactics were never necessary. Then again, I do live in the real world.

The truth is, I have no way of knowing if Guv's grenade worked this time. Whether it affected the White House decision-making process or sped things up or added a dash of urgency. What happened next might have been a total coincidence, completely unrelated to Governor Richardson's phone call.

What I do know is that after the governor dropped that grenade, Joey and Paula Reed received a call from White House assistant Jake Sullivan, informing them that the president had authorized him to take action that would bring Trevor home.

It would take about five more days, the Reeds were told. On April 27, Roger Carstens, the special envoy for hostage affairs, would facilitate a prisoner exchange with the Russians, Konstantin Yaroshenko for Trevor Reed.

It was the day the Reeds had been waiting for. It was an answer to their most heartfelt prayers. It was the one-for-one deal that we had collected in Moscow and delivered to Washington.

It would be the first—but certainly not the last, we hoped—of such prisoner exchanges approved by the Biden administration.

And yet with every win, there is a loss, just as with every loss, there are some small wins.

I was elated for Paula and Joey Reed. And, of course, for Trevor. I was devastated for Elizabeth and the Whelan family. This marked the third time an American administration had had a deal in hand for Paul's release—and failed to bring Paul home. And now the very same Russian prisoner who in 2019 had been offered in return for Paul Whelan was freed in exchange for Trevor Reed.

Paul and his family would have to wait some more.

PART V
LESS
THAN A
GRAM OF
HASH OIL

20 BIG PRIZE

Two lessons I keep learning about this work we do: First, never assume you know everything that's going on. And second, it is never, ever finished.

By the time Guv, Cameron, and I were in Moscow, at the end of February 2022, trying to find a way to bring Paul Whelan and Trevor Reed home, a whole new storm was already brewing in the Russian capital. One we knew absolutely nothing about. Another American citizen was under arrest. And this time, it wasn't an obscure military veteran. It was a superstar professional athlete, Brittney Griner, the towering center for the Phoenix Mercury of the Women's National Basketball Association. On February 17, the six-foot-nine-inch Griner had landed at Sheremetyevo International Airport to play in the Russian Premier League, her regular WNBA off-season gig. While passing through customs, she was detained by uniformed officers from the Russian Federal Security Service, who searched her luggage and said they found vaping cartridges for an electronic cigarette. Those cartridges contained less than a gram of hashish oil.

At that moment, Brittney Griner became the highest-profile American to be jailed in Russia since—well, maybe ever.

Everything about Brittney was impressive, not just her height.

Now thirty-one, she had been a standout player almost from the day she learned to dribble a ball. A three-time All-America at Baylor University, she was the only NCAA player to score 2,000 points and block 500 shots. In 2011–12, she led Baylor to an undefeated 40–0 season, the most wins in NCAA history, and the Division I Women's Basketball

Championship. With an arm span of 87.5 inches and a men's US size
17 shoe, she had a Nike endorsement deal (their first with an openly
gay athlete) and a lucrative future. A two-time Olympic gold medalist, Brittney was now in her ninth season with the NBA's Mercury, her
eighth with the Russian Premier League's UMMC Ekaterinburg. The
seven-time WNBA All-Star seemed almost unstoppable.

How quickly things can change when hostilities between nations are
running hot! Without a word of warning, one of America's (and Russia's)
top professional athletes was all of a sudden under arrest just as Russia
was heading to war in Ukraine. She was facing many years in prison on a
minor drug-possession charge.

The Kremlin didn't announce the arrest of the American basketball
player. Neither did the US government. Neither did Griner's family or
her representatives. None of the Russian officials we met in Moscow
mentioned any of this to Guv, Cameron, or me.

It wasn't until March 5 that a short report from Russian News
Agency TASS was picked up by the *New York Times*: "Brittney Griner,
Star W.N.B.A. Center, Is Detained in Russia: Russian customs officials
said a U.S. basketball player had vape cartridges containing hashish oil
in her luggage. A Russian news agency identified the player as Griner."

What?

Was this Putin's idea of retribution? Had the Russians grabbed a
high-profile American just in time to slap back at the Biden administration for its support for the Ukrainians? I couldn't help wondering if
this was yet another step in Russia's grab-a-prisoner escalation. When
the Americans had refused to trade Paul Whelan for Konstantin Yaroshenko, the Russians had upped the ante by detaining Trevor Reed.
Now, as Washington showed fresh reluctance to negotiate for Whelan
or Reed, the Russians had grabbed Brittney Griner. There was no denying that their latest American prisoner offered a whole different class of
leverage: an Olympic champion, a WNBA superstar, Black, gay...plenty
of new constituencies to enflame there.

A couple of weeks later, Brittney's agent, Lindsay Kagawa Colas, emailed me, connected by a mutual colleague. "We saw you guys were in Moscow a few weeks back and looked at your history of success," Lindsay opened.

I was happy to talk, I wrote back.

Brittney wasn't Lindsay's only client. Her agency represented many other top players, and her experience was vast. I would soon see why the sports agent excelled in her business. But one thing she and her team had never dealt with before was a client taken as a political prisoner. What was so amazing about Lindsay was how quickly she learned to navigate this new space, its hard-to-read government officials and its constantly shifting dynamics. Lindsay was smiley and friendly. She was trim and had long, black hair. She projected a high-watt intensity that made it absolutely clear: *You do not want to be on Lindsay's bad side. Ever.* But for now, in late March, she and I were just getting to know each other and discussing what might happen next.

"For us to be directly involved," I explained, "we'll need a simple note from Brittney's family asking for our help. That note will never be made public, but it is the only mandate we have to get involved. Of course, this is done at no cost to the family."

Lindsay, as I would learn over the next nine months, is always direct. No bullshit. Straight to the point...and fast. No apologies. I liked that a lot.

She said: "Let me discuss this with Cherelle," Brittney's wife. "I am not sure we are ready to ask formally for help. We have a lot of moving pieces right now, and we are just learning this."

"Whenever you are ready," I said.

"But Mickey, can we keep this line of communication open? What we discussed has already been extremely helpful, and I would like to continue talking as we figure all this out."

"I am always available," I told her.

It was April 27 when news broke about Trevor Reed's release. Trevor's parents, Paula and Joey, issued a public statement that thanked Governor Richardson. It was that same day that Cherelle Griner sent us a simple note, asking for the Richardson Center's assistance in bringing Brittney home.

Of course we'd help. Now we were officially on the case.

* * *

Even if Brittney Griner's possession of vape cartridges was a technical violation of Russian law, the offense couldn't possibly justify *this*. There *had* to be something more to it. Brittney even had a prescription for medical marijuana. She found that the drug eased the pain of her sports injuries. While Russia didn't explicitly permit the use of medical marijuana, the sensible solution would have been to confiscate the minuscule amount Brittney carried, issue a warning, and send her on her way. After all, the American athlete was a frequent traveler to Russia and had never been in trouble before.

With our recent efforts on behalf of Reed and Whelan—one a success, the other an incomplete—we had established multiple channels of communication with the Russians, both formal and informal. That was a plus. At the same time, the fact that the two governments had ultimately dealt directly with each other to facilitate the Yaroshenko-Reed exchange gave the two governments some positive momentum. At least that's what I was hoping for. But weeks turned into months, and it felt to me as if any momentum was all but lost. We saw no signs that negotiations were progressing through the official channel—no evidence that the two governments were even talking about Brittney Griner as the worsening war in Ukraine soaked up everyone's attention.

But that in itself might be an opening. As we had learned in Venezuela, when government-to-government discussions aren't possible, independent channels can be even more important.

"We don't want to do anything right now that will give legitimacy to Vladimir Putin," a friend in the State Department said to me, noting that President Biden had just called the Russian leader a war criminal. "Putin would love a chance to look like a legitimate leader to the outside world. We can't afford to give him that opportunity."

Frustrating as that was, I did understand where the State Department aide was coming from. The US government—any government—has a complex relationship with its rivals and a wide range of issues on the agenda. That's one of the main reasons an independent group like ours is so important in a case like this. Since we have no government authority, there's no point discussing policy demands with us. All we are able to talk about is humanitarian issues, including the release of prisoners. And talking can often help. Talking to our rivals. Talking to our friends. Talking to our own government. Talking to anyone, anywhere around the world, who might be helpful.

"Do you think the Russians are ducking us?" Guv asked me on the phone after our attempts to arrange a new round of meetings in Moscow kept falling short.

Did he need to pull the pin on another of his high-pressure hand grenades? No, not yet. The Russians were asking for a signal from the US government that we were authorized to negotiate for the prisoners. But we *weren't*. We weren't "authorized" to do anything. The Russians knew that. We were always clear with them. Our objective was to look for pathways out of the crisis and to have honest and open discussions. Open discussions that government officials often cannot have. Especially not in a time of war. And those discussions needed to happen in person. Zoom wasn't the same.

"Maybe I need to do an advance trip," I told the governor. "Just me this time. So I can calm everyone down and pave the way for a larger visit."

Guv agreed. "But I don't think it's safe for you to go into Moscow on a commercial flight right now," he said. He'd had similar worries about my safety when I went without him to North Korea. But when my flight back from Pyongyang was delayed, Guv had called Robin to say, "Don't worry, he's fine." And I was. But this time, I had to admit he might be right.

"I can go to Yerevan," I told him. "Ara will host me. He could include some of his Russian friends. We can have the meetings at his place."

Vitaly, Ara's trusted friend and translator, immediately started working on the logistics. After all the delay, I felt like we were finally on the move again.

* * *

"Bill, I saw you might be heading into Moscow," said an email in the Richardson Center inbox. It was from John Podesta, who'd been chief of staff to President Clinton and was an old pal of the governor's. "A friend of mine, Jennifer Dudley, has a nephew also being held in Russia, accused of crossing the border illegally after the Ukraine invasion."

Uh-oh!

"I know Jenny," I told Guv after forwarding the email to him. "We were together at the Clinton Foundation, when I worked on the Global Initiative. Let me talk with Jenny and see what this is about."

She brought me up to speed on her nephew, Taylor Dudley. A thirty-four-year-old navy veteran, he'd been in arrested at the end of April crossing into Kaliningrad Oblast, an extraterritorial region of Russia that borders Poland and Lithuania. He'd been at a music festival in Poland. Exactly why he had been crossing into Russia was a little murky. It didn't sound great. And the emails that Jenny shared with me between the American embassy in Moscow and the Dudley family—well, they made clear that the US officials felt extremely constrained in the assistance they were able to provide. The information was partial at best. No surprise there. That's often true in these cases. But no one had seen or heard from Taylor Dudley since he was detained. Not his family and not the US diplomats in the region. It had been almost three months.

Unfortunately, Jenny's nephew's wasn't the only new case that landed in our inbox. The cases of two other imprisoned Americans surfaced at more or less the same time. One had been held since shortly before the invasion of Ukraine. Another had been captured as he was volunteering to assist the Ukrainian forces. Our plate was certainly getting full. But no case is like any other. Each brings a unique set of circumstances, and therefore a unique set of challenges, opportunities, and possible solutions, all of which need to be fleshed out.

We would try to stay on top of all of them. Clearly these were volatile times in and around Russia. Lindsay, Cherelle, and I remained in close contact, speaking on the phone and meeting in person. Cherelle was just as impressive as you would expect. An attorney and terrific advocate for her wife, she had an amazing presence that drew people toward her as soon as she stepped into a room. I encouraged Cherelle to come to the Foley Foundation gala in Washington in early May.

"I think you would benefit from meeting other families who are in this club with you," I told her. "A club no one wants to belong to. But it can be helpful. It's a loving and supportive group."

Cherelle and Lindsay came. Family members of other hostages introduced themselves to Cherelle and instinctively hugged her. She seemed overwhelmed by the encounters. She was welcomed with so much warmth and sympathy. But she was also meeting person after person—daughters, sisters, brothers, spouses, parents—who'd been fighting for the freedom of their loved ones for two, three, four, even nine years!

"You know, Cherelle," I said to her when we sneaked a quiet moment together, "these people you are meeting, they are in a marathon. I believe, with a little luck, you are in a sprint."

I couldn't say for certain. No one could. And things weren't moving quickly...yet. But Brittney's high profile did affect the dynamics of her imprisonment. It made her harder to ignore or forget, by the Russians or the Americans. And I wanted to ease Cherelle's anxiety. Hearing that the nightmare she was living through might last for years—that was a difficult realization. But I truly believed her nightmare would be shorter.

Cherelle was clear with me from the start. "I don't need the feel-good conversations," she said. "Those don't help me. I don't need to vent or waste anybody's time, including my own. I just want to talk, when there is a tangible update or something I need to do."

I didn't push. People find different ways to cope with trauma.

Lindsay and I spoke frequently. Three or four times a week. Never long calls. That was not Lindsay's style, any more than it was Cherelle's. Always to the point and geared toward decisions and actions. She kept me updated on their legal strategy and the support they were rallying from Brittney's fellow athletes and other supporters. We coordinated the public communications they were putting out. We discussed the timing of the public effort Lindsay would muster to get Cherelle in front of President Biden.

"Just like what you did with Reed," Lindsay said, "we want to make sure we don't mount the pressure prematurely." I agreed. I had no doubt Lindsay could get Cherelle into the Oval Office. She'd already demonstrated her ability to galvanize NBA stars, faith leaders, community activists, and Brittney fans. But a presidential sit-down needed to wait until a feasible deal to get Brittney home was cooked enough for a presidential decision. We weren't there yet.

"So you tell me, Mickey," Lindsay said, "if and when you and Richardson get a sense that such a deal is refined enough."

21 | AH, SYMMETRY

IN EARLY JULY, BRITTNEY PLEADED GUILTY TO THE CHARGES AGAINST her—in hopes of winning leniency from the court. Though she emphasized that she'd had "no intention" of violating Russian law, she didn't deny that the vape cartridges had been in her luggage or that they were hers. She'd been stressed after recovering from COVID-19, she explained to the court, and had been rushing to get ready for her flight to Moscow and accidentally left the cartridges in her bag.

"She decided to take full responsibility for her actions, as she knows that she is a role model for many people," said defense lawyer Alexander Boykov. "Considering the nature of her case, the insignificant amount of the substance, and BG's personality and history of positive contributions to global and Russian sport, the defense hopes that the plea will be considered by the court as a mitigating factor and there will be no severe sentence."

Brittney's guilty plea confused some Americans. If she was guilty, then she should pay the price, people started saying on social media. To me, that view didn't only lack empathy. It was an extremely narrow way of thinking...and dangerous. Dangerous because it could quickly turn the public narrative and produce an ugly result.

Lindsay was right on top of that. So were we.

"Any prisoner in a situation like this needs to do what they believe can help them survive the ordeal," Guv said on CNN. "She is fighting for her life." The people at the Richardson Center were trying to secure the safe return not just of Brittney, he added, but of Paul Whelan too.

Brittney's guilty plea was not aimed at freeing her. It was aimed at helping her survive captivity and, hopefully, shorten it. The first part worked. The second part did not. Despite her compliance and show of remorse, Brittney received the maximum sentence allowed by Russian law, nine years.

* * *

JUST BEFORE I WAS ABOUT TO LEAVE FOR YEREVAN, THOSE PLANS CAME to a screeching halt. On July 27, Secretary of State Tony Blinken announced that he'd be speaking with Russian Foreign Minister Sergey Lavrov "in the coming days" to discuss Paul Whelan and Brittney Griner.

"We put a substantial proposal on the table," Blinken told the media.

That's great!

Then I heard what Blinken intended to propose. The details leaked immediately.

Ugh!

The US proposal? Swapping Viktor Bout, the Russian arms dealer imprisoned in Illinois, for Griner *and* Whelan. One Russian for two Americans. As much as the Russians wanted the arms dealer home, I knew the minute I heard it that the deal would never fly. The Russians would never agree to swap one Russian for two Americans. Their pride wouldn't allow it. Lack of symmetry! In my head, I could already hear the howls of outrage from Moscow. *Biden thinks a Russian life has half the value of an American!*

In fact, when Blinken and Lavrov got off the phone two days later, all the US Secretary of State could say about the call was that it had been a "frank and direct conversation," Washington-speak for *We didn't agree on anything, but at least we spoke.* Actually, it was worse than that, as my contacts in the Russian foreign ministry made clear when I caught up with them.

"Two for one?" one of them declared indignantly. "That's an insult, a double smack in the face. First of all, negotiating in public like that? Leaking the proposal to the media at the same time they were sharing it with us? It was clearly done for domestic consumption. That wasn't an actual negotiation from someone who wanted to make a deal. And secondly—are you really offering us one for two? *One for two?* Where's the symmetry in that? We could never agree to that."

Ah, symmetry again.

Without a doubt, this proposal was going nowhere. In fact, it might have set us back. I hoped we could get back quickly on track, but that wasn't looking likely at all.

It turned out the irritated Russians had a strategy of their own. They came back with their own out-there offer: Griner and Whelan for Viktor Bout and Vadim Krasikov.

Krasikov was a new name on the swap list—and quite a disreputable-sounding character. A fifty-seven-year-old former colonel in Russia's Federal Security Service, he had been convicted in a German court of assassinating Chechen rebel leader Zelimkhan "Tornike" Khangoshvili, who was shot to death in broad daylight in a park in central Berlin in the summer of 2019. The German prosecutor called the hit a "state-mandated murder" and a severe breach of German sovereignty, so severe the German government expelled two Russian diplomats. After being convicted of murder, Krasikov was serving life in a German prison.

This was the prisoner the Russians wanted the US to free to help resolve a minor pot case? A hit man locked up in Germany?

Just as surely as the Russians objected to Blinken's two-for-one deal, I knew the Americans would never go for this. First, Krasikov was a convicted international assassin. And second, he wasn't even in US custody. To include him in a prisoner swap for Griner and Whelan, Washington would need to intervene at the highest levels of the German justice system, which would be hugely complicated at the very least, perhaps impossible.

And with that, the "negotiations," if that's what you could call them, completely stalled. It seemed as if the two sides weren't even talking anymore, much less hammering out a deal. It was no and no, and no more.

If there was ever a time for fringe diplomacy, that time was now.

So much to sort out, and it wasn't going to be done over Skype or WhatsApp. We would need the support of the Russian foreign ministry, and that meant sitting down and negotiating with top people there. But so far, all we'd been getting was excuses and delays. The war in Ukraine. The challenge of scheduling. Disgust at some passing comment some politician in Washington had thoughtlessly tossed off. Those might not have been the *reasons* for the delay. But they made easy excuses. Some weeks, all we heard was ghostly silence in response to our *Hey, let's talk* emails. All through July, the days had ticked by with no real progress. Brittney was still in the lockup in Moscow. Paul Whelan was in harsh Lefortovo Prison.

It was clear: we had to do *something.* We weren't getting anywhere with all this sitting around. Thankfully, a month after Blinken's speech, Ara said he was ready again to see me in the Armenian capital of Yerevan.

* * *

YEREVAN WASN'T MOSCOW. ARA ABRAMYAN WASN'T RUSSIAN FOR-eign minister Sergey Lavrov. And I certainly wasn't Governor Richardson. But still. I trusted Ara, his political savvy, and his vast network of friends and associates at the highest levels of the Russian power structure. So when, through Vitaly, he sent me the message, *Come see me in Yerevan,* I knew that was the path forward.

Ara alone couldn't approve a prisoner swap on the Kremlin's behalf, any more than Guv and I could approve a swap on behalf of the White House. But he had proved he could play the influential middleman. Ara was the one I needed to work with in order to find a way to get a Moscow visit for Guv and me back on track. He would be the one hosting us and coordinating with the Russian leadership.

I landed in Yerevan on August 21 with one hope and two fears.

My sincerest hope was that together, Ara, his colleagues, and I could come up with a realistic idea, a Russian-US prisoner swap that both nations could agree to. Names. We needed names. It was clear which prisoners the Americans wanted. But who was on the Russian wish list to be exchanged for Paul Whelan and Brittney Griner? As far as I was concerned, as far as the White House was concerned, certainly as far as the Whelan and Griner families were concerned, the two Americans had already been behind bars in Russia for far too long.

At the same time, I was worried about two hardballs that I imagined Ara and colleagues might throw at me. First of all, I was concerned they might insist on leaving Paul Whelan entirely out of the equation. Again. Even before we sat down together in Ara's large office, I could imagine him saying: *We're ready to trade Griner for Bout, but* not the spy. *Whelan is off the table.*

That would've been really, really difficult to swallow, even putting aside the question of whether Paul Whelan was a US agent or not. (He was not.) After he had been skipped on the Trevor Reed deal, it wouldn't only be cruel. It would also be terrible politics for the Biden administration, I thought—though if I were Putin, it might look like a tempting way to torture the American president. I could already imagine the headlines back home: "Biden Fails Again to Free Former U.S. Marine from Russian Prison."

My second fear was that the Russians would bring up that assassin again, the one being held in Germany. I knew the Biden administration would never agree to a deal that included the release of Vadim Krasikov.

Our eight-hour meeting started with some familiar choreography: me being lectured by my Russian counterparts for a couple of hours about the state of world affairs. "As we are sitting here," it started, "the world is being carved into two spheres of influence. One led by the US and its NATO allies, the other led by Russia and China. And guess what? We already have about seventy percent of the world's population in our bloc. We have Russia, China, India, Saudi Arabia, almost all of Africa, and a big chunk of South America."

I listened politely. If I'd been a US diplomat or an official government representative, I suppose I would have had to raise an objection to the content and the tone. But I was neither. For me, this was gold! I was hearing the authentic Putin narrative on world affairs. What the Russians were doing. Why they were doing it. And the intended outcome.

I just nodded. Grasping this was critical for me. If I could genuinely understand how Putin saw the world and Russia's role in it, that would give a me big advantage as I sought fresh areas for engagement and pathways to tangible results. I'd be better able to predict how Russia would respond to my overtures and how I should respond to theirs. What might work and what certainly wouldn't. I could better avoid the land mines.

The war in Ukraine wasn't going well for the Russians. But for Putin, I realized, Ukraine wasn't the entire game. He was not a checkers player. Putin was a chess player. And his board was the world order. His legacy, as he saw it, was breaking down Western hegemony and placing Russia back in its rightful position as a superpower, toe-to-toe with the United States. And from Putin's perspective, this was the time to do it. The NATO alliance was fragile, he believed. America's standing in the world was already compromised, he believed, by its rivals and its allies. And America was rife with domestic divisions, to which he was happily contributing. In Trump, Putin believed, America had had a president who saw the world as he did. In Biden, Putin believed, America had a president who was old and tired. A president who would be reluctant to have a confrontation with Russia as he tried to reunite his own country.

As I sat there in August 2022, I could easily have argued that Putin had badly miscalculated Ukraine's resolve—and the North Atlantic Treaty Organization's. I didn't, but I could have. But was Putin succeeding in the larger fight for a new world order? That was harder to tell. Three months later, when Saudi Arabia would sign a deal with Russia that countered American interests in the energy field, I would recall that August conversation and think to myself, *So that's what the Russians were talking about...*

In between the stories and the comments that day in Yerevan, I thought of something else that kept me wondering. How was it that Putin seemed to hold such strong support from his political and military elites, as well as vast chunks of the Russian population? After all, he was the absolute leader of the nation, and he hadn't delivered economic prosperity to his people. And now he'd gotten them into a surprisingly difficult war against a nation and people that were an integral part of the Russian culture and history.

I already knew about the Russians' narrative regarding World War II and their unrecognized sacrifices. But what I was picking up now was an additional layer. Putin was providing the Russian people with an answer to the question of why they'd lost the Cold War. That national humiliation that had brought down the Soviet superpower. It was not that the Soviet system was inferior to the West's. And it was not that the Russian people were inferior to the Americans. Putin argued that Russia had lost the Cold War because of the tragic deficit of the twenty-eight million people who had died in the Second World War. These were not just ordinary people. These were the talented young men who could have been Russia's next engine of growth. Their loss was a profound handicap at the start of the Cold War. And the West had exploited that handicap to keep Russia down. That was the whole purpose of NATO. And now, with NATO's bold attempt at consuming Ukraine, the Russians finally had to respond.

Does that sound far-fetched? To an American ear, it does. But to a Russian national who'd been suffering for years, it was a narrative that said, *It's not your fault. It's not because of you. It's because others took advantage of your courage and your bravery and your sacrifice.* Those were receptive ears.

That look inside the Russian mindset would guide my understanding of Russian behavior from the moment I recognized it. But I wasn't in Yerevan for philosophical discussions. I was there to find a way to get American prisoners home. And when we finally got onto the prisoners, Ara didn't throw either of the hardballs I feared. When I asked for names, Ara went straight to a two-for-two deal, then put an entirely new name on the table.

Alexander Vinnik.

The proposal was Brittney Griner and Paul Whelan for Viktor Bout and Alexander Vinnik.

I already knew Bout from our last round of prisoner-swap discussions. Vinnik was new to the equation. A forty-three-year-old computer whiz, Vinnik had cofounded BTC-e, a Russia-based cybercurrency trading platform with servers in the United States. He'd been hit by a flurry of accusations from France, New Zealand, the US, and (surprisingly) Russia. Fraud. Money laundering. Ransomware attacks. At the request of the US government, he was taken into custody at a vacation resort in Greece, was convicted in France of laundering ransomware funds, and on August 4 was extradited to California to face charges that he'd laundered $4 billion through BTC-e and operated an unlicensed money service in America.

Now, apparently, the Russians wanted him home. To jail him in Russia? To set him free? I didn't know, and I didn't ask.

But before we got to Vinnik, I had to know: "What about Krasikov, the guy in Germany? I thought he was the one you wanted."

Ara laughed.

"Why are you laughing?" I asked.

"Well," he said, "that was just a fuck-you to Blinken for his fuck-you to us, when he said he wanted two for one."

What a relief!

"Does the official channel know that you've moved beyond that name?" I asked.

"The official channel is not really communicating well," was the answer I got.

Obviously I couldn't speak for the White House or the State Department, but from where I stood, my very first reaction was: *This is a feasible deal.*

Not an easy deal, maybe, but absolutely doable.

Vinnik had been in US custody since August 5. That made things easier right there. He'd been charged, but he hadn't yet been convicted of anything in the United States. And not to downplay the seriousness of money laundering or cybercrime—but it wasn't quite the equivalent of traveling to another country and assassinating a political opponent in broad daylight in a public park. As for Viktor Bout, he wasn't a Boy Scout either, but he'd already been vetted in Washington, and compared to the Berlin assassin, Vinnik could be a Brittney Griner slam dunk.

I was also able to figure out what was holding up Guv's visit to Moscow. There was a presidential directive from Putin that no Russian officials should meet over the prisoners outside of the official channel. I guess that following the Reed-Yaroshenko exchange, Putin believed the official channel would suffice in getting the results and did not want confusion. Made sense. Especially coming from a political system where decisions are made and executed by a single leader. Well, the US government is quite different. But that presidential directive explained why we were having difficulties being welcomed to Moscow.

As I'd learned so many times before, when you meet face-to-face and have an honest discussion, you learn things. You can find solutions. This was no exception. Within the course of a few hours, Ara and I came up with a formula for bypassing the latest obstacles. Guv would send a note to his old friend Lavrov asking to meet him privately, not formally, to discuss bilateral issues and explore some ways of mitigating the crisis between our two nations in the near and long terms. Not a formal or official meeting. Just a friendly encounter between a couple of old colleagues who wanted to figure out how to solve some serious problems.

The rest of the private meetings, we figured, could be added later.

Of course, the issue of the prisoners would be raised in these conversations. But this wouldn't be a "negotiation," just a chance for us to listen to the Russians and see if we could help. We also agreed that a copy of that note from Guv would be sent to Ambassador Antonov at the Russian embassy in Washington, making sure no one was surprised.

I left Yerevan with a smile on my face, eager to deliver the encouraging news to Guv.

22 DOUBLE-TALK

IT WAS SHORTLY AFTER I GOT BACK TO WASHINGTON THAT GOVERNOR
Richardson and I went to see Jonathan Finer, the deputy national security advisor, at Guv's favorite early-morning Washington hangout, the
elegant breakfast room at the Hay-Adams. No need to pass through
White House security. No need to cram into a stuffy West Wing office.
No reporters snooping around. And just a short walk for Jon, right
across Lafayette Square.

That's where I floated Alexander Vinnik's name and Jon seemed so
surprised, wondering why the Russians would deliver such a message
through *me* and not the official channel. I explained to him the benefits of using a free agent to propose deal terms. *Fringe diplomacy!* I don't
think Jon was entirely convinced, but that part didn't really matter.
What mattered was the name the Russians were floating and how the
White House would react to a potential prisoner swap involving Brittney Griner and Paul Whelan. Vinnik, the Russian computer whiz and
convicted money launderer, sure sounded like a much easier lift than, say,
a paid international assassin or some other more violent thug.

I reminded Jon that the negotiations still had a long way to go. That
the Russians were still angry that President Biden had called Vladimir
Putin a war criminal. That they still felt insulted by Secretary of State
Antony Blinken's one-for-two prisoner-swap plan. They were still in the
fuck-you stage.

So were both sides finally ready to get beyond all that? I didn't want to
lose the momentum we had.

"Jon," I finally said, "I understand your skepticism, and it is absolutely possible they are playing me. But in a couple of weeks, Governor Richardson and I will go to Moscow, and I suspect we will hear the same thing there. Either you want to do the deal or you don't want to do the deal. Or maybe you have another deal to propose." I waited a moment, then said, "It would be nice if you could get us some indication of what might be acceptable *before* we go to Moscow."

The White House aide was noncommittal but agreed to try.

A couple of days later, I sat with Roger Carstens, the special envoy for hostage affairs, to update him on our efforts. "Mickey," Roger said firmly, "if the deal ends up being Vinnik and Bout for Griner and Whelan, I'm going to praise you for bringing it up."

"That's not the point," I laughed, "and you know it."

Roger smiled. He knew what I needed. I needed a clear signal from the Biden administration that the president would agree to that deal.

And now we were almost there. There were positive indications from both the deputy national security advisor and the special envoy for hostage affairs that, in their view, this would be a favorable deal if we could get it. Was it a binding commitment? No. Absolutely not. We don't wait for binding commitments. We can't. We'd be waiting forever. But it was more than enough for us to press forward with the Russians and try to nail down that Ara and his colleagues in Yerevan were speaking for the people who could actually deliver this deal, officials at the highest levels of the Kremlin.

I also needed to fill Guv in. The deal Ara had floated was the one we were potentially agreeing to. I didn't want there to be any doubt about any of this. I wanted the Russians to tell the governor the same names they were telling me. I wanted him to hear it directly from *them*. One step closer. One step closer to bringing two American citizens back home. With Richardson involved, I knew, there'd be a whole lot less wiggle room. And, I knew, the more time passed the more wiggle room they'd have.

"We need to go to Moscow," Guv said. "Make it happen. As soon as you can."

* * *

TRAVELING TO RUSSIA WAS GETTING HARDER BY THE WEEK. THIS WAS, after all, a country at war, even if officials in the Kremlin were doing everything they could to avoid using that term. The Ukrainian forces had been far fiercer than the Russian military was prepared for. Tight sanctions were in place and getting tighter, enforced by the United States and no small number of our European allies. This had sparked bitterness and logistical difficulties inside the country, not to mention special challenges for anyone hoping to travel there. For starters, there were no more Aeroflot nonstops from Dulles to Sheremetyevo. What we had instead was a dire-sounding advisory from the State Department: "Do not travel to Russia due to the unprovoked and unjustified invasion of Ukraine by Russian military forces, the potential for harassment against U.S. citizens by Russian government security officials, the singling out of U.S. citizens in Russia by Russian government security officials including for detention, the arbitrary enforcement of local law, limited flights into and out of Russia, the embassy's limited ability to assist U.S. citizens in Russia..."

I certainly didn't want to end up sharing a cell with Paul Whelan. But we had the invitation we wanted. And the State Department hadn't actually said Americans couldn't travel to Russia. It was just, I figured, an advisory. The approach Ara and I devised in Yerevan had worked. After Guv sent a carefully worded note to Foreign Minister Lavrov, our visit to Moscow was approved. But the logistics were still up to me and, thankfully, Steve Menzies. The strategically minded businessman who'd helped us arrange our mission to Venezuela stepped up again.

But State Department advisories aside, we had other issues. With such strict sanctions in place, we couldn't fly straight from the United States to Russia, even in Steve's private jet. We had to divide the journey in two. We headed first to Istanbul. Steve's plane had more than enough room for all six of us: Guv, Cameron Hume, Ara's two associates (Ian Brownlow and Vitaly Pruss), Steve, and me. Next, Steve arranged for a locally chartered jet to meet us in the Turkish capital and fly us the rest of the way to Moscow. The local jet was smaller. Much smaller. The six of us could barely squeeze aboard with the pilot and copilot. I got the cramped seat beneath a tall, shaky stack of luggage and spent most of the flight praying that we didn't hit turbulence and those suitcases wouldn't tumble down on my head.

Though the flight was smooth, it was far from quick.

Istanbul to Moscow *should* take about two hours, straight across Ukraine. But with so many missiles in the air, the Ukrainian airspace was too dangerous. We had to follow a roundabout route over the Black Sea and the Caspian Sea—then shoot up to the Russian capital. But we got to Moscow eventually, and I was happy to see Ara waiting for us at the private terminal.

Guv breezed through Russian customs. So did Cameron, Steve, and I. So did Ara's associate Vitaly—but there seemed to be an issue with Ian, the ever-positive British American who was Ara's other guy. The scowling Russian immigration officers stopped him at the processing window. Soon they were grilling him intensely, and they didn't look anywhere near satisfied.

"Hey," I whispered to Ara, "they just took Ian to the other room. That can't be good."

Ian was in there for a while. I tried texting him. I got no answer. Ara was working the phones, seeking outside help.

The problem, it turned out, was that Ian had an incorrect date of birth on his visa. Apparently a clerk at the Russian consulate in Washington had written April 22, not April 27. And that didn't match the date of birth on Ian's passport. A tiny bureaucratic error, big real-life obstacle. And since this was a Sunday afternoon, there were no customs supervisors on the scene to help resolve the matter.

Our visit wasn't getting off to a very smooth start.

Meanwhile, Ara had made some headway. At least he had people to call. I don't know any of their names or how he managed to reach them on a Sunday. But he must have dropped a name or two or barked at a duty officer somewhere. And all of a sudden, the customs officers were wishing Ian well, urging him to enjoy his stay in Moscow, and saying he was free to leave the airport. It turned into a nice moment for Ara, who was able to show the rest of us that he really did have influence in war-time Moscow among people who could actually get things done.

I couldn't help but wonder: *Can that influence include arranging more prisoner exchanges?* We could hope.

It was a minor stumble overcome. A minor calamity averted. But to me, it felt like a triumph worth celebrating. During dinner at Ara's lavish home outside Moscow, I made a deadpan announcement: "I just sent out a press release saying, 'We've been in Russia for six hours, and we've already gotten one prisoner released.'"

Not to be outdone, the governor had a deadpan quote for my imagined publicity grab. "Our team started the mission with a deficit," he said. "At least now we're back to even."

* * *

ON MY PREVIOUS TRIP TO RUSSIA, MOSCOW HAD FELT ALIVE. THE hotel was busy. Even though it was February, there were festivals in the streets. Not too many foreign tourists, but plenty of Russians visiting the capital. Now, in September, nearly seven months into the war, everything was far quieter. *Sober* is the word I would use. Except for us and a business delegation from India, the hotel was almost empty, and it wasn't the Ritz-Carlton anymore. It was just the Carlton now, though it still seemed fairly ritzy to me. Cameron and I did a visitors' tour of the city to get a quick feel for things. We walked around Red Square and stopped at the Kremlin. We saw Catherine the Great's silver-silk coronation gown. So many diamonds...all for Christ's sake! After the tour, we went with Guv to view the changing of the guard at the Tomb of the Unknown Soldier. I had to assume our every step was being observed. I thought it was important to demonstrate to the Russians that we respected the nation's sacrifice during World War II. Important for them to see and important because I truly did appreciate how they felt. I wouldn't say the city felt completely depressing. But in September, it was definitely darker and grayer and emptier than in February, the opposite of what you'd expect.

Ara was an excellent host. He knew exactly how to navigate the Russian bureaucracy, and he already had meetings set up for us. I asked him about Taylor Dudley, Jenny's nephew, the navy vet being held in Kaliningrad Oblast. "Is there any chance we can pick him up on this trip?"

Ara didn't say yes, but he didn't rule it out either.

Since Taylor hadn't been designated by the US government as wrongfully detained, he'd never been mentioned in the media, and Washington had never formally asked for his release. No one in Moscow seemed to know much about him, which gave us an open field. In the Griner and Whelan cases, we were working outside the official channel. With Dudley, there *was* no official channel.

"Let me handle the Kaliningrad kid," Ara said to me. "I am sending my person there and he is meeting with the local judge today." Ara seemed to have a person everywhere. "Let's not elevate this to the national level," he urged.

A couple of hours later, Ara reported that the judge was asking for a letter from Dudley's family confirming that they'd authorized us to act on their behalf. It was 3:00 a.m. in California, where Taylor's brother, Louis, lived. I didn't think he'd mind if I woke him. "I need you to write a letter and sign it, authorizing the Richardson Center to deal with the Russians on Taylor's case." I gave him the wording. "Oh, and I need it notarized." I have no idea how he found a notary in the middle of the night. But within two hours, we had a notarized letter from Louis Dudley.

And we had a follow-up idea. Up to this point, no one had seen or heard from Taylor since his arrest almost five months earlier. Not his family and not representatives from the US embassy. "Ara," I said, "ask the judge to let Taylor call or email his family. They will confirm that we are authorized."

Within an hour, the Dudley family received their first communication from Taylor since his arrest. *What a relief!*

Steve Menzies and I started plotting logistics, in case we got a green light to collect Taylor in Kaliningrad Oblast. "This is complicated," Steve cautioned. Airspace restrictions over western Europe made it illegal for a Russian plane to fly over Lithuania and illegal for a Western plane to fly over Belarus. To reach Kaliningrad, we would normally fly over both.

Now, Steve told me, the only legal route would take an extra four hours each way and require us to return to Moscow with Taylor, something we were certainly hoping to avoid.

"The very difficult, we will do right away. The impossible will take us a little time." That's one of my favorite air force slogans. It should be Steve's motto. After a few more hours of careful conspiring, he and I finally figured out a way to pick up Taylor in Kaliningrad Oblast. But we never got to use it. His release, Ara's person reported back, was going to take a couple of weeks. "My person will stay on it," Ara assured us.

I had no doubt.

At least the Dudleys had heard from Taylor, and now we had a plan.

* * *

ARA HOSTED A LUNCH FOR HIS FRIEND GOVERNOR RICHARDSON AT an out-of-the-way Moscow restaurant. He invited a couple of his Russian friends to join him. "That way, you'll have a relaxed environment where you can talk more openly," he said.

I liked the way Ara thought.

Foreign Minister Sergey Lavrov arrived with his top deputy, Sergei Ryabkov, whose portfolio included keeping a close eye on the United States. Both men knew the governor from their New York and Washington postings, and both spoke excellent English. The conversation was informal and friendly and a bit meandering.

We more or less followed the note from Guv to Lavrov that had helped set up the meeting, touching on quite a few topics before we ever got to the American and Russian prisoners. The US and NATO sanctions, which the Russians hated. The Ukrainian orphans who'd been relocated to Russia, as well as the Russian and Ukrainian prisoners of war. The Russians' desire to revive the strategic-stability dialogue with Washington, which had been sidetracked by recent hostilities. And finding a way to adjust the United Nations' Ukrainian grain agreement so fertilizers were treated differently. With such a change, they said, the grain agreement would have some actual meaning. That last part, which sounded a bit arcane, seemed especially important to the Russians.

Neither Lavrov nor Ryabkov raised the topic of a prisoner swap. So Guv did.

The primary objective for our visit was for the governor to hear the Russian officials repeat what I'd been told in Armenia three weeks earlier. But Lavrov was cagey at first. "Well, you know, Bill," he said, "all this will be negotiated with the official American channel. You're not authorized for this."

If the governor felt dissed by that, he didn't let on.

"I get it, I get it, Sergey," he said. "I'm listening to *you*, what it is *you* want. Then maybe I can help make it happen...or something like it."

That was Guv. Supremely confident. Ignoring potential roadblocks. Showing no equivocation, as if he had no doubt at all that he could help advance the deal.

That's when Ryabkov spoke up. "I get it," the deputy said. "If you talk to the people that you talk to, not on our behalf, but if you talk to them, and if you are able to convince them to raise this specific deal, two for two, Vinnik and Bout, through the official channel, I believe it will be positively received on our end."

Yes, there were some ifs there, a lot of ifs. But to me, it sounded exactly like what we had come all this way for—a direct confirmation of the deal terms and another step toward the deal.

"I think we can be helpful," the governor said, nodding in that slow way of his.

"To be clear," the deputy foreign minister emphasized, "I'm not *asking* you to do it. But if...*if* the Americans raise it, I think it will be received well."

"I get it, I get it," Guv said.

He did, and they did. Vladimir Putin and the Russian government would not be the side proposing a deal for the imprisoned Americans. The proposal would come from the American side.

But if the Americans raise it, it will be well received.

Now we had something to bring back to Washington, something even the White House national security aides would have to take seriously. Delivered by the highest-ranking officials in the Russian ministry of foreign affairs. And handed not to Mickey Bergman, whoever he was, but to Governor Bill Richardson, the former US representative to the United Nations, the famous rescuer of American prisoners abroad and a decades-long pillar of the Democratic foreign-policy establishment.

Even with all of that, now came the even thornier part.

Executing the plan.

Much as we'd like to, that was something we absolutely could not do alone.

*   *   *

On September 17, a couple of days after our return to Washington from Moscow, Guv called Jonathan Finer at the White House and delivered a thorough briefing about our trip. He told Jon that the prisoner-exchange proposal I'd learned about in Yerevan had now been confirmed by Foreign Minister Lavrov and his deputy, Ryabkov. Guv described to the deputy national security advisor exactly what the White House needed to do if there was still an appetite for the two-for-two exchange, Bout and Vinnik for Griner and Whelan.

"Jon," Guv said, "the deal is there to be made."

It just needed to be presented correctly. The US had to propose it. The proposal had to come through the *official channel*. If that happened, the Russians had indicated clearly, they would say yes.

"You need to have a clean bill on this one," Guv emphasized. "No add-ons. No caveats. Two for two, and that's it. We have every reason to think you'll get a positive response."

Silence on the other end of the call.

"Try them," Guv urged.

I think I might have held my breath. One second. Two. Three. Jon Finer answered. "Sounds good," he said.

And then...*nothing.*

23 GETTING CLOSE

WHAT WAS IT WITH THE BIDEN ADMINISTRATION AND ALL THESE delays?

Days passed. Then weeks. Then almost a month passed, and we weren't hearing anything.

Maddening!

But this time, it turned out, my assumption was unfair. It wasn't the White House that was refusing to make a decision and causing frustrating delays while American citizens sat needlessly in Russian prisons and, yes, Russians sat in American prisons too.

This time the Russians were refusing to act.

We learned this only after returning to the Hay-Adams Hotel near the White House for another breakfast with Jonathan Finer. He was joined by Josh Geltzer from the National Security Council.

"We offered it," Jon said. "The Russians didn't go for it."

"What do you mean they didn't go for it? Did they say no?"

"Not in so many words. We just didn't hear from them."

"Did you follow up?"

"We haven't heard," he said again.

So the answer wasn't really no. The answer, as far as Finer and Geltzer were concerned, was, *We don't have an answer. Yet. And we didn't really push.*

I didn't want to get into an argument. None of this could happen without the White House. Prisoner trades were not something the Richardson Center could do alone. Government to government, the official channel, was the only way to go. But maybe we could still be helpful.

"I'm not sure what the issue is," I said to Jon and Josh. "I'm not sure why they aren't answering you." What I didn't say was: *And I don't know why you aren't pushing harder.* "But why don't you let *us* try and get an answer from the Russians? We get responses from them. If the *official channel* isn't working, let's try the alternative."

"No," Josh said emphatically. "We don't need that kind of help."

That was frustrating to hear. But then again, it's complicated for the government to authorize an out-of-government actor to negotiate. I wish it weren't. So much more could be achieved with just a little flexibility and creativity. Harness the awesome power of fringe diplomacy! But that's not where we were. Unfortunately, pressure had built between us and the White House over months of pushing for prisoner trades. That had clearly led to an erosion in trust.

Truth be told, Guv, Cameron, and I didn't know for sure what the issue was on the Russian side. Were they playing us or not? But we figured we'd come this far. Maybe we ought to find a way to tell the story of our efforts. It might piss off the White House a little more. But at the moment, honestly, what did we have to lose?

I offered Governor Richardson to CNN. They were happy to talk with him. He was booked on *State of the Union* on October 9.

And the governor laid it all out there.

"I am cautiously optimistic on the Griner-Whelan negotiations," Guv told Jake Tapper. "I think it's gonna be a two for two. I don't want to get into who I met with. It was senior Russian officials, individuals close to President Putin. I've coordinated with the White House. I've coordinated as much as I can. Sometimes they are a little nervous about me doing this on my own. But we *have* had success recently."

Guv mentioned Trevor Reed. He mentioned Danny Fenster.

"I know what I'm doing," the governor emphasized. "At the same time, it is important that we recognize that I work, our foundation, for the families. We don't work for the US government. We do everything at no cost to the families. At the same time, we do coordinate with the administration. And we are doing that. Look at my track record over the past thirty years. I'm gonna continue these efforts."

Despite our last breakfast, Guv remained hopeful that Brittney would be free by the end of the year. "I do think so," he said on CNN that Sunday. "Now, I hate making predictions, but yes. I know they are very despairing. We work very closely with families. With the Whelan family, the Griner family....All I can say is the Biden administration is working hard on this. So am I." Guv knew exactly what he was doing. Through the power of TV, he was talking directly to President Biden and, at the same time, letting the American people know where to direct their own frustrations about the prisoners stuck in hostile nations. "We coordinate and not always agree with every tactical decision. I am not going to interfere with their process. I'm just giving you an assessment after two visits to Russia on behalf of American hostages. By the way, there are forty-seven other hostages around the world....We as Americans have an obligation to bring back, whether it's the government or private humanitarian groups."

* * *

The third week in October, I was in Israel for Yom Kippur with my daughter, Noa, who was almost nine, when I got the call from a contact of mine at the National Security Council. There'd been a lot of internal discussion about how to proceed. I could tell that just from my contact's cautious tone.

"Here is the message that we have for you," he said. "We want you to convey to the Russians that the White House told you that they agree to the exchange, the two for two. And they want to know, Who should they call in order to make arrangements? Say, 'That was the message they wanted us to convey.'"

I thanked my contact for the response.

Of course, I called Guv and Cameron right away. The second part of the White House message left all three of us a little uncomfortable, the way it was framed. Now they wanted names? Didn't asking that leave room for endless back-and-forth and endless delays? "If we say it that way," Guv said, "then the Russians will tell us, 'The White House should go through the *official channel.*' And we'll all be working in circles. The White House will go back to the *official channel.* When they hear nothing, they will throw up their hands again and say, 'Well, we tried.' We'll have to go back to the Russians, and the Russians will say the same thing to us: 'They should go through the *official channel.*'"

Guv made the decision. "It's time to do something more practical."

So we decided to put a twist in the message. The twist was a very tight deadline.

We didn't do that freelance. I went back to my contact at the National Security Council and said, "Here's what we want to say to the Russians. *The White House is interested in the deal we discussed, two for two, and they are prepared to make the exchange in ten days in Yerevan.*" Armenia was an easy three-and-a-half-hour flight from Moscow—even in these tense days. US aircraft could fly freely in and out of the airport there. So could Russian aircraft. And Ara, I knew, could help with the logistics.

"We'll say, *The two Russian prisoners will be brought to Yerevan in ten days. The White House wants to know exactly who they should call to make the arrangements.*"

It was a subtle difference but a crucial one, we thought.

As I said to my National Security Council contact, "By giving them such a tight deadline, we'll know quickly if the Russians are serious or not. The deadline will call their bluff."

Clearly there were people in the State Department who didn't want to engage with the Russians in any way as long as the war continued in Ukraine. At a time like this, they were loath to do anything that might make the Russians look good. The governor and I certainly couldn't do any of this alone. We needed the White House *and* the Russians to agree. We couldn't deliver the Russian prisoners on our own.

We didn't have to wait long for an answer. Guv reached out to Jon Finer, and Finer didn't only have a quick answer. He had an encouraging one.

"You can do that," he said. "Go ahead."

We really might be getting somewhere this time. That's how it felt, anyway. The next question was how we should convey the White House answer to the Russians. I didn't want our hard-earned yes from the White House to languish in some corner of the Moscow bureaucracy somewhere, going stale. But we didn't have time to fly to Russia again or time to fly to Armenia and meet with the Russians there. So we decided to do three things at once. First I drafted a short memo detailing the White House response and addressed it to the deputy foreign minister in Moscow, Sergei Ryabkov. As a backup, I also decided to hand-deliver the same memo to the Russian embassy in Washington, and, as a very last option, I would send a copy to Ara. If all else failed, I knew he could get it into the right hands in the Kremlin. I didn't know which of those avenues would be swiftest or the most effective. But with all three going at once, I was fairly confident the White House response would find its way to the highest levels of the Russian government without too much delay.

* * *

WHAT HAPPENED AT THE RUSSIAN EMBASSY IN DC SURPRISED ME. Lately, when I visited, I was dealt with by a young woman named Larisa. She replaced my old contact, Igor, who was sent back to Moscow after the US ordered the deportation of some Russian diplomats. Igor was on the pack-your-bags list. Larisa was always pleasant. She'd always accepted whatever I had to deliver and promised to pass it on.

This time, when I arrived at the embassy on Wisconsin Avenue, Larisa was joined by two senior officials, stoic-looking men who obviously knew why I was there. We didn't speak for long. But in our brief exchange, they said something interesting.

"Mr. Bergman," one of the men said to me, "I want you to know that we appreciate this. It is not normally our way to work in the gray areas, but these are extreme circumstances. We understand that you are not acting in a formal role. There is an official channel. But we appreciate that you are trying to convey this information to us. We will pass it on to

Moscow immediately. Please also remind the White House that we do wish to pursue the other topics that we discussed."

Yes, *those*.

The issues that the Sergeis, Lavrov and Ryabkov, had raised with us in Moscow, especially the two they seemed most animated by, reviving the strategic-stability dialogue and finding a way to get fertilizers out of the UN's Ukrainian grain agreement. I understood. Those other issues were part of the reason the Russians were engaging with us on the topic of prisoners. They knew how eager the Biden administration was to get Brittney Griner and Paul Whelan home. The Russians, like the Americans, were always finding ways to leverage the other side. So of course, they didn't want us to forget those "other topics."

After I got home from the Russian embassy, I had a Zoom call with Ara. I reached him in Moscow. He had already read the deal memo I'd sent to him.

"We conveyed the message," he said.

That was fast.

I pushed as hard as I could. "Would you talk to Lavrov?" I said to Ara. "Would you talk to Ushakov? Would you talk to Patrushev?" Yuri Ushakov, who'd been the Russian ambassador to the United States, remained a trusted advisor to President Putin. Nikolai Patrushev directed Russia's national security council and had been a staunch proponent of the "special operation" in Ukraine. When it comes to Russia's relationship with the rest of the world, no one had Vladimir Putin's ear any more than Lavrov, Ushakov, and Patrushev. "Will you call them? These are your friends. This is the same deal we discussed a month and a half ago. Now we have a commitment from the White House. We have ten days to get it done."

* * *

WHETHER AN EXCHANGE LIKE THIS COULD REALLY BE CONSUMMATED in ten days, I did not know. But the tightness of the deadline was already having the effect I'd hoped it would. It brought an urgency to everyone.

Ara felt the pressure. He knew the environment we were operating in.

This was the time. If not now, when? "If we can make it happen, it will happen in Yerevan," I said to him. "Will you be there?"

"Absolutely."

"This is your backyard."

"I know."

None of this really surprised me. Ara loved being in the middle of a high-stakes negotiation. I could see what made him a successful businessman. He wouldn't miss this for the world.

He'd been planning to leave Moscow the next day. But after our call, he decided to delay his departure so he could get to work on the plan. He said he would be back in touch as soon as he heard anything.

The wait wasn't long, less than a week, though it felt like an eternity as we counted down the days and waited to hear something from Ara, from the foreign ministry, from the embassy, from anyone who might know anything on the Russian side. Maybe we wouldn't get any further than the White House had. But we had a good plan. A workable plan with advantages for both sides. I wasn't losing hope.

One thought did occur to me: Even if the Americans and the Russians were willing to make this two-for-two deal, Moscow might want to drag it out for longer than ten days. Perhaps to just past the US midterm elections, which were set for November 8. With the sanctions in full force and US military aid pouring into Ukraine, the Russian government did not seem eager to do any political favors for Joe Biden and his Democratic Party. The Russians could read American politics as well as anyone could. They understood that getting Brittney Griner home would be a political plus for the Democrats. I figured, Why not wait until after the elections? The vote was barely three weeks away.

* * *

At 2:00 p.m. on Monday, October 17, I got a message from Ara. He said he had met with General Patrushev at the Security Council. Ara said that Patrushev had asked him to deliver a message to us. Ara read it carefully to me.

"The message," he said, "is that the American national security advisor, Jake Sullivan, needs to call General Patrushev, the Russian national security advisor—call him directly—and suggest the two-for-two prisoner swap in ten days in Yerevan, just as we discussed it. And that suggestion will be approved. But it has to be set up at that level."

National security advisor to national security advisor. Man to man. Symmetry.

I thanked Ara and told him I would share the message with Guv and Cameron and take the next steps. This certainly sounded promising. But could we take it at face value? I was optimistic. The governor wasn't so sure.

"How much do you think this is accurate?" Guv asked when I spoke with him and Cameron. "Is there more to it than what we are hearing from Ara?"

"It sounds authentic from Patrushev," I said. "It makes sense. Security advisor to security advisor. The Russians want both sides to have some skin in the game. That part makes sense to me."

"And what about Ara?" the governor asked.

"Is Ara exaggerating a little bit and forcing something that might not quite be there yet?" I considered the question. "Possibly. But that's not necessarily a bad thing. We've done that before. That's fine. It gives everyone deniability. They sent a message. We pass it on exactly as Ara delivered it to us. I say we go for it. What's the worst that can happen? And if Jake Sullivan actually talks to Patrushev, that's a good thing. Maybe they actually get a deal done. It really is good for both sides."

"Fine," the governor said. "Let's get that together. I'll talk to Jake Sullivan."

24 WILD CARD

I sent an email from Governor Richardson's account to Jon Finer and Jake Sullivan. "We need a call tomorrow. It's important. Bill."

An hour later, before I'd heard anything back from the White House aides, I got an email with an official response from the Russian embassy.

"Dear Mickey," the email said. "We received the message from Moscow. It is as follows: 'The Russian side, of course, highly appreciates the desire of the governor to help American and Russian prisoners return home. However, as we have repeatedly said, the dialogue of the specific exchange schemes goes strictly through the channel of the respective special agencies. In this regard, everything remains unchanged until the White House notifies us on paper about a change in this format by investing Bill Richardson with the appropriate powers by the National Security Council and the State Department. We cannot have a substantive conversation with him on the topic of the prisoners. At the same time, we emphasize that we are ready to discuss other topics of interest to both sides. Please confirm receipt of this email.'"

Uh-oh!

Had we just been blown off by the Russians? That was my initial reaction. But as I thought about it, I wasn't so sure.

On the one hand, the official Russian channel was saying that the White House needed to go through the official American channel, as circular as that might be. But I also saw a glimpse of encouragement in there, like we were getting another message too. This was the formal reaction, sent after we had received the informal one.

The Russians were very specific. There was nothing in this message that contradicted the message from Patrushev because Patrushev wasn't saying, *Bill, call me*. He was saying that the national security advisor should call him. It stayed in a formal channel. But this message being sent via cable—they must have assumed the White House would intercept it. That way, the Russians could show they were maintaining the official channel. They weren't playing around.

"What do we do?" the governor asked.

"Well...," I said, "when you have the call today with the White House, you can't avoid telling them about the formal message because they already know it. They intercepted it. Just lay out both messages, the informal and the formal one."

The instructions from the Russians were as clear as can be, I said. The US national security advisor, Jake Sullivan, needed to call the Russian national security advisor, Nikolai Patrushev. "We have to make sure Jon and Jake understand that, as we agreed in our precall call," I told Guv.

Soon enough, Jon Finer was on the phone from the White House. Guv quickly got him up to speed.

"As we discussed last week," he said, "we have received a return message from the Russians. Two separate messages, actually." One, he explained, was a formal message that had come through the embassy. "That message acknowledged gratitude for our efforts and reiterated that the official channel is the channel in which the deal will be negotiated." The second message, he said, came from Patrushev and wasn't conveyed through the embassy.

"His message was that the US national security advisor should call Patrushev directly as soon as possible and offer the specific two-for-two exchange we discussed"—Bout and Vinnik for Whelan and Griner in Yerevan in ten days. "The deal will be approved, but it needs to be set up at that level. That is the message from them."

The White House official listened carefully and seemed to take it in. He answered in his usual noncommittal way. "OK, thank you," Jon said. "We'll discuss it internally and act on it."

I still had some lingering doubts about the timing. I kept thinking: *If I'm Putin, and I know I have a deal in my pocket, why give Biden a win before the midterm elections on November 8?* My best guess was still that the Russians would sit on the deal for a couple of weeks. Antonov, the Russian ambassador, had visited Viktor Bout in prison the week before. The ambassador must have had some kind of message to deliver. Moscow clearly wanted this. But the Russians didn't feel the same urgency that the Americans did.

Still, I felt proud and confident in where we were, what we had delivered to the White House, a deal that everyone thought was doable, an exchange that really could bring Brittney Griner and Paul Whelan home. That was the goal we'd been intently focused on. And now, even if the timing lagged, we'd wrapped it up in a neat little package and delivered it directly to the White House.

Not bad.

The only question now: Would the Biden administration move decisively enough to make it happen? Soon enough, we would know.

* * *

I HAD NO DOUBT THAT JOE BIDEN WANTED TO BRING BRITTNEY GRI-ner home, ideally before the midterms. Paul Whelan too. But keeping that top of mind at the White House and the State Department required a careful campaign of public pressure, slowly building up. We couldn't allow Brittney's captivity to slide too far out of view.

After an early-July call from President Biden and Vice President Kamala Harris, Brittney's wife, Cherelle, and agent Lindsay Kagawa Colas agreed to give the president some "quiet space" to see if the White House could bring Brittney home. By late August, when Lindsay and I spoke, they were ready to ramp up the public pressure again. Lindsay just wanted to make sure the timing was right. Like an orchestra conductor, she had assembled an array of supporters and advocates with many different instruments. She would signal to each section when it was time to play, how loudly, and at what pitch. Of course, Lindsay was a natural at this.

After I returned from my advance mission to Yerevan in late August, she and Cherelle asked me if it was time to really strike up the band. "We are getting there," I told them. "We've identified a feasible deal. We're not quite there yet. But it might be a good idea to get Cherelle in front of the president."

"We will get it done," Lindsay said with confidence. I had no doubt she would.

On September 16, two days after Guv, Cameron Hume, Steve Menzies, and I completed our mission in Moscow, Cherelle met with President Biden at the White House, adding fresh urgency to Brittney's return. But here we were in late October, a deal in sight but still frustratingly slow in coming together.

Lindsay pushed on her end, summoning other sections of her orchestra. And we pushed on ours.

We knew what the deal was. It wasn't savory, but it was feasible. And yet the two governments were still having trouble communicating directly and wrapping everything up. We knew that both sides wanted it to happen. They both kept telling us as much. But like a couple of adolescents smarting from schoolyard grudges, they couldn't seem to get together and just talk things out.

Partial information was part of the problem.

This was getting very frustrating.

Guv got a message from Jonathan Finer, referring to Jake Sullivan's *latest* attempt to speak directly with his Russian counterpart, Nikolai Patrushev, as requested by the Russians. "Jake tried to call twice, but the call was declined."

What does that mean? I wondered. *Did Jake try to call Patrushev's iPhone and the Russian pressed* decline? *Did someone answer the phone and say, "Nikolai doesn't want to talk?"* We knew the two national security advisors had each other's numbers and spoke periodically. *Do we have to dial for them?*

So we did what we often did when we needed to nudge the Russians. We went back to Ara. "We gave the White House the message you conveyed to us," I said. "And they said Patrushev declined the call."

Ara had the same question I had. "What do you mean 'declined the

call'?" Truth was, we didn't know what it meant. That was all the information we had. Ara agreed to call his friend Patrushev to find out. The
result was not great. Not great at all. Ara reported back that Patrushev
said Jake never called him. The Russian national security advisor told
Ara he thought the Americans were playing him. This was a blow for
Ara. He too felt hurt by this failed attempt. He couldn't deliver what
he'd promised, and that undermined his credibility with his colleagues
in Moscow. I was upset. Not only because I couldn't figure out who was
playing whom, but now because my friend Ara, who had put his neck out
on this, was upset. And I wasn't sure how to fix any of it.

We had two top-level officials saying to us privately that the solution
we presented was acceptable to them and that they were eager to speak
to each other. Now one of them was claiming that the other refused to
take the call, and the other one was claiming the first one never called.

Come on!

Misinformation was also part of the problem. But that's where we
were.

Guv, Cameron, and I spent hours trying to figure out where the truth
was. As Americans, we tended to believe our White House. Why on
earth would US officials lie about something like that? But we also had
to wonder: While it was certainly possible the Russians were trying to
manipulate us, to what end? What would the Russians gain from sending us these messages and not following through? Could there be some
misunderstanding in the chain of communication that could still be
resolved? And how about this: Had the conversations already happened
and both sides had decided to keep us on the outside? Anything was possible, but we couldn't figure it out.

* * *

NOVEMBER 17. BREAKFAST TIME. A COLD AND GRAY MORNING IN
Washington. A full month since Ara had tried to connect Jake Sullivan
and Nikolai Patrushev. Guv and I were back at the Hay-Adams to meet,
one more time, with Jon Finer and Josh Geltzer.

We wanted to explore how we might salvage what was starting to feel like a fleeting opportunity to bring Brittney Griner and Paul Whelan back home. We were still in the dark. We'd run out of calming and positive words for Cherelle Griner and Elizabeth Whelan. Had the Americans called Russia? Had they not called? Had the call been refused? Should we coordinate the damn call ourselves, allowing each side to demonstrate it was not bluffing? What if the Richardson Center scheduled a simple conference call and invited both sides? Would the Russians and the Americans both show up? If they did, we could drop off and let the two sides communicate directly.

This shouldn't be so hard!

It sounded so simple and so silly, but we were running out of ideas. The election was over. The Democrats had done much better than anyone expected them to. No one had seriously challenged the merits of the deal at hand. Was it really just a matter of getting the two security advisors to talk to each other on the phone?

Every day that passed, the families were getting more desperate. Lindsay had called me on November 14, sounding especially distraught. "Mickey," she said. "We were hoping to get in touch with a well-known Russian wrestler who was close to Vladimir Putin." She explained that they had reached out to Dana White, president of the Ultimate Fighting Championship. "We hoped Dana could ask one of his Russian-born mixed-martial-arts fighters to speak with Putin about Brittney."

Like Guv and me, Lindsay was constantly on the lookout for something that hadn't been tried yet. I knew almost nothing about the UFC, but I was open to using every imaginable asset to bring Americans home. You know, fringe diplomacy.

"Well," Lindsay continued, "Dana said he would try. But when he called back, he said, 'Look, I did you one better. I called Trump. I told him, "Maybe you could be helpful with this Brittney Griner thing." He seemed open to the idea.'"

I went silent. *The ex-president? Back in the game?* Actually, I guess he'd never left it. Scenarios and calculations went running through my head. Was this a brilliant idea? Was it a terrible idea? I'd have to think some more.

"We did not ask Dana to do that," Lindsay emphasized. "He did it on his own."

"So what exactly did Trump say?" I asked her, trying to get all the information I could to feed my thoughts.

"He said he needed to think about it, but he seemed inclined to do it, according to Dana."

"Does the White House know?" I asked Lindsay.

"Yes," she said. "I sent a message to the president's chief of staff and to Geltzer at the NSC."

Good...*I thought.*

"What was their reaction?"

"Pretty mellow, actually," Lindsay said. "If they were rattled, they certainly didn't show it."

"Well," I said after a few seconds of contemplation, "the good news is I think Brittney will be home by the holidays." Lindsay certainly liked the sound of that! One of two things would happen, I said. Either Trump would jump into the case and strike a deal with Putin, who'd be happy to hand Brittney to Trump and leave Biden out in the cold. Or the prospect of Trump getting involved would create enough urgency in the White House that it would move quickly to strike a deal.

"That *is* good news," Lindsay said. "Is there bad news?"

I nodded. There was. Not directly for Brittney, but bad nonetheless. "The bad news," I continued, swallowing hard before finishing the sentence, "is that Paul Whelan is screwed." In bringing home Brittney Griner, Trump would see an electoral upside: women, Blacks, gays, and athletes were all constituents. Whelan, electorally speaking, didn't give Trump much. The race would be to bring Brittney home.

I asked Lindsay if it was OK for Guv and me to address this in our upcoming meeting with Finer and Geltzer.

"Of course," she said.

So we had plenty to speak about with Jon and Josh when they joined us at Guv's early-morning hangout near the White House.

The Hay-Adams discussion that morning focused on urgency. "You need to be more urgent about this," Guv pushed the foreign-policy aides.

"We are doing everything we can," Jon protested. "We tried your thing. It didn't work. What else can we do?"

We discussed some ideas, but nothing seemed to be clicking.

"And now you have the former president possibly getting involved," Guv added to the mix.

"We heard," Jon Finer responded. "If the former president calls and wants to help, we will see if he can be helpful."

I was a little taken aback by the response. More than a little. "Do you think that is how Trump will play this?" I asked skeptically. "Just trying to be helpful to the current administration? If I'm Trump, I call Putin, and I say: *Mr. President, I am going to come visit you next week in Moscow. You know, I announced that I am running for president again. I need you to do me a favor. When I come, I need you to give me Brittney Griner. When I get her back to America, I will do a press conference. I will explain that I flew to Moscow because that is what leaders do at times like this. I will explain that Vladimir Putin is a serious leader who is willing to make deals. Vladimir Putin gave me Brittney Griner, and he didn't demand anything in exchange. And I will add that Vladimir Putin told me he was willing to make a deal for Paul Whelan. So if Biden wants to make a deal, he should come to Mar-a-Lago, and I will help him make a deal for Paul Whelan.*"

Was that so far-fetched?

Jon Finer and Josh Geltzer both looked at me. I couldn't really tell what they were thinking, but I believe the picture was sinking in.

"Wow," Josh finally said with a small smile, "you can give good advice to bad people. Do you think the former president could really come up with all that?"

"I don't think he needs to," I answered. "As soon as he calls Putin, Putin will put it together for him. He'd be happy to."

That would be a huge win for Trump. He would get Brittney Griner released. In his mind, it would win him support from Black voters, gay voters, women voters, and all the sports fans in America. If he wanted to take it an extra step, he could bring his friend Herschel Walker with him to Moscow. The former All-Pro NFL running back was facing a critical runoff election for a US Senate seat in Georgia. And a scenario like that would have one other major advantage: it would be a big embarrassment for Joe Biden.

In all honesty, I have no idea if that conversation at the Hay-Adams and the wild scenario I spun out played any role at all, directly or indirectly, in what happened next with the Americans wrongfully imprisoned in Russia or any of the decisions that were made inside the White House. I don't even know if Jon Finer and Josh Geltzer ever mentioned that breakfast conversation to anyone. I will never really know. But in more than seventeen years in the dirty trenches of fringe diplomacy, I have learned that I never really know which of the multiple efforts was the one that made the difference. The decision makers themselves don't always know what tipped a decision or shifted an approach. All I know is that when enough levers are pulled and a certain critical mass is achieved, the world can look very different on the other side. Something tipped the balance. It doesn't really matter which straw was the last one.

* * *

On December 6, Lindsay Kagawa Colas and I met for lunch in Washington.

We had just ordered and hadn't gotten our food yet when both our phones lit up. Brittney had been moved from her prison in Mordoviya. No one seemed to know *where* the American prisoner had been moved or *why* she had been moved. Lindsay and I looked at each other and began a ritual that by now was as familiar to her as it was to me, questioning the credibility of these latest reports and trying to figure out what they might mean. You know, partial information. But it was hard not to be hopeful.

"Is this what I want to think it is?" Lindsay asked me, very tentatively. I didn't answer directly.

I could tell what she was thinking. The same thing I was. *This could be it…at last.* But neither of us was ready to say that out loud, not wanting to jump on the emotional roller coaster as it climbed higher and higher because, too many times before, we'd also ridden it all the way down. The pieces seemed to fit. The timing felt right. But both of us knew: even if our lunch hunch was correct, it would still take twenty-four to thirty-six hours, minimum, until Brittney was in the hands of American officials and breathing free air. So many things could happen in that time, things neither of us wanted to contemplate. Lindsay and Cherelle had had enough surprises already to last a lifetime. We also knew that all this was out of our hands now. The White House would close this deal… or it wouldn't. All we could do was sit silently and let the next steps play out. Well, that was all *I* could do. Lindsay? She had plans and backup plans and contingencies and spreadsheets and I don't know what else, just in case Brittney was really coming home.

Always thinking. Always prepared.

It's the best feeling in the world, when I know that someone I have worked hard to free is finally coming home. It's best of all when we are there to greet the freshly freed prisoner. There's a special moment of elation in cases like that. But there's no such thing as a bad prisoner release. They are all filled with joy, whether I am standing on a faraway tarmac or watching the final moments from home on TV. I have never forgotten something a friend of mine said about football that applies just as well to getting Americans out of foreign prisons. In football, everyone focuses on the last two yards as the player carries the ball over the goal line. That's when the cheers are the loudest. But in fact, that's not where most of the real work gets done. The real work is delivering the ball to the two-yard line…so someone has the chance to carry it into the end zone. That's what we did for Brittney Griner. That's a lot of what we do. And you know what? I'm OK with that. I know how we got here. I'll skip the final round of cheers…as long as our people are coming home.

I think about their families. I think about their lives ahead. I think about the terrible pain and all the time that's been stolen from their lives. Over the next few hours, Cherelle Griner was constantly on my mind. So was Brittney's father, Raymond. And Brittney's teammates in Phoenix. And her millions of fans. And Lindsay and her amazing team.

At the same time, I couldn't stop thinking about Elizabeth Whelan. About the Whelan family.

About Paul.

The deal that was struck between the US and Russian governments, when it finally came together, wasn't the two-for-two prisoner swap we had delivered to Washington on a platter. It wasn't Alexander Vinnik and Viktor Bout for Brittney Griner and Paul Whelan. It was one for one: half the deal I had carried from Yerevan, half the deal Guv and I had confirmed in Moscow, half the deal that had seemed to brighten the mood of our contacts in the White House. In the end, it was the Russians who weren't ready to free Paul Whelan, still insisting he was a spy. So maddening! The deal that was made, Bout for Griner, left Paul behind.

Again.

There are no wins without losses in fringe diplomacy, as I tried to remind myself. And here we were again, right on the verge of a hard-won victory, still living in the shadow of terrible loss. How much more could the Whelans take? We wouldn't give up in our efforts on their behalf. We'd keep at it as long as it took to bring Paul home. But for the fourth time now, by my count, a genuine opportunity to free him had slipped away. And that made me angry. I could only imagine how Paul and the Whelans were feeling as Brittney's family experienced such elation. I wanted to hug Elizabeth. I cried to myself. I felt devastated by the Whelans' pain.

* * *

CHERELLE WAS AT THE WHITE HOUSE WHEN BRITTNEY WAS FINALLY freed, on December 8, 2022, after ten months in Russian custody. As we had predicted, she'd be home for the holidays. "She's safe, she's on a plane, she's on her way home," President Biden announced with Cherelle at his side. "After months of being unjustly detained in Russia, held under untolerable circumstances, Brittney will soon be back in the arms of her loved ones, and she should have been there all along."

The president did give voice to the "mixed emotions" all of us were feeling, caused by the tragedy of leaving Paul Whelan in prison as Brittney Griner headed home. "This was not a choice of which American to bring home," he said. "Sadly, for totally illegitimate reasons, Russia is treating Paul's case differently than Brittney's. And while we have not yet succeeded in securing Paul's release, we are not giving up. We will never give up."

Cherelle said she was "overwhelmed with emotions." How could she not be? She vowed that she and Brittney "will remain committed to the work of getting every American home, including Paul, whose family is in our hearts today."

If anyone understood what the Whelans were going through, it was the Griners.

For his part, Paul Whelan told CNN in a phone call from prison that he was happy about Brittney's release, even as he felt deep frustration about his own situation. "I was led to believe that things were moving in the right direction and that the governments were negotiating and that something would happen fairly soon." His disappointment was palpable. "I don't understand why I'm still sitting here," he said.

It was our friend Roger Carstens, the special envoy, who carried the ball across the goal line. He was waiting at the airport in Abu Dhabi when the plane carrying Brittney Griner arrived from Moscow. The Russian arms dealer Viktor Bout, who'd served fifteen years in an American prison, was also heading home. The exchange took less than a minute. Off came Brittney Griner, on went Viktor Bout. So much effort and commitment to get here—and it was over just like that.

EPILOGUE

Brittney Griner was doing her best to put all this behind her, which wouldn't happen quickly or easily. It never does. Brittney had no time for victory laps, and neither did we. Barely a month after her release, the whole Richardson Center band was back together again, thousands of miles from home.

It was a frigid January night. Two rented silver Toyota minivans were careening along the narrow farm roads of far-northern Poland. I was at the wheel of the front vehicle, my phone balanced precariously on my lap, as I tried to follow the winding Waze directions from the Russia-Poland border to the Gdańsk airport. That's where Steve Menzies's plane was waiting for us with a rapidly narrowing departure permit. There'd been delays on both sides of the border. We were already five hours late. From the front passenger seat, Governor Richardson was yelling at me as we bounced through the darkness on these rugged rural roads.

"Did you get the press release out? We need to get back to the reporters!"

News was already breaking back home that Taylor Dudley, the US Navy veteran who'd been held in the Russian enclave of Kaliningrad Oblast for the past nine months, was being released from prison. Which was true. But it was crucial that we get the facts out as quickly and accurately as we could...and that we get Taylor out too.

Steve was in the seat behind me. Next to him was Anna Tunkel, an old friend from Georgetown. Just forty-eight hours earlier, I'd enlisted Anna to help with Taylor's extraction when Vitaly Pruss, the Belarussian American businessman who worked closely with Ara Abramyan, fell sick. We needed a translator, and Anna was Russian born. Though she was now a top executive at the policy-affairs consultancy APCO Worldwide and was swamped organizing its upcoming global economic forum, which was just a week away, she'd agreed to come along.

Taylor was in the minivan behind us. He'd been turned over to our group at the Bagrationovsk-Bezledy border crossing after six months of intense negotiations by Ara, Guv, and me. Ara had made Taylor's release a personal cause of his. The case had gotten almost no publicity in the US or in Russia. In a way, that made Taylor's plight more typical than Brittney Griner's or Paul Whelan's. But believe me, he was just as thrilled to be coming home.

In the van with Taylor was his mother, Shelley, and a doctor who'd agreed to conduct a postincarceration medical evaluation on the go. Next to them was the communications strategist and all-around creative thinker Jonathan Franks. Guv and I had convinced Jon to join this mission a few weeks back.

My phone kept pinging with texts and calls from reporters asking for details and comment. Not grasping that we were still driving the extraction vans with the freshly released prisoner. And with each new ping, the Waze map on my phone disappeared from the screen. I had to fumble to get the app back up without missing a turn in the three-and-a-half-hour drive along these unlit roads. And Guv was still yelling at me: "Did you get the release out?" "Can you call the *Washington Post*?" "Did you see the text from the *Wall Street Journal*?"

I'm still not sure how we made it to Gdańsk.

But fifteen hours later, with one engine lost over the Atlantic, we were back on US soil. Taylor could finally return to his family in Lansing, Michigan, though his journey back to normalcy, like those of so many other freshly released Americans, had only just begun.

There had been no prisoner swap this time.

We were able to bring Taylor home because his case stayed out of the media. We were able to bring him home because he was never designated by the United States government as "wrongfully detained." Therefore, his release was never officially requested by Washington. And we had

Ara Abramyan. Don't underestimate that. The Armenian Russian businessman knew how to navigate the system in Kaliningrad Oblast and do it under the radar. He was willing to risk a lot for the release of Taylor Dudley. And we had Steve Menzies, who stepped up again and provided exquisite organizational and logistical resources to help execute the extraction mission. We were able to bring Taylor home because his family had been relentless in pursuing his freedom. So many pieces had to come together seamlessly, and this time they did.

It was a clean and satisfying win that could hardly have gone any better for Taylor Dudley...or for us, the hair-raising extraction aside. But it was just *a* win, not *the* win. In this always-challenging business of ours, as we keep discovering in far-flung countries around the world, there is no permanent or total victory. We have to celebrate our successes one by one by one.

There is always another strongman somewhere, ready to snatch an innocent American.

Another aggrieved leader, eager to make a point by poking a finger in the eye of the most powerful nation on earth.

Another head of state, seeing some advantage in incarcerating a vulnerable tourist, a hardworking journalist, a hotheaded military veteran, an apolitical business executive—any ripe target whose arrest might provoke international attention and, perhaps, extract a concession or two from Washington.

And many of these foreign leaders, I know from experience, convince themselves that their actions are entirely justified. So we're exploring shades of gray again.

The good news is that our independent campaigns have brought enormous attention to the issue of Americans unjustly imprisoned abroad. We have helped to focus the White House, the State Department, the National Security Council, and Congress on these heartbreaking cases and have helped Washington policymakers develop more effective strategies. Our fringe-diplomacy campaigns, the quiet ones and the loud ones, are rarely as quick or as easy as we would like them to be. But often we are the last, best chance these families have. We step forward when others are unable or unwilling to. Working alone or in concert with the US government, we keep showing unprecedented results. By now, there's a long list of Americans we've helped to bring home to their families, people who may have never made it home otherwise.

It's a record we have every right to feel proud of. But there is also a lingering frustration: these unjust incarcerations never seem to stop. And until they do, our work remains undone. We've been at this long enough to see the patterns. Prisoners freed, prisoners taken, prisoners freed, prisoners taken…when will it ever end? Though our efforts keep easing individual tragedies, the issue of unjustly imprisoned Americans doesn't go away. Even in the wake of our successes, someone is about to be grabbed somewhere.

Yes, I am tempted sometimes to throw up my hands and declare, *Our world is broken. Innocent people are being abused. Why can't we make this madness end?* All legitimate causes for deep frustration, as much as I try to keep those feelings at arm's length.

Then my phone rings.

Or an email lands in the Richardson Center inbox.

Or we get an initial inquiry from a friend of a friend.

An American is in custody overseas for no good reason. The family is desperate. They don't know where to turn. And all of a sudden, we are back in action again.

WILLIAM BLAINE RICHARDSON III
1947–2023

Early Saturday morning. September 2, 2023. Washington, DC. So early, it was still dark outside. I had just begun my morning run on the winding Mount Vernon Trail beside the Potomac River. If I don't get these runs in early, my day gets away from me, and I'll have a million excuses why I have no time to exercise.

My phone began to vibrate in the little pouch on my left arm.

Damn it, Guv! I thought to myself. *You know this is my time!*

Guv had some kind of sixth sense. He loved to call me just as I was starting my run. *I'm not answering,* I decided. *I'll finish running first.*

I knew he'd give me shit for that: "Why don't you answer your phone?!"

Just give me a minute, OK?

As soon as I completed the twenty-mile loop and made it back to the parking lot, I slipped the phone out of its pouch and glanced at the screen. But the missed call wasn't from Guv. It was from his wife, Barbara.

My heart sank.

Ugh!

Guv had his minor ailments. He carried a few extra pounds. But his health wasn't *that* precarious for a seventy-five-year-old man. Yet somehow or another, I knew exactly what his wife was going to tell me as soon as I returned the call. I just knew.

Within two hours, I was on my way to National Airport for a flight to Cape Cod and the Richardsons' summer house in Chatham, Massachusetts. The next week and a half was a blur of arrangements and sadness.

Preparing statements for the media. Chartering a plane to fly Guv's body home to New Mexico. Planning a funeral at the historic Cathedral Basilica of St. Francis of Assisi in Santa Fe. All the while bathed in my own deep, very personal grief.

This was the man who had changed my life in a single phone call: "I need you to pack your stuff and get your ass to Santa Fe. We're leaving for Khartoum." He'd focused my talents and my passions in a direction I never would have found on my own. He'd built up my confidence. He'd put me in the middle of some of the most fascinating human dramas in the world. He drove me crazy sometimes. Sometimes, I just wanted to shake him and shout, "Can I *please* have five minutes to myself?" But he'd set me on a path I knew I'd be following for the rest of my life.

And now he was gone, much sooner than I'd expected him to be.

I suppose I always knew this day would come...but *now*? Guv and I had a packed schedule ahead. In two weeks, we were set to fly with Steve Menzies to Venezuela, the second-to-last step in a long-running campaign to bring seven American prisoners home, including Eyvin Hernandez, a public defender from Los Angeles who'd been wrongfully detained in a Venezuelan prison since March 2022, and two former US Army Green Berets, Luke Denman and Airan Berry. We were so excited about the positive signs for them that, just the day before, Guv had authorized me to share our optimism with the prisoners' families, something we are normally reluctant to do while negotiating with a government as volatile as the one in Caracas.

Though Guv was gone now, I knew those efforts had to continue.

"We can't give up on these families," I told Steve when we spoke that fateful Saturday morning. "The substance for this mission is already set. It doesn't rely on Guv's input. Then again, the access that got us the meeting with Venezuelan leadership? That was all Guv."

"So, what if we find a replacement, someone to stand in for the Governor?" Steve asked.

Good luck, I thought.

"It would have to be someone similar to Guv," I found myself saying.

"Someone acceptable to the Venezuelans. Someone willing to rub the Biden administration the wrong way. And most important of all, someone who won't go running to the White House to check if they support the mission since the White House doesn't know anything about it and will definitely be opposed if we ask."

I didn't know anyone who could check all of Guv's boxes, someone who also knew how to navigate at the highest levels of international diplomacy. The fact was, the White House did *not* know about our imminent mission to Venezuela. And if they did, they'd almost certainly try to shut it down immediately. They'd say the left-wing government of Nicolás Maduro was no friend to the United States. But as I like to say, we don't work for the White House...or for any government.

Of the Americans held in Venezuela, the Biden administration had never designated the two Green Berets, Denman and Berry, as "wrongfully detained," meaning the US government was not formally negotiating for their release. Even if the American and Venezuelan governments had somehow struck a prisoner-exchange deal—no sign of that on the horizon—that deal would exclude our two war heroes. But unbeknownst to the White House, Guv and I had already gotten a written promise from the highest authority in the Maduro government that they would go for a seven-for-one prisoner exchange.

Seven for one.

And, yes, the seven Americans would include the two Green Berets.

The one? That would be Alex Nain Saab Morán, a wealthy Colombian-born financier and "special diplomat" for Venezuela's Maduro government. Over the years, Saab had been accused of drug smuggling, money laundering, consorting with terrorists and doing business with the Venezuelan government in violation of international sanctions. In October 2021, he was extradited from the island of Cape Verde off the coast of Africa to South Florida, where he was now being held pending trial for conspiring to launder money tied to a Venezuelan housing program.

"He's off the table," Deputy National Security Advisor Jon Finer had snapped at us when Guv and I raised Saab's name between omelet bites at the Hay-Adams.

"But you released Victor Bout for one American...," Guv pressed. "An arms-dealer!"

"Well," Finer answered with a soft chuckle. "Next to Bout, I guess I'd have to call Alex Saab a Boy Scout."

In a private conversation a few days later, a friend of mine from the Department of Justice left more room for hope. "If Saab pleads guilty, it's likely that our objection to his release in return for innocent Americans will be withered." He quickly added: "But we cannot ask for that."

"*You* can't, but we can," I responded, not saying anything too specific but knowing that, if we set something up on our own, the administration would be hard pressed to walk away from a solid deal. "Not on your behalf. Just as our idea. And if the Venezuelans agree, then we might have something to work with."

That was the clear direction we were heading when Guv died.

Alex Saab would take a plea bargain at the federal courthouse in Miami, then be released in exchange for the release of the seven Americans. It was the exact same mechanism we'd used four years earlier to get Princeton graduate student Xiyue Wang out of Iran. But just because Guv was gone, that didn't have to mean all future deals were off. It couldn't mean that. Sure, we'd been counting on Guv's unique presence, relationships and commanding personality. But the prisoners and their families were counting on *us*. We couldn't just throw up our hands and abandon them. Guv wouldn't want that. And we couldn't live with ourselves if we shrugged and told these families, "Too bad."

I was determined to honor Guv's life mission and his remarkable legacy by making every single effort, using every single point leverage, to see this deal through. Steve felt exactly the same way.

I texted Jorge Rodríguez, the head of the Venezuelan National Assembly and a close confidant of President Maduro. Jorge and I had met in Caracas in the midst of the pandemic. We'd stayed in touch since then.

> Dear Jorge, I began. As I am sure you saw in the news over
> the weekend, we lost our friend Governor Bill Richardson.
> Such a huge loss.

Then, I quickly got down to business.

> We were all confirmed to come see you and the President
> in two weeks with a very solid idea and plan to resolve the
> mutual detainees' issues in a way that serves both of our
> nations in the best possible way. I am determined to honor
> Governor Richardson's life and legacy by doing everything we
> can to complete this last mission of his.

I wasn't sure how Jorge or the Maduro government would react. But I just kept typing:

> Jorge, I would like to request that in honor of our friend, you
> and the President consider allowing us to continue with our
> planned mission to Venezuela, September 21-23. The idea
> Governor Richardson wanted to share with you in person
> is still very valid, and this visit is a critical step in our effort
> to get it done. Our discrete mission will be led by former
> Ambassador Cameron Hume, senior advisor and confidant of
> Governor Richardson. I will be accompanying him, along with
> Rodrigo Aguilar and Steven Menzies (who were with us on our
> last mission in 2020).

Three minutes. That's how long it took Jorge to respond.

Hi Mickey, he wrote. We certainly deeply mourned the loss of Governor Richardson and he shocked us because, as you know, we were expecting him on September 22nd. We will gladly wait to serve you and, from our humble position, pay tribute to that man of peace who was Bill Richardson.

What a relief! The mission was on!

We would fly to Caracas right on schedule. I could feel it. We were going to bring these prisoners home. There might even be a couple of other Americans we could add to the mix in Venezuela. Guv, I knew, had gotten us this far. Now it was up to the rest of us to carry that mission from here.

* * *

In the months to come, we would map out a whole new post-Richardson future for this work we shared. I had no doubt we would do more than sustain our crucial mission. We would expand on it. Even before we lost Guv, Steve and I had been talking about the long-term future, readying ourselves for the inevitable. A little sooner than we expected, that day was here.

The work of the Richardson Center, I'm thrilled to say, will continue in Guv's name, doing the independent diplomacy and round-the-world negotiating we've always done. Only now, we are gathering a small, talented team of former high-level diplomats, top professionals with experience and contacts in some of the world's diciest corners, filling the high-profile role Governor Richardson had so brilliantly played. Veteran ambassador Cameron Hume has already signed on to this A-team. So has Robert O'Brien, the savvy national security advisor from the Trump administration. Others will join too. Guv is not replaceable. But with this unmatchable team, we will have the extraordinary talent and depth that we need.

This exciting new organization is called Global Reach. It is funded by Steve Menzies. And I have the humbling responsibility of leading it. Going forward, this private foundation will take on individual cases and design and implement strategies to bring Americans home. It will also support the work of the Foley Foundation, HostageUS, and others who are every bit as dedicated to the cause. Looking after the needs of these anxious families. Rallying political support around the world. All of us working together, freeing as many American prisoners as we possibly can.

We will grow and expand and adapt as we need to. We will welcome support from generous partners everywhere. We will keep doing whatever it takes to free Americans unjustly imprisoned, no matter where they are.

As long as the need is there, our work will go on.

ABOUT THE AUTHORS

Mickey Bergman directs the Richardson Center for Global Engagement, a nongovernmental, nonprofit organization that negotiates the release of political prisoners and hostages around the world. He has spent the past decade freeing Americans from some of the most complex and insular countries on earth, including Iran, North Korea, Venezuela, Russia, Syria, Gambia, and Sudan. Bergman is an adjunct professor at the Georgetown University Walsh School of Foreign Service, where his graduate-level courses focus on the art of emotional intelligence in international relations. He was nominated for the Nobel Peace Prize in 2019 and 2023 alongside former governor Bill Richardson.

Ellis Henican is a Pulitzer Prize–winning journalist and a multi–*New York Times* bestselling author. His website is www.henican.com.